Capturing a Locomotive

Also from Westphalia Press
westphaliapress.org

The Idea of the Digital University

Criminology Confronts Cultural Change

Eight Decades in Syria

Avant-Garde Politician

Socrates: An Oration

Strategies for Online Education

Conflicts in Health Policy

Material History and Ritual Objects

Jiu-Jitsu Combat Tricks

Opportunity and Horatio Alger

Careers in the Face of Challenge

Bookplates of the Kings

Collecting American Presidential Autographs

Misunderstood Children

Original Cables from the Pearl Harbor Attack

Social Satire and the Modern Novel

The Amenities of Book Collecting

Trademark Power

A Definitive Commentary on Bookplates

James Martineau and Rebuilding Theology

Royalty in All Ages

The Middle East: New Order or Disorder?

The Man Who Killed President Garfield

Chinese Nights Entertainments: Stories from Old China

Understanding Art

Homeopathy

The Signpost of Learning

Collecting Old Books

The Boy Chums Cruising in Florida Waters

The Thomas Starr King Dispute

Salt Water Game Fishing

Lariats and Lassos

Mr. Garfield of Ohio

The Wisdom of Thomas Starr King

The French Foreign Legion

War in Syria

Naturism Comes to the United States

Water Resources: Iniatives and Agendas

Designing, Adapting, Strategizing in Online Education

Feeding the Global South

The Design of Life: Development from a Human Perspective

Capturing a Locomotive

A History of Secret Service in the Late War

by Rev. William Pittenger

WESTPHALIA PRESS
An Imprint of Policy Studies Organization

Westphalia Press
An imprint of Policy Studies Organization
1527 New Hampshire Ave., NW
Washington, D.C. 20036
info@ipsonet.org

ISBN-13: 978-1-63391-546-6
ISBN-10: 1-63391-546-8

Cover design by Jeffrey Barnes:
jbarnesbook.design

Daniel Gutierrez-Sandoval, Executive Director
PSO and Westphalia Press

Updated material and comments on this edition
can be found at the Westphalia Press website:
www.westphaliapress.org

A RAILROAD CHASE.

Frontispiece.

CAPTURING A LOCOMOTIVE:

A HISTORY

OF

SECRET SERVICE

IN THE LATE WAR.

BY

REV. WILLIAM PITTENGER.

"Storm'd at with shot and shell,
  Boldly they rode and well;
Into the jaws of death,
Into the mouth of hell,
    Rode the six hundred.

   *   *   *   *   *   *

"They that had fought so well
Came through the jaws of death
Back from the mouth of hell,
All that was left of them—
    Left of six hundred."
        TENNYSON'S *Charge of the Light Brigade.*

WASHINGTON:
THE NATIONAL TRIBUNE.
1885.

NAMES OF THE ADVENTURERS.

EXECUTED.

J. J. ANDREWS, *Leader*....Citizen of Kentucky.
WILLIAM CAMPBELL.......Citizen of Kentucky.
GEORGE D. WILSON.........Co. B, Second Reg't Ohio Vols.
MARION A. ROSS.............Co. A, Second Reg't Ohio Vols.
PERRY G. SHADRACK......Co. K, Second Reg't Ohio Vols.
SAMUEL SLAVENS............Thirty-third Reg't Ohio Vols.
SAMUEL ROBINSON..........Co. G, Thirty-third Reg't Ohio Vols.
JOHN SCOTT.....................Co. K, Twenty-first Reg't Ohio Vols.

ESCAPED IN OCTOBER.

W. W. BROWN[1] (*Engineer*) Co. F, Twenty-first Reg't Ohio Vols.
WILLIAM KNIGHT[2]..........Co. E, Twenty-first Reg't Ohio Vols.
J. R. PORTER[3].....................Co. C, Twenty-first Reg't Ohio Vols.
MARK WOOD[4]...................Co. C, Twenty-first Reg't Ohio Vols.
J. A. WILSON[5]....................Co. C, Twenty-first Reg't Ohio Vols.
M. J. HAWKINS[6].............Co. A, Thirty-third Reg't Ohio Vols.
JOHN WOLLAM[7]...............Co. C, Thirty-third Reg't Ohio Vols.
D. A. DORSEY[8].................Co. H, Thirty-third Reg't Ohio Vols.

EXCHANGED IN MARCH.

JACOB PARROT[9]...............Co. K, Thirty-third Reg't Ohio Vols.
ROBERT BUFFUM[10]............Co. H, Twenty-first Reg't Ohio Vols.
WILLIAM BENSINGER[11]......Co. G, Twenty-first Reg't Ohio Vols.
WILLIAM REDDICK[12].........Co. B, Thirty-third Reg't Ohio Vols.
E. H. MASON[13].................. Co. K, Twenty-first Reg't Ohio Vols.
WILLIAM PITTENGER[14]......Co. G, Second Reg't Ohio Vols.

RESIDENCES IN 1881.

[1] Perrysburg, Ohio.
[2] Minnesota.
[3] Carlisle, Arkansas.
[4] Dead.
[5] Hoskins, Wood County, Ohio.
[6] Topeka, Kansas.
[7] Unknown.
[8] Jefferson, Wisconsin.

[9] Kenton, Ohio.
[10] Dead.
[11] McCombs, Hancock County, Ohio.
[12] Unknown.
[13] Unknown.
[14] Woodbury, N. J. A member of the New Jersey Conference of the Methodist Episcopal Church.

4

PREFACE.

WAR has a secret as well as a public story. Marches and battles are open to the popular gaze; but enterprises of another class are in their very nature secret, and these are scarcely less important and often much more interesting than the former. The work of spies and scouts, the enterprises that reach beyond the lines of an army for the purpose of surprise, the councils of officers, the intrigues by means of which great results often flow from apparently insignificant causes, and all the experiences of hospitals and prisons,—these usually fill but a small place on the historian's page, though they are often of romantic interest, and not unfrequently decide the course and fate of armies. The enterprise described in these pages possesses all the unity of a drama, from the first plunge of the actors into the heart of the enemy's country, through all their adventures and changing fortunes, until the few survivors stood once more under the old flag! No single story of the war combines so many of the hidden, underground elements of the contest against rebellion as this. Disguise and secrecy, the perils of a forlorn hope, the exultation of almost miraculous success, the sufferings of prisoners, and the gloom of despair are all mingled in a varied and instructive war-picture.

In telling the story all fictitious embellishments have been rejected. No pains have been spared to ascertain the exact truth, and the reader will find names, dates, and localities so fully given that it will be easy to verify the prominent features of the account.

In narrating those events which fell under his own eye, the writer has waived all scruples of delicacy, and used the first personal pronoun. This is far more simple and direct, while an opposite course would have savored of affectation.

This is not a revision or new edition of the little volume published by the present writer during the rebellion. DARING AND SUFFERING, like a number of similar sketches published in newspapers, magazines, and pamphlets, was a hasty narrative of personal adventure, and made no pretence of completeness. CAPTURING A LOCOMOTIVE is broader and more historic; a large amount of valuable material is now employed for the first time; and the story is approached in an entirely different manner. No paragraph of the old book is copied into the new.

WOODBURY, NEW JERSEY January, 1882.

CONTENTS.

ILLUSTRATIONS.

8

CAPTURING A LOCOMOTIVE.

CHAPTER I.

A SECRET MILITARY EXPEDITION.

As the writer looked up from the manuscript page on a warm March afternoon of 1862, a very busy, and occasionally an amusing scene was presented. I was seated on a gentle, wooded slope which led down to the clear and quiet stream of Stone River, in Tennessee. Not being at that time " on duty," I had strolled away from the tents which whitened the level fields above, and was passing an hour in the pleasant task of preparing " war correspondence" for the *Steubenville Herald.* Now and then I lifted my eyes to watch the work in progress a few yards farther down the stream. A large bridge, burned by the enemy on their retreat a few weeks before, was now being rapidly repaired, or rather rebuilt. The chief director of the work was General O. M. Mitchel, of astronomical fame, in whose division I then served. He was in every respect an able officer, and understood the construction of railroad bridges as well as observing the stars, or moulding raw recruits into veteran soldiers. But all his skill and science did not save him from becoming a little ridiculous at times. The Union soldier found no difficulty in loving his commander and laughing at him at the same instant. General Mitchel was now most impatient to complete this bridge, and thus maintain a

9

northern line of communication, while he penetrated farther into the South. Being now, for the first time, possessed of an independent command, he wished to signalize himself by some great blow struck at the most vulnerable point in the enemy's line. He could, therefore, scarcely endure the necessary delay caused by burnt bridges, and worked like a beaver, and chafed and fretted, and caused the men of his command to perform more hard labor than was agreeable. As I saw him running from place to place, urging on the idlers, and taking hold of any piece of work that presented itself as if he had been a common laborer, shouting and scolding, but always knowing just what ought to be done, and making surprising progress, I could not help admiring the man, even while I laughed at some exhibitions of superfluous zeal. Mitchel's scientific education, his practical experience, and his inventive genius stood him in good stead, as was proved by the rapid growth of the bridge before me. The soldiers almost idolized their skilful and zealous commander, but this did not deprive them of the soldier's privilege of grumbling without stint at his restless activity. He was to be found along the guard lines at almost any hour of the night, and woe to the sleepy sentinel who failed to give the proper challenge or to " turn out" promptly. No severe punishments had yet been inflicted, but some of the indolent had been terribly frightened, and were accustomed to declare that " Old Mitchel" had been watching the stars so long that he could not sleep at night himself, and was not willing that anybody else should ! But the discipline of the troops steadily improved, and the hearty commendation of their commander, who knew how to praise as well as blame, made amends for seeming harshness.

As I watched the working-parties, my attention was attracted to one strong-looking soldier who was obviously shirking. Before many minutes General Mitchel saw him too. The man pretended to lift and work,

GENERAL O. M. MITCHELL.
(From Harper's Magazine.)   Page 11.

while really doing nothing, and thus became a great
hindrance, for his example was contagious. Stealthily
the general stole towards him, and when I saw him take
a piece of rotten wood in his hand I looked for a scene.
It came. He dealt the idler a sudden blow that covered him all over with rotten wood, and nearly took
him from his feet, but did him no real injury. The
fellow turned furiously to avenge himself on his assail-
ant, but stood abashed when he saw the face of his commander, and heard the exclamation, " Go to work, you
lazy rascal !" The spectators enjoyed the man's look
of blank amazement greatly, and the work went forward more promptly than ever. But in a few moments
the tables were turned. Large framed masses of timber
were first floated near the position they were to occupy
in the bridge, at the end of the trestle-work, and then,
with ropes and pulleys, were slowly and painfully
hoisted into place. One of these was approaching the
perpendicular, and the general, in his eagerness, ran to
the end of a log, which extended over the water, and
began to encourage the laborers by loud cries of,
" Heave, O ! heave, O !" as they pulled at the ropes.
Another party of workmen passed by the shore end of
the log on which Mitchel stood, carrying a load of
timber. Just as they reached the log,—the lazy man
among them, now lifting as much as any other,—I
could not see just how it was done, but probably by a
quick motion of the foot, the general's log was turned
so suddenly that he had no choice but to plunge in the
water. I expected a fearful explosion of indignation,
and perhaps the summoning of a guard to arrest the
offender, but was greatly surprised to see Mitchel, as
soon as the splash enabled me to see at all, stand up in
the water, which was not more than two feet deep, and
without even turning towards the shore, continue calling, " Heave, O ! heave, O !" as vigorously as ever.
There was some laughing, but the soldiers had great
respect for such coolness and presence of mind. The

general made no effort to discover the author of his
sudden immersion, though he must have known that it
was not accidental. "'Old Stars' can take a joke,"
was the approving remark of a soldier close to my
side.

I had just finished reading to a friend the newspaper
article I had been writing, when Captain Mitchel, a
distant relative of the general's, and commander of one
of the companies in the Second Ohio Regiment,—the
regiment in which I served,—came and sat down by
me, and asked what news I had been writing to the
papers. This was always a matter of great interest to
the officers and soldiers of our volunteer armies, for the
public letter served to give the families at home a great
deal of news, and thus to fill out the accounts conveyed
by private letters. I read the sketch over to him, and
it suggested a general conversation on the prospects of
the war. These we regarded as eminently favorable.
McClellan was about to move towards Richmond with
an overwhelming force, and we expected him to easily
capture the rebel capital. Buell, who had been with
us in our march through Kentucky, had gone Southwest to join Grant. That they would, when united, be
able to drive the enemy far down the Mississippi, even
if they did not open that river to the Gulf, seemed
equally sure. But where were we going, that we, with
only ten thousand men and an adventurous general,
were being hurried Southeast? There was no enemy
in our front now, but we could not continue to march
in that direction very long without finding foes enough.
We were striking directly between the great armies of
the Rebellion, and, if we went on far enough, would
totally sever their connection. At this point in the
conversation Mitchel exhibited some constraint, as if
afraid of saying too much. I declared my own opinion,
which I shared with the greater part of the army, that
we were bound for Chattanooga, and possibly for Atlanta, but that the rebels would be sure to run in heavy

bodies of troops by rail, and give us all the fighting we wanted before reaching even the former place.

"Possibly they may," said Mitchel; "but there are ways of looking out for that."

"How?" I asked, with interest, for I knew that he was usually well informed and very intelligent.

He smiled, and said that "I might find out some time."

His manner, much more than his words, piqued my curiosity. Besides, there was another matter I had resolved to question him about at the first opportunity. A few days before several of the best soldiers of our regiment had suddenly disappeared. Four of the missing men were from the company to which I belonged, and two others from Mitchel's company. They had been seen in close and apparently confidential conversation with the regimental officers, and then, without any leave-taking, were gone! No one of the private soldiers could tell anything about their destination. In a moment the hints of Mitchel connected themselves, in my mind, with the absence of these men. Had not some secret enterprise been set on foot in which they were engaged? If there was any such scheme, I would like to find it out, and, if still possible, take a part in it. In addition to this motive for curiosity, one of the absent men was a young cousin of mine, in whose welfare I was deeply interested.

"Mitchel," I said, turning sharply on him, "I understand that Frank Mills and those other men have been sent into the enemy's lines to perform some important and dangerous service. I want you to tell me all about it."

As soon as I uttered the words I knew I was right. Mitchel was silent for a moment, and then asked who had told me so much.

"No matter about that," I returned. "You can trust me fully. Tell me what you know."

"I will," he answered, "for I am anxious about the

boys myself, and want to talk the matter over with some friend. I am not sure that we did right in letting them go."

Rising, we strolled up the stream until we reached a solitary place far away from the bridge and the noisy workmen. Then getting a seat on a large rock, I listened to Captain Mitchel's story. This conversation is one of the most important epochs of my life. So strange and romantic were the particulars to which I listened, that it was difficult at first to give them perfect credence.

Said Mitchel, " Do you remember a Mr. Andrews, a Kentuckian, who was about our camp last fall ?"

At first I did not, but a moment after, I recollected seeing a fine-looking, well-dressed man standing on the street-corner in the town of Prestonburg, up in the mountains of Eastern Kentucky. He held carelessly on his arm a beautiful Winchester rifle, which I, in common with many others, had examined with great admiration. I therefore answered Mitchel's question in the affirmative, though I thought he was beginning rather far away from the subject in hand. He continued,—

" Some of you maintained that he was a rebel citizen, and possibly a spy, who was only pretending to be a unionist because our army was at hand."

I said that such had been my own opinion when I first saw him, for he was the very ideal of a magnificent Southern gentleman, but that I had afterwards learned that though he was a spy and secret agent, it was on the Union side, and that he was high in the confidence of our officers, adding that I had seen the same man in our camp again, but had not spoken to him after the first occasion.

" Well," continued Mitchel, " he was, and is, a spy, and has been of great service to us. But I sometimes fear that we may have trusted him a little too far. Our boys are now in Georgia with him."

I sprang up from my seat. This was startling

news. It had, indeed, been asserted by the camp-fires
—where all events are discussed, and where conjectures
too often pass for facts—that the missing men had
turned spies, but I had scouted the idea. I thought
that at most they might have been sent on ahead of us
a short distance, to seize some important post in connection with similar details from other regiments, and
supported by cavalry. But we were a hundred and
fifty miles from the nearest point of the Georgian State
line.

I looked at my companion in astonishment, and exclaimed, " What on earth are they doing in Georgia ?"

" Andrews has taken them there," he said, " disguised
as Southern citizens, with the intention of capturing a
railroad train. He has also engaged a Southern man,
who is an engineer on the same railroad, to run their
locomotive, and when they get their train they will start
for our line and burn every bridge they pass over.
They will cut all the telegraph wires, and thus leave the
enemy in helpless rage behind them."

My imagination took fire at the picture his few words
had sketched. A train surprised by a handful of bold
men in the heart of the enemy's territory ; the passengers and train hands forced to get out under threat of
instant death, and possibly a desperate fight before this
was accomplished ; then the wires cut, so that no
lightning message could be flashed ahead ; the secret
confederate—whom there might be a show of compelling by force to mount the engine—set to his work ;
the train rushing on its way through a hostile country,
past the towns and camps of the enemy, but rendered
secure by the two elements of surprise and speed ; the
great bridges (like those at Green and Stone Rivers
and other places, which had cost us weary delays and
hard work in repairing),—all these bursting into flames
as they were passed, and possibly other damage done before the daring adventurers returned in triumph to our
own lines. I knew enough of war to understand, at a

glance, the great military importance of thus severing
railroad communications, for had I not seen our whole
division brought to a halt, and General Mitchel rendered almost furious with impatience over a single
burnt bridge? Besides, it required no particular insight to reveal the immense moral effect upon an enemy
of such a bold stroke far in the centre of his territory.
It would tend to diffuse distrust and fear through all
the rebel armies if they were thus made to feel that no
place in their whole country was safe from the presence
and the blows of a daring adversary.

"Well, what do you think of it?" said Mitchel, as
he saw my preoccupation.

"Why, it is the grandest thing I ever heard of!"
was my enthusiastic reply. "I wish I was with them.
But do you think that spy can be trusted? Spies are
all the time betraying the confidence of one party or
the other, and if he should be false to us, he has the
lives of our boys in his hands. I have heard that he
has been over the lines several times, and if he has
been a secret rebel all the while, it would be a nice
stroke of business for him to lead down a party of our
best men and deliver them to the rebels."

"I have no fear of the fidelity of Andrews," said
Mitchel. "He has been too well proved. But I am
not so sure that he will be able to carry through all
that he has undertaken, or that our boys can preserve
their disguise until they reach the right point and are
ready for the blow. If they should be detected while
pretending to be rebels, it is not at all unlikely that
they will be treated as spies and hung up. I wish they
were back in camp again. But if they get through all
right and burn the bridges, we will make for Chattanooga as fast as our legs can carry us. This is one of
the reasons that makes the general so anxious to have
that bridge done. If we should hear to-morrow, as
we may at any moment, that those Southern bridges
are smashed, it would be a race for Chattanooga with

all the odds in our favor. But you must not breathe
a word of this to one of the soldiers, or especially
write of it to the papers, or to any of the relatives of
the poor fellows, till they are back with us,—if they
ever come back! Give me your candid opinion, was
it right to let them take such a risk?"

Without the slightest hesitation I declared that it
was right, giving the reasons that seemed most weighty.
War is full of risks. In an obscure skirmish, or by a
chance shot from the picket-line, the most valuable life
may be put out. Now, if by a little additional risk a
few men can do the work of thousands,—the work that
if done in the ordinary mode would certainly cost a
score times as many lives as are imperilled,—the risk is
worth taking. Of course, it would not be right to send
men on such an enterprise without their consent, but
in the Union army it was never necessary to force men
into any dangerous enterprise. Volunteers were always
plenty enough.

I asked, further, how many men were engaged, and
learned with additional astonishment that the detachment from our own regiment—only eight men—was
all. This force seemed totally inadequate to the greatness of the work, but I understood that the risk of
detection would multiply with the increase of numbers.
The very smallest number that could serve was, therefore, selected. If they succeeded, few were better than
many.

After a long conversation, Mitchel and I returned to
the working-party down the river. The burnt rem-
nants of the old railroad bridge and the rapidly rising
timbers of the new had now a deeper interest than
ever. The completion of this bridge and the burning
of some others far in the South were the two events
for which that whole division, whose tents dotted the
meadows behind us, was unconsciously waiting. My
head was full of conjectures and plans as I walked
back through the twilight to join my messmates in the

tent. I could talk to no one of what I had heard, but as I lay awake that night a most important resolution took shape. I was weary of the slow movement of the army, and of the monotony of a private soldier's service. While trying carefully to do all my duty, and winning a fair degree of approval from my officers, I yet had no taste for military affairs. If by a little extra hazard I could do more for the country, while getting rid of distasteful routine and entering into a new sphere of work, I was more than willing to accept all the hazard involved. It was too late to take part in the present attempt, but I resolved to be prepared for any opportunity of the kind that might again offer.

Accordingly, in the forenoon of the next day I went up to regimental headquarters and told Colonel L. A. Harris, of the Second Ohio, that I had a favor to ask of him. Major (since General) Anson G. McCook, in whose company I had served during the first three months of the war, was also present. I told them I had ascertained that some of our men had been sent out on secret service lately, and that if any similar details should be made in the future, I wanted the opportunity of being included. Major McCook, while saying some kind things about me, intimated a doubt whether my defective vision—I was very near-sighted—might not be a hindrance on any perilous service. Colonel Harris, however, took a different view of the matter, saying he thought that if I dressed in citizen's clothes, and wore my spectacles (as I was accustomed to do even in the ranks), no person in the South would suspect me of being a soldier, and I was thus only the better fitted for any secret service. McCook did not press his objection, and after learning the reason for my request and trying in vain to find the source of my informa tion, Colonel Harris said,—

"Pittenger, I don't know that we will ever send an more men out of camp in this manner, but I will gi· e my promise that if we do, you shall be the first man called upon."

This was perfectly satisfactory. I returned to my duty, and in the routine of camp-life waited for several days in impatient anxiety. I dreamed at night of burning bridges and startling adventures. Duty on picket and in the camp lines, however, with other excitements, began to weaken the impression, as day after day rolled by with no recurrence of the subject. But one day it was told me by a friend that one of the missing men, a member of Company C, was back again in his usual place in line. For some time attempts to get him to say where he had been, and whether alone or in company, were in vain. He would speak no word by which any one could divine the nature of his errand while away from us, or the degree of success he had met with. I was much disquieted by his return alone, but having no special acquaintance, I did not like to try to get any information directly from him. But I soon learned that he had gone as far as Chattanooga and had turned back,—some of his comrades afterwards thought because he became so sensible of the difficulties of his attempt that he resolved to go no further in it,—a determination which he had a perfect right to make, and which in no way impugned his character as a soldier. His own explanation, afterwards given, which I saw no reason to doubt, was more dramatic. He said that he had gone in disguise as far as Chattanooga, but had there been recognized by a rebel soldier, who was an old acquaintance, and who knew that he belonged to the Union army. This man heard him telling his false story in a public place without contradicting him, but as soon as he could do so unobserved, drew him aside and declared that he remembered him, and knew he was down there disguised for some bad purpose; but that if he would pledge himself to return immediately to the Union lines, he would, for the sake of their former friendship, refrain from denouncing him, otherwise his own sense of duty would require him to report all he knew to the commander of the post. Under such circumstances our comrade judged it most prudent to give and keep the pledge required.

At length the bridge over Stone River was completed, and there was great rejoicing as the first train, laden with army supplies, passed over it from Nashville. Next morning the order was given to the whole division to prepare three days' rations. This was invariably the signal for a decided movement. Our lost comrades were still away, and no word had reached the rank and file of the army of any unusual occurrence southward. The uneasiness of General Mitchel and the regimental officers of the Second Ohio, and especially of Captain Sarratt, who commanded the company to which I belonged, and my friend, Captain Mitchel, was apparent to any careful observer.

Just before the march began, while we were standing in line early the next morning, with the camp all broken up, our knapsacks swung, and our haversacks filled with rations, waiting only for the word "forward," Captain Mitchel came over to me and uttered a sentence, in a half whisper, that went through me like an electric shock. His message was simply this: " Mills is back, and has gone up to headquarters to report." While standing in my place in the ranks I could give no answer, nor could I ask any question, but my mind was full of surmises. Had the adventurers succeeded, and were we now on our way to do our part in the great plan,—to strike swift and far into the South, while the enemy's communications were broken? That would involve hard fighting and stirring scenes not far ahead. Had they failed? If so, there would probably be other attempts,—that is, if the secret had been kept,—and then I would have a part in the risk and the adventure. At any rate, I was exceeding glad of Mills's return, and I knew that I would find out all

about it as soon as I could get to talk with him alone.
As Company K—Mitchel's—was next my own in the
line, that opportunity, even on the march, would not
be long delayed.

Soon the command to march was given, and the
column moved southward towards Shelbyville, about
twenty-five miles distant. Before noon I dropped
out of my place, sought and found Mills, and as we
plodded along, in the loose order allowed on long
marches, we had no difficulty in remaining together,
and yet far enough from other soldiers to talk in
perfect security. The whole history of my relative's
adventures was fully laid open before me. I found
that all Mitchel had narrated was perfectly accurate,
but the enormous obstacles to be encountered by such
an expedition were now brought much more plainly
into view. Mills said that he and his companions had
first of all exchanged their uniforms for citizen's clothes,
and made provision for the safety of their arms and
personal effects in the camp. Then, under the direction
of Andrews, they had scattered in the mountains, to
the eastward of our camp, representing themselves as
refugees from the oppressions of the Union troops in
Kentucky, and had journeyed thus to Chattanooga.
That town had been reached in about four days. My
friend pictured in lively colors the manner in which
he had been compelled to verbally abuse the Union
cause, and join in praise of the leaders and principles
of Secession. The squad to which he belonged had no
particular difficulty in passing themselves as good
rebels. The man who first returned had been less
fortunate. At Chattanooga they took passage on the
cars for Atlanta, and in due time reached that place,
where they scattered themselves among the several
hotels and lived plentifully (they had an abundant
supply of money) for three days longer. Each hour
Andrews anticipated the arrival of that Confederate
engineer of whom Mitchel had spoken to me. But he

did not come. All possible inquiries were guardedly
made concerning him, for it was not safe to appear too
inquisitive.

"How did you feel while thus waiting in suspense?"
I asked.

"I felt as if I wanted to be back in camp, and had
no business to be in that town any longer," replied
Frank. "To hear the curses and threats made against
everything that belonged to the Union, and to be
obliged to keep perfectly quiet, or to agree with them,
was more than I could easily endure. And the folks
about the hotel were more anxious every day to know
who I was, and I had to tell them lies without number.
I resolved not to stand it much longer."

"Were you really afraid of being found out,
Frank?" I queried. "Did you consider yourself in
much danger?"

With great emphasis he answered, "No money could
hire me to put myself in such a position again. I
would have run away if we had been obliged to stay
much longer."

This man was as brave as any human being. I had
seen him perfectly cool and serene under circumstances
of great danger, when every one else in the company
betrayed some sign of fear. I did not suspect him of
exaggerating the perils of the situation in which he
was placed, and, having a deep personal interest in the
matter, I put the question bluntly,—

"If men should be wanted to try this thing again,
would you not go?"

"Never!" was the unequivocal response. "If Andrews and Mitchel want bridges burned, they can go
themselves and burn them! I will do my duty as a
soldier, but as to going out among those——"

The terms applied, and the energy given to the accompanying description of the horror of being alone
among blood-thirsty enemies, feeling that, sleeping or
waking, a rope was around one's neck, just ready to be

tightened on the utterance of a single careless word, it is not necessary to transcribe here.

"But why did not that man come to help you? Did you find out anything about him?"

"Andrews told us, on the third day after we had reached Atlanta, that he had heard through some of the railway officials that the engineer had been transferred to the Mobile and Ohio Railroad to help in running troops to Corinth" (this was a short time before the battle of Shiloh). "But my own opinion is that the man got scared and had himself transferred there to get out of a bad scrape."

"But how did Andrews take this disappointment?"

"He was very much cast down. He asked each of us if we had ever been engineers or firemen. But no one had ever occupied such a position. He hated terribly to give up; but, as nothing more could be done, he at last told us we might work our way back to camp."

"Where are the other boys?"

"I suppose they are on their way. It was harder getting back than going down. Everybody seemed to think it natural for us to be going South; but we had to make all kind of excuses for ' heading the wrong way,' as they called it. We had to scatter to avoid observation, and travel part of the way by night; and if some of them are not discovered and either put into the rebel army or hung, I will be very glad."

"Do you think Andrews will now give up the job of burning those bridges, or will he try again?"

"If he can get men to go, you may be sure he will keep at it until he succeeds or dies. But I would never go again or advise any one else to do so. Why, he said he would stay down several days after we left and make a complete survey of the line, for the very purpose of trying over again."

"What do you think of Andrews himself? Can he be trusted?"

"Yes; he's as true as steel, and very smart. But I am afraid he will venture a little too far, both for himself and for those with him, one of these days."

I have omitted the many striking incidents that Mills narrated to me in the course of this conversation, which was more interesting to me than any romance, because adventures very similar in their general character to those he described will be fully narrated in another place.

I found my way back to my proper place in the regiment, feeling sure that another attempt to destroy the Southern communications would be made, in which I must engage if I did not positively "back out"; convinced, also, that it would involve hard labor, much peril, and, even with these, great risk of failure.

The next day others of the Andrews party returned to us, and corroborated the accounts given by Mills. The day following the remainder arrived in safety. They were all glad to get back, and were unanimous in declaring that they would not again venture disguised into the enemy's country under any circumstances. They spoke very sparingly about their experiences, for the officers had cautioned them to say but little, in view of the possibility of a new venture of the same character.

On Saturday evening, the 5th of April, we camped on the banks of Duck River, in some pleasant meadows about a mile from the town of Shelbyville. The next day was delightful. The spring of 1862 opened very early, and now the meadows were verdant and the birds singing. The calm, quiet, and beauty of that Sabbath, with the white tents dotting the level fields, and the soldiers luxuriating in one day of rest after the hard march, which had been rendered more fatiguing by the accompaniments of rain and mud, form a very pleasant picture in memory. The next Sabbath came to me under entirely different circumstances. I felt the pressure of a vague melancholy resting upon me,—

possibly it was only that pensive feeling often inspired
by a fresh, bright, and quiet day in early spring; possibly the faint shadow of coming evil. I devoted the
greater part of the day to writing letters to friends and
newspapers,—the last I wrote for weary months. On
this same day—though we knew it not till afterwards—
began the great battle of Shiloh, or Pittsburg Landing,
one hundred and fifty miles west of us.

On Monday Andrews himself returned to our lines,
and asked, as I had anticipated, for permission to renew
his enterprise. He had spent several days along the
line of the Western and Atlantic Railroad, learning the
number of trains, their times of running, and everything else likely to be useful. He had then started for
camp, and being provided with passes, so that he could
take the most direct road, besides being well mounted,
he came in almost as soon as the private soldiers who
started much sooner.

But not one of the first party would return. They
were tired of feeling, as one of them expressed it, that
their necks depended upon a lie. Like Schiller's diver,
they had plunged once into the abyss and returned in
safety; but, unlike that venturous youth, they would
not make the second and fatal trial.

The new expedition, as proposed by Andrews, differed
in three particulars from the first. He wanted a larger
force,—twenty-four men instead of eight. He had seen
that it was possible to carry a considerable number of
men in disguise to the scene of action, and the number
now requested was none too large for the capture of a
full-railway train or the overpowering of guards at important bridges. He also wanted some engineers to be
detailed, in order that no mishap might leave them
without the power of running their train. Five were
secured, thus leaving an ample margin, as it was believed, for the possibility of capture on the way down,
or of death by the enemy's bullets in the hour of conflict. It thus became an enterprise completely fitted

out in Federal lines, without any reliance on help from the South.   The third point of difference was of more importance than a casual glance revealed.   The first expedition had an abundance of time.   A week's delay, even after the soldiers were in the enemy's country, would have involved no risk, save that of discovery,— would, indeed, have been an advantage, as it would allow less time for the repair of damages done to the Southern railroads before Mitchel's arrival at Chattanooga.   But now it was different.   The whole division was ready to advance, its course being clearly indicated to the enemy, and moments became precious.   By making the utmost speed it was still possible to have the bridges burned at the right time, but every hour's delay would render the work more difficult, and its success more uncertain.   The bearing of this question of time will be made painfully apparent in our story.

General Mitchel received the report of Mr. Andrews (which also embraced all the information the most skilful spy could have brought concerning the nature and disposition of the enemy's forces), approved his prudence in ordering the return of the soldiers, and sanctioned the second attempt.   He, however, advised caution, saying that Andrews must not strike unless he saw a good prospect of success; but he made no objection to the increase of force, provided volunteers could be obtained.   It was easy to secure the five engineers asked for without going beyond the limits of the three Ohio regiments composing General Sill's brigade.   Of the detail as finally made out, nine men belonged to the Twenty-first, eight to the Thirty-third, and seven to the Second Ohio Regiments.

CHAPTER II.

MIDNIGHT CONSULTATION.

ON Monday, April 7, while I was inside my tent engaged in some of the little details of work which occupy a soldier's time in camp, a comrade pulled open the canvas door and called out,—

" Pittenger, Captain Sarratt is looking for you."

I went out and met the captain, and together we walked up the street formed by the two rows of tents to the larger tent occupied by the company officers, which stood across the street at the upper end. He took me inside, and then said, with a sigh,—

" Colonel Harris has just sent me word that you are to go with Andrews down to Georgia. I do not know why he has selected you, but I advise you not to go. You have perfect liberty to refuse."

I told him that so far from refusing my mind was fully made up to accept, and that I had already arranged with Colonel Harris to that effect. Sarratt was surprised to hear this, but urged every argument in his power to dissuade me; telling me that the safe return of the four who had been out on the former expedition had lifted a great burden from his heart; but that if I went, it would be no better than before. I was deeply moved by his evident concern, but had gone too far to retract. I asked if any other member of our company was to go. He answered in the negative, saying that he understood that but one from each company was to be detailed. Finding persuasion in vain, he gave me a pass to Shelbyville, where I could see Andrews and procure all necessaries for the journey. I left him, deeply impressed by the kindness of the man, which

led him to regard the soldiers under his command as
children, for whose welfare he felt himself in a great
degree responsible.

No one of my comrades yet knew of the intended
expedition. In the afternoon I took a friend with me
and strolled into Shelbyville, a well-built village of a
few hundred inhabitants, and purchased some articles
of clothing, but was not able to find a complete suit.
A number of persons were engaged in making similar
purchases—among others, the sergeant-major of our
regiment, Marion Ross. By watching the character
of his purchases and by a few careful questions, I found
that his business was the same as my own. No side-
arms could be found, but I knew that all lack in that
direction could easily be supplied in camp. Getting
away from all other company, Ross and I strayed
through the town for some time, keeping a sharp lookout, until, at length, we saw Andrews. His striking
personal appearance made it easy to recognize him, and,
approaching, we told him that we were ordered to report to him. After scrutinizing us a moment, and asking us the company and rank we held, he told us that
it would not be prudent to talk much in so public a
place, but to overtake him after dark a mile or more
east of Shelbyville, on the road toward Wartrace, and
he would there give us full explanations, and allow us
to return to our regiments if not satisfied with his
plans. With these few words we parted from him, and
went back to our tents for final arrangements. I borrowed the additional clothing I needed from one of the
former adventurers. All my arms and equipments I
put carefully in order, packed my uniform in my knap-
sack to be left in the care of the proper authorities, arrayed myself in citizen's clothes, and stepped out of my
tent. The soldiers who were idling around passed the
word to their comrades who were in their tents, reading, playing cards, or amusing themselves in the various
ways incident to camp-life, and soon almost the whole

company—indeed, all who were not absent on guard duty—thronged around and commenced all kinds of questions. " Pittenger, going to desert? Going home? Going out as a spy? Got a discharge? Got a furlough?"—were a few of the inquiries that rained from every quarter. At the same time I heard it asserted that several other men were dressing up in the same manner. I answered all questions in the affirmative, and stepped over to the company street adjoining our own—that of Company K—and sought the tent in which Frank Mills messed. He had a very good revolver which I wanted to borrow. As I entered, he read the situation in a glance.

" So, you are going with Andrews."

I nodded, and hastened to add, " I want your revolver."

" You are welcome to the revolver, but if you know when you are well off you will stay where you are. Because I was fool enough to go, it does not follow that you need be."

I did not argue the question, but he saw that it was settled, and he gave me the weapon, with a liberal supply of cartridges. I was now ready, and the gravity of the situation forced itself more clearly upon my apprehension. I did not expect to return to camp until the proposed enterprise had been accomplished. Considering, therefore, that so much was already known in camp from the report of the former party, and from seeing me arrayed as I was, I could not understand that it would be any advantage for me to steal away unnoticed. With this view, I went up to Captain Sarratt's quarters and bade him good-by. He was almost overcome with emotion, and could not muster a single one of his accustomed good-natured jokes. Then came the farewells to tried comrades. Few of them had any distinct conception of the nature of my errand, but they knew it was secret and dangerous, and this was enough to excite their apprehension. They labored

3*

hard to dissuade me. The devotion of one of their
number, my inseparable companion, Alexander Mills,
was especially affecting. Though he had been lying
in our tent very sick all day, he now crawled to the
door and begged me not to go. Finding that I was
fully determined, he hurried as fast as his tottering
steps would allow to headquarters, for permission to go
along! Notwithstanding his physical inability, he persisted in his request until the colonel threatened to
have him put under arrest. Had he been well he
would not have been refused, as he was a most excellent soldier; but in the trying times that followed, it
was a great satisfaction to me that he was left behind.
Poor fellow! he lost his life while carrying the flag
of the Second Ohio at the battle of Lookout Mountain,
eighteen months later, and now sleeps in the beautiful
National Cemetery at Chattanooga,—that town towards
which our steps were now bent.

When all the farewells were over I strolled back to
Shelbyville, meeting Sergeant Ross as we had arranged,
and passed the time pleasantly with him in looking
about the village until about dark, when we inquired
the road to Wartrace, and started for the rendezvous
that Andrews had appointed. We walked very leisurely, expecting that some of our number, who were
probably behind, would soon overtake us, and having
a curiosity to ascertain whether we could recognize
them by speech or manner as belonging to our party.
We saw several persons, but they were travelling the
opposite way, and we began to be apprehensive that
we had taken the wrong road.

As we journeyed on, we noticed a house surrounded
by a yard, and Ross proposed getting a drink of water.
Crossing the fence we went up to the house, but before
we reached the door, a dog came up silently behind my
companion, and, biting his leg, ran under the house
before a revolver could be drawn.

The bite was not severe, and I laughed heartily at

his mishap; but after drinking, and before reaching the fence, the same dog rushed out once more. Ross saw him in time, and sprang over the fence, but I sat on the top of it in fancied security. The malicious creature sprang at me, seized my coat, and tore a large piece out of it. The same coat, thus torn, I wore during the whole of the year through which our adventures extended. The incident was trivial, but in the deepening darkness, with a thunder-storm, which now began to mutter in the distance, approaching, uncertain as to where our comrades were, and at the beginning of a desperate enterprise, it stands out in memory with lurid distinctness. To a superstitious person it might have seemed ominous of the results of that expedition in which Ross perished, and from which I returned a shattered and disabled invalid.

A pistol-shot easily cleared us of the dog, and we pursued our way,—not rejoicingly, for our situation grew every moment more perplexing. Not one of our comrades was visible, and we were almost certain we had taken the wrong road. Finally, we resolved to retrace our steps, and try to get in Shelbyville some better clue to our journey. Unless we could obtain further instructions, we knew not how or where to go. We did not like to return to camp, for that would probably delay us too long to take part in the enterprise, and the failure to go, after our affecting leave-taking, would have formed a ludicrous anticlimax, and probably have been charged to cowardice. At a cross-road in sight of Shelbyville, where we felt sure that any of the adventurers who obeyed the directions we had received must pass, we sat down and waited nearly an hour longer.

Our patience was rewarded. We had started too soon, and from this miscalculation all our perplexity arose. A few men, whom we recognized almost instinctively as belonging to our party, came along the road in the right direction. A little guarded conversation showed us that we were right, and we strolled slowly on with them. Shortly afterwards others overtook us, among whom was Andrews. This was a great relief, as we now had a guide. Soon we were as far from Shelbyville as Ross and I alone had been, and a few hundred yards farther on fell in with still other men. Our party had so greatly increased as to be quite conspicuous, and it was advisable to add still further security to the cover of the night. Accordingly, we left the road for some distance, and, marching silently, were soon at the appointed rendezvous.

A little thicket of dead and withered trees, a short distance from the road, and sufficiently open to assure us that no listener was near, was the place of our assemblage. Never was a consultation preparatory to some desperate deed held under more fitting circumstances. The storm which had been gathering all the evening was now near. Black clouds covered one half the sky, and the young moon, low down in the west, was soon obscured. The frequent flashes of lightning, more vivid in the darkness, and the low roll of thunder that followed, grew continually more emphatic, forming most startling interruptions to the earnest but suppressed words of our leader. It is very singular that amid these ominous surroundings, which fitted so well the character of the business in hand, one ordinary sound stands out in my memory, far more clear and distinct than any part of the scene. Far off I heard the bark or howl of a dog,—no doubt at some farm-house,—roused either by the coming storm which began to sway the leafless boughs above us, or by the passing of some belated traveller. Popular superstition would probably have considered such a sound as ominous of evil; and most of us are superstitious when young, in the dark, and entering upon unknown dangers.

. We formed a close circle around Mr. Andrews while he revealed to us his daring plans. In a voice as soft and low as a woman's, but tremulous with suppressed

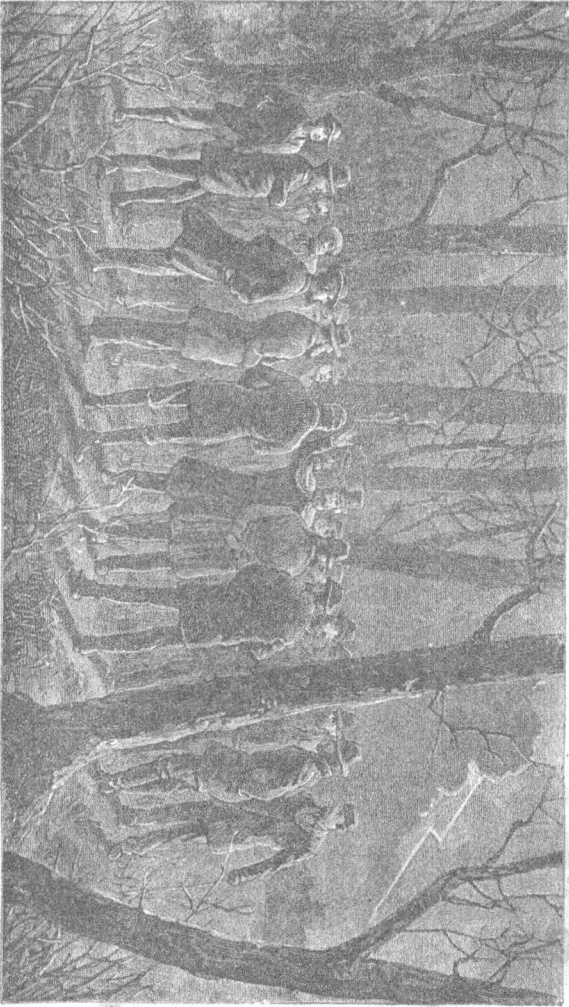

MIDNIGHT CONSULTATION.

enthusiasm, he painted the greatness of the project we were to attempt, the sublimity of rushing through a hostile country at the full speed of steam, leaving flaming bridges and raging but powerless foes behind. But he did not disguise the dangers to be encountered.

"Soldiers," he said, "if you are detected while engaged in this business, the great probability is that you will be put to death,—hung as spies, or massacred by a mob. I want you to clearly understand this, and if you are not willing to take the risk, return to camp, and keep perfectly quiet about it."

A murmur all around the circle conveyed the assurance that we would follow him to the last extremity.

"Our plan," he continued, "is simply this: you are to travel on foot, or by any conveyance you can hire, either to Chattanooga or some station not far from that point on the Memphis and Charleston Railroad; then you can take passage on the cars down to Marietta; that will be our next place of assembling, and not Atlanta. You must be there by Thursday evening, ready to take passage on the cars northward again by Friday morning. I will be there as soon as you, and tell you what more is to be done."

"But how about money to pay our way?" was asked.

"I have plenty of Confederate money, and will share it among you before we part. As to your story, you cannot do better than to tell everybody that you are Kentuckians coming South to get away from the Yankees, and to join the Confederate army; only be careful to have always some plausible reason for going farther before joining. A great many Kentuckians have gone South by this route, and are very heartily received. If you will go eastward through Wartrace and Manchester, you will get into the track they usually take, and by then turning south, you will not appear to be heading from the Union army. If any one of you are questioned closely, you may say you are from

c

Fleming County, for I happen to know that no soldiers from that county are in this part of the country."

All of these directions were eagerly listened to, but the closing one afterwards bore disastrous fruit.

One of the soldiers asked, " If any of us are suspected, and find we can't get away, what would you advise us to do?"

" Enlist without hesitation in the rebel army," was the response. "You are fully authorized to do that, and no one of this party will be accused of desertion, even if captured among the rebels. I would be sorry to lose any one of you, but it will be far better that you should serve awhile with the enemy than to acknowledge who you are, and thus risk the disclosure of the enterprise."

"But is it likely that we could get the chance thus to enlist?" it was further asked.

"Most certainly," said Andrews. " They are taking all the prisoners out of the jails and enlisting them. They are picking up men who have run away from the conscription wherever they can find them, and serving them in the same manner. If you tell your story and stick to it, even if they are not satisfied that you are telling the truth, they will put you into the service. You can stay until some dark night on picket. But I hope you will escape all trouble, and all meet me at Marietta safely. Break this party up into squads of three or four, and don't recognize each other on the way. I will ride along the same country you are travelling, and give you any help or direction in my power. But you must not recognize me unless sure that we are not observed."

There was but one subject on which I cared to ask any questions, and that related to a distant contingency. I was well informed as to the first part of the intended enterprise.

"Suppose we succeed in capturing the train," I said, "and in burning the bridges, are we then to leave the train, and try to steal back to our lines in the same way we are now going South?"

"By no means," replied Mr. Andrews. "We will run the train right through Chattanooga, and westward until we meet Mitchel, who by that time will be coming eastward on the road from Memphis. If we should not quite reach him, we will get so close that we can dash through in a body."

This was satisfactory as far as it went, but there was still another contingency. More than anything else I dreaded being left alone in an unknown country.

"If we fail to run the captured train through Chattanooga, will we then disperse or stick together?"

"After we meet at Marietta, we will keep together, and, if necessary, cut our way back to our own lines. Form your squads now, and I will give out the money."

Swiftly we selected our companions. There was little time for choice. Most of the men were strangers. The darkness was intense, and the thunder-peals almost overhead. In a moment we formed six or seven little groups. My former comrade, Ross, stood with another man or two beside Andrews. Two men from Captain Mitchel's company and one from the next company to that in the regimental line stood by my side. Andrews went from group to group, giving out the money freely, and answering questions that were still asked. When this was accomplished, he addressed himself once more to the whole number, and we crowded around to listen to his parting words. They gave us the fullest insight into the whole plan we had yet received.

"To-morrow morning," said he, "Mitchel, with his whole army, will start on a forced march right south to Huntsville. He will capture that town not later than Friday (it was now Monday night), and will then turn east towards Chattanooga. We must burn the bridges south of Chattanooga the same day, for after that, the road will be crowded with trains bringing reinforcements against him and running property away, and

our task will be very much harder. So we have no
time to lose. We must be at Marietta on Thursday
evening. The last train for that station leaves Chattanooga at five o'clock in the afternoon. Be sure to catch
it. Good-by."

He gave each of us his hand with a hearty pressure
and fervent good wishes. Not many moments after, the
storm broke over us with all its fury. The rain fell in
torrents. The last glimpse I caught of Andrews as
my party of four hurried on their prescribed course
was by means of a broad glare of lightning that made
the drenched landscape for a moment as bright as day.
He had just parted from the last group and was gazing
after us.

CHAPTER III.

COMPANIONS AND INCIDENTS.

WHO was this Mr. Andrews, from whom we had
just parted in storm and darkness,—the man from
whose brain sprang the Chattanooga Railroad Expedition, and to whose keeping we had so fearlessly committed our lives? Few of us knew much about him at
that time, but became wiser afterwards. As he is the
hero of the earlier part of this story, it may be well to
give the reader the benefit of all the information as to
his character and history subsequently obtained.

Mr. J. J. Andrews was born in that part of Western
Virginia known as the "Pan Handle," on the eastern
bank of the Ohio River, and only separated from my
own county of Jefferson by that stream. While quite
young he had removed to the mountains of Eastern
Kentucky, settling in Fleming County. Here he acquired considerable wealth, but at the outbreak of the

civil war lost most of it again. While in business here
he travelled over much of the South, and became acquainted with many men whom the war afterwards
threw into prominence. At the first outbreak of hostilities he joined the Union army, not as a soldier, but
in the still more useful and dangerous character of a
spy and secret negotiator. He accompanied General
Nelson in his Eastern Kentucky campaign, on which
occasion I had seen him at Prestonburg, and afterwards
he journeyed back and forth two or three times from
Nashville before the capture of that city. He also
spent several days in Fort Donelson during the week
preceding its capture by General Grant. At this place
he narrowly escaped detection. Subsequently he visited Atlanta and brought back much valuable information. By representing himself as a blockade-runner,
and carrying southward through our lines articles of
small bulk but of great value to the enemy, he secured
their confidence and brought back information a hun-
dredfold more valuable. This business was pecuni-
arily profitable to himself as well as very serviceable
to the Union army. A Mr. Whiteman, of Nashville,
afterwards testified that he had paid him ten thousand dollars for one cargo, the most of which was clear
profit. Some of the Southern officers with whom he
was intimate had bestowed upon him passes authorizing
him to come and go through their lines at pleasure. It
is not my intention to offer any apology for a man who
thus betrays the confidence even of rebels. What justice requires to be said on this subject will find a more
appropriate place in explaining the position of those
who accompanied him in his last and most perilous
journey. His occupation was one of the utmost danger, and he could not expect much mercy if detected.
He had even gone the length of taking the oath of allegiance to the Southern Confederacy, though he was
passionately loyal to the old government. Indeed, his
hatred for secession and everything connected with it

had become the more intense from the very disguise he
so frequently assumed ; and the desire to work all possible injury to that cause had far more influence in inducing him to pursue his perilous vocation than any
hope of reward. I have since been told by Southern
authorities that he acknowledged being promised fifty
thousand dollars reward in case he succeeded in destroying the bridges from Atlanta to Chattanooga, but
I never heard of such a contract. Certainly no reward
whatever was promised directly or indirectly to the
soldiers who accompanied him, and I never heard
Andrews himself speak of expecting any pecuniary
recompense.

Mr. Andrews was nearly six feet in height, of powerful frame, black hair, and long, black, and silken
beard, Roman features, a high and expansive forehead,
and a voice fine and soft as a woman's. Of polished
manners, stately presence, and more than ordinary personal beauty, wide information, great shrewdness and
sagacity, he was admirably fitted to win favor in a
community like that of the South, which has always
placed a high value on personal qualities. He had also
the clear forethought in devising complicated schemes,
and the calmness in the hour of danger necessary for
the perilous game he played. Carrying his life in his
hand whenever he ventured beyond the Union pickets,
involved continually in dangers, where a single thought-
less word, or even an unguarded look, might lead to
detection and death, he had learned to rely absolutely on
his own resources, and to contemplate with easy famili-
arity enterprises that would have looked like sheer
madness to one without this preliminary drill.

But it was said that even he had grown tired of this
perpetual risk, and intended, if successful in this last
and most difficult enterprise, to retire to peaceful life.
A tender influence conspired to the same end, and im-
parts a dash of romance to his story. He was engaged
to be married in the following June, and intended then

to retire from the army. Alas! June had a far different fate in store for him.

At our interview in the afternoon, as well as in the midnight consultation, Andrews impressed me as a man who combined intellect and refinement with the most dauntless courage. Yet his pensive manner, slow speech, and soft voice indicated not obscurely what I afterwards found to be almost his only fault as a leader, —a hesitancy in deciding important questions on the spur of the moment, and in backing his decision by prompt, vigorous action. This did not detract from his value as a secret agent when alone, for then all his actions were premeditated and accomplished with surpassing coolness and bravery; but it was otherwise in commanding men in startling and unforeseen emergencies. This trait of character will be more fully developed in the course of the story.

How were the soldiers selected who assembled that evening at the rendezvous? This question was asked with curiosity and wonder by the enemy, and is of great importance in estimating the treatment of such of their number as were afterwards captured. The enemy could not, by their utmost exertions, obtain correct information on this subject; but there is now no reason for reticence. The nature of the enterprise was such that it could not be publicly explained and volunteers called for, as it was quite possible that spies of the enemy were in our camp; neither was it right, according to the laws of war, to divest soldiers of their uniform and place them under the orders of a spy without their full consent. A medium course was adopted, which avoided the opposite difficulties as far as possible. The captains who were ordered to furnish each a man gathered a few of their soldiers about them in a quiet way, and stated that a volunteer was wanted for a very dangerous enterprise. Of those who professed willingness to go one was selected, taken aside from the others, and told simply that he was to be sent

disguised into the heart of the enemy's country, under
the orders of a Southern citizen, whom the commanding officers trusted fully.   If they felt like engaging
in this service, with all its risks, they could see this
man and learn more; but if not, they would be at liberty to decline the dangerous honor.   In one or two
cases these preliminary explanations were so vague that
the men addressed did not fairly understand the matter,
and subsequently declared that if they had been more
fully informed they would not have taken the first
step.   After they met Andrews, however, they felt that
their reputation was at stake, and were not willing to
"back out."   In one or two other cases the men were
merely selected by their captains and ordered, without
any preliminary explanations, to report to Andrews
outside of the lines.

Twenty-four men were thus detailed, twenty-three
of whom met at the rendezvous.   The twenty-fourth
we never heard of; whether he tried to reach us and
failed, or whether some one of the captains who was to
furnish a man was unable to induce any one to accept
the dangerous honor, is uncertain.   Indeed, there must
have been a failure of two men, for we had one with
us who was not originally expected to go.   Captain
Mitchel had one man to furnish, and Perry G. Shadrach was chosen.   William Campbell, a native of
Salineville, Ohio, but for many years a citizen of Kentucky, a man of wild and adventurous habits, was visiting Shadrach, and at once asked and obtained permission to go with him.   Though he was only a civilian,
we always spoke of him as an enlisted soldier of Captain Mitchel's company.

While we are splashing along in the darkness and
under the fast-falling rain, it may be a good time to describe the members of the squad with whom I travelled.
Shadrach and Campbell were two of its members.   The
former was small but roundly built, a merry, reckless
fellow, often profane, easily put out of temper, but very

kind, and willing to sacrifice anything for a friend. Campbell was physically the strongest man of the whole party and possibly of Mitchel's division as well. He weighed two hundred and twenty pounds, was perfectly proportioned, very active, apparently fond of danger for its own sake, and as true as steel. Neither of these two men possessed much skill in duplicity or shrewdness in planning. They were willing to leave the task of asking and answering questions to their comrades, but were always ready to bear their full share in action.

The third, George D. Wilson, of Cincinnati, was of very different character. He was not highly educated, though he had read a great deal, but in natural shrewdness I have rarely, if ever, known his equal. He was of middle age, whilst most of us had just passed out of boyhood. He had traveled extensively, and had observed and remembered everything he encountered. In the use of fiery and scorching denunciations he was a master, and took great delight in overwhelming an opponent with an unmeasured torrent of abuse. In action he was brave and cool; no danger could frighten him, no emergency find him unprepared. The friendship I felt for him grew steadily until his tragic death. I depended on his judgment and advice more than on that of any one in the whole expedition.

The writer was first corporal in Company G of the Second Regiment of Ohio Volunteers, and had just been promoted to the position of sergeant. I was twenty-two years of age, a native of Jefferson County, Ohio, had been reared on a farm, had taught school in the winters, and more recently had entered on the study of law. My opportunities for acquiring knowledge were very limited, but had been tolerably well improved. I had read a good many volumes and gained a fair English education. For war and warlike affairs I had not the slightest taste, and was indeed so near-sighted that it was very doubtful whether I

could ever make an efficient soldier. When the call
for three months' troops was made at the bombardment
of Fort Sumter, I felt that the emergency was so great
as to require the services of every patriot, and immediately enlisted. I did not then contemplate a longer
term of service, as I believed that the government
would be able to organize an adequate force within that
period from those who were better adapted to the profession of arms. My decision to enter the ranks was
not made without some forethought. Just previous to
putting my name to the enlistment paper, I took a solitary night walk and tried to bring up in imagination
all the perils and discomforts that were possible in
military service, asking myself whether I was willing
to endure any of them that might fall to my lot as the
result of the step I then contemplated. Having decided, I returned to the mass-meeting (convened in the
court-house of Steubenville, Ohio) and entered my name
as a volunteer. The company formed that night was
hurried to Washington, and on the route was organized
with others into the Second Ohio Regiment. During
the three months' service our only experience of fighting was in the badly-managed battle, or rather skirmish,
of Bull Run. On the battle-field, when the tide of
fortune turned against us, I concluded that I ought to
re-enlist for two reasons. It was hard to quit the army
with no experience but that of defeat, and the country's
need of men was still urgent. When the Second Ohio
was reorganized for three years' service, I therefore continued in the ranks. We were sent to Eastern Kentucky, and succeeded, after some trifling engagements,
in clearing that part of the State from rebels. We were
then ordered to Louisville, and greatly to my delight
were put under the command of the astronomer Mitchel.
A few years before I had studied astronomy enthusiastically, and had even gone so far as to construct a ten-
foot telescope for my own use. This similarity of
tastes led me to feel greatly delighted, and almost ac-

WILLIAM PITTENGER.

[1882—twenty years later.]

Page 42.

quainted, with our new general. His fame as an astronomer did not guarantee his success in war; but the ability displayed in one profession was a hopeful indication for the other. Our division participated in the advance upon Bowling Green and afterwards upon Nashville. This service offered no hardship except wintry marches, for the capture of Fort Donelson by General Grant had broken the enemy's resistance. During this march there was not perfect accord between Mitchel and his less energetic superior, General Buell. Even the soldiers learned something of their disputes, and were much gratified when, at Nashville, Mitchel was detached from the main army and left to operate independently. In three days he marched to Murfreesborough, where this narrative opens.

On parting from Andrews we worked our way eastward, keeping not far from the railroad leading to Wartrace. We did not wish to travel very far through the rain, which was almost pouring down, but only to get well beyond the Federal pickets, so as to have a clear track for a long journey on the following day. We wished to elude our own pickets, not only to avoid detention, but to gain a little practice in such work. It was our intention to get that night beyond Wartrace, where our last outpost in that direction was stationed; but our progress was so slow and fatiguing that we changed our minds, and determined to find a lodging at once. This resolution was more easily made than accomplished.

For a long time we searched in vain. It seemed as if the country was uninhabited. At length the barking of a dog gave a clue, which was diligently followed. The better to prosecute the search, we formed a line within hearing distance of each other, and then swept around in all directions. A barn was our first discovery, but we were so completely wet and chilled that we resolved to persevere in hope of a bed and a fire.

Shortly after, finding a rude, double log house, we

roused the inmates and demanded shelter for the night. The farmer was evidently alarmed, but let us in, and then began to investigate our character.

I narrate minutely the events that accompanied our first setting out, not so much for their intrinsic interest, as for the sake of giving a vivid idea of the conduct required by the nature of our expedition. This may also be a good place to answer a question often asked, "How can the equivocation and downright falsehood that follows be justified?" I am not bound to attempt any formal justification; but it is easy to show that all the moral question involved is only a branch of the larger question as to the morality of war. In its very nature, war is compounded of force and fraud in nearly equal quantities. If one of the necessary ingredients be wrong, the other can hardly be right. The most conscientious general thinks nothing of making movements with the sole purpose of deceiving his adversary, or of writing absolutely false despatches for the same purpose. If it be right to kill our fellow-beings, I suppose it is also right to deceive them in order to get a better chance to kill them! The golden rule, which is the basis of all morality, has but little place as between hostile armies or nations. To find where some unsuspecting persons are asleep, and steal upon them, begin to shoot and stab before they can wake to defend themselves, would, in peace, be thought a crime of the most dastardly and ferocious character; but, in war, it is only a surprise, and, if successful, confers the greatest honor upon those who plan and execute it. Are there two sets of morals, —the one for peace, the other for war? "But," the objector may continue, "is not a constant resort to falsehood in a secret expedition peculiarly dishonorable?" Let us look this question fairly in the face. All armies employ spies, and the old adage, "The receiver is as bad as the thief," is here fully applicable. A general who induces a man, by the hope of money or promotion, to go disguised into the enemy's lines.

with a lie in his mouth, for the general's advantage, is a full partner in the enterprise, and cannot throw off his share of the guilt. It is true that the laws of war throw all the odium on the spy. But the generals, and not the spies, made the laws of war. Besides, there is no necessary connection between the laws of war and the laws of morality. The former are merely the rules men construct for the regulation of the most tremendous of all their games, and can never affect the essence of right and wrong. I do not wish to argue the abstract right of deceiving an enemy, or of deviating from the strict truth for any purpose whatever. It is enough for my purpose to show that deception is an element in all war. The candid reader will also consider that most of us were very young. The common sentiment of the camp was that deceiving a rebel in any manner was a meritorious action. With the full sanction of our officers, we had entered upon an expedition which required disguise and deception. We had been expressly told that we were not even to hesitate in joining the rebel army,—which implied taking the oath of allegiance to the Confederacy,—if that step became necessary to avoid detection. In the whole of this expedition we were true to each other and to the mission upon which we had entered, but we did not hesitate at any kind or degree of untruthfulness directed towards the enemy. Such was the effect of our resolution in this direction that no one, so far as I remember, ever expressed any sorrow or remorse for any of the falsehoods that were so plentifully employed. Indeed, while the war lasted, I did not find a single person, in the army or out, who ever criticised our expedition from the *moral* stand-point. There seemed to be some kind of an instinctive feeling that the revolted States had forfeited all their rights by rebellion,—even that of having the truth told to them. I confess that deception was very painful to me at first, and from inclination, as well as policy, I used it as sparingly as possible. But practice made it comparatively easy and pleasant, within the limits indicated above.

We did not wait for all these reasonings before we began to practise deception upon our host. He was informed that we were Kentuckians, disgusted with the tyranny of the Lincoln government, and seeking an asylum in the free and independent South. His reply was a grateful surprise. "Oh," said he, "you come on a bootless errand, and might as well go home again and make the best of it. The whole South will soon be as much under Lincoln as Kentucky is."

"Never!" we answered. "We'll fight till we die, first!"

At this the old man chuckled quietly, but only said, "Well, we'll see, we'll see." We found him to be an enthusiastic Union man, but firmly maintained our own assumed character. He provided us with a good supper, late as it was, and with good beds, which we refused to occupy until he had promised not to betray us to the Union pickets.

The next morning we were early on our way, reaching Wartrace in the midst of a pelting storm. Attempting to pass directly through, our soldiers on guard were too vigilant for us, and we enjoyed another opportunity for "diplomacy," in the endeavor to represent ourselves as innocent citizens from the adjoining country. But it was more difficult to deceive our own men than the enemy, and, to avoid detection, we were obliged to reveal our true character, which secured our immediate release.

We plodded onward through the deep mud and splashing roads, and were now outside our own lines. Our only safety, from this time, lay in our disguise and in our false tongues. We felt not unlike the landsman who for the first time loses sight of the shore, and feels the heaving of the broad ocean under his feet. To the average Northern citizen a vague mystery and terror had rested over the whole of the Southern

States, even before the beginning of the war. During
the existence of slavery no Northern man dared make
his home in the presence of that institution and express
any views unfavorable to it. Many tales of violence
and blood were reported from that region long before
hostilities began, and as the passions which led to the
contest grew more fierce, the shadows still deepened.
When war began the curtain fell, and only reports of
wild and desperate enthusiasm in behalf of the cause
of disunion and slavery, with stories of the most cruel
oppression of the few who dared to differ with the
ruling class in still loving the old flag, reached Northern ears. No doubt there were many exaggerations,
but there was a solid basis of fact. The South was
swept with a revolutionary frenzy equal to any that
history recalls, and the people were ready to sacrifice
any one whose life seemed dangerous to their cause.
Even exaggeration was potent as truth in aiding to invest the region beyond the Union lines with mysterious
horror. Into this land of peril and fear and frequent
outrage we were plunging as the secret but deadly enemies of the whole people. Now, when Chattanooga
and Atlanta are brought into such easy communication
with Northern cities, it is difficult to recall the feelings
with which they were regarded in the dark days of
eighteen hundred and sixty-two. But hope and courage outweighed apprehension in our hearts, and we
pushed rapidly forward.

Others of our party were occasionally seen trudging
along in the dreary rain, and sometimes we went with
them a little way, but mostly we kept by ourselves.
Shortly after noon we crossed Duck River, and entered Manchester, stopping just long enough to get the
names of some of the prominent secessionists along our
proposed route, that we might always have some one
to inquire for, and be recommended from one influen-
tial man to another. Nightfall this evening (Tuesday)
found us still several miles from Hillsborough, and we

began to fear that we would be behind time in reaching our destination. Each one was weary and stiff, but we resolved to make every effort, and, if necessary, travel a whole night rather than be too late. I have always been sorry that this night journey was not required of us.

At the place where we lodged that night I first heard a slave-holder talk of hunting negroes with blood-hounds. In conversation after supper our host said to us, as a mere matter of news, "I saw some persons dodging about the back of the plantation just as it was getting dark, and in the morning I will take the hounds and go out and hunt them up. I will be glad to have you go along and see the sport, if you can afford the time. If they prove to be negroes I will make something."

"What will you do with them?" I asked.

"Oh, turn them over to the authorities and get the reward," was the answer. "I have caught a considerable number, and it pays to keep on the lookout."

Of course we had to agree outwardly; but the idea of hunting human beings with the ferocious-looking dogs we had seen about his door, and that for money, thrilled me with detestation and horror. Soon afterwards we found that blood-hounds were not kept for negroes alone.

After a sound night's rest we continued our journey, and were fortunate enough to find a man who was willing, for the good of the Confederacy, and for an extravagant price in money, to give us a short ride. The conveyance was an old wagon, with a wood-rack for a bed, four mules, with a scanty chain harness, ropes for bridles and lines, a driver black as ebony, who rode the lead mule, with a straw bag for a saddle, and flourished a fine black-snake whip,—the latter the only really good article in the whole "turnout." Seven or eight of our party were now together, and we rattled merrily over the stony road, holding on to the sides of the old wool-rack, and agreeing that this was much better than walking. About the middle of the forenoon we came in sight of the Cumberland Mountains. It was now Wednesday, our second day outside of our own lines.

Never have I beheld more beautiful scenery. For a short time the rain ceased to fall and the air became clear. The mountains shone in the freshest green, and about their tops clung a soft, shadowy mist, gradually descending lower, and shrouding one after another of the spurs and high mountain valleys from view. But the beautiful scene did not long continue. Soon the mist deepened into cloud, and the interminable rain began again to fall. To add to our discontent, our wagon could go no farther, and we once more waded in the mud.

At noon we found a dinner of the coarsest fare at a miserable one-roomed hut. One of our men, not belonging, however, to the squad I usually travelled with, managed to get possession of a bottle of apple-brandy, which he used so freely as to become very talkative. He was placed between two others, who kept him from all communication with strangers, and walked him rapidly on until he became sober. This was the only instance of such dangerous imprudence in the whole journey.

From the personal narrative of J. Alfred Wilson, who was with us by this time, I will make frequent extracts, though by no means always indorsing his opinions as to military affairs, or the hopefulness of our enterprise. He was a man of great resolution and endurance, though by no means of hopeful temper. He says,—

"Not till fairly away from the sight of the old flag and of our regiments, and entirely within the enemy's line, could we begin to realize the great responsibility we had incurred. To begin with, we had cast aside our uniforms and put on citizen's clothes, and assumed all the penalties that, in military usage, the word *spy* implies, which is death the world over. Again, our mission was such that concealment was impossible. We were sure to

arouse the whole Confederacy and invoke the brutal vengeance
of its frenzied leaders in case we did not make good our escape
after doing our work. The military spy, in the ordinary line of
his duty, is not compelled to expose himself to detection. On
the contrary, he conceals, in every possible way, his identity.
This we could do until in the heart of the enemy's country, the
very place where we would be in the greatest danger."

Some of the groups fell into the natural error of
overdoing their part, and by the very violence with
which they denounced the United States government
excited suspicion. One party of five or six made a
narrow escape from this kind of danger. Their talk
was too extravagant and their answers to some questions somewhat contradictory. As none but citizens
were then present, no objections were made to their
statements; but a company of rebel guerillas was secretly summoned, and they were pursued. The guerillas
arrived at a house where this party had passed the
night but a few moments after they had resumed their
journey in the morning. The pursuit was continued;
but growing somewhat weary, and receiving more re-
assuring accounts of the travellers ahead, the chase was
abandoned, and our comrades escaped.

Two others of our number were less fortunate. They
became involved in the same manner, were followed,
overtaken, and arrested. They told their Kentucky
story in vain, but as they professed their willingness to
enlist in the rebel army, that privilege was granted
them. They were sent to the nearest post and duly
sworn in. Not long afterwards they took the step that
had been in their minds at the hour of enlistment by
endeavoring to desert. One of them succeeded, but
the other was arrested, and had to suffer a long and
severe imprisonment. Finally, however, he was sent
back to camp, and his next attempt at desertion was
more successful.

In conversation my own group was careful to take a
very moderate though decided Southern tone. It was
agreed that Wilson and myself should, as far as possible,

do all the talking when in the presence of the enemy. On entering towns it was our custom to go directly to the street corners and the groceries, inquire for the latest news, tell our Kentucky story as often as it seemed necessary, deny some of the reports of Union outrages and confirm others, assuring the bystanders that the Yankees were not half so bad as reported, and especially that they would fight, as otherwise they would never have conquered our great State of Kentucky, and then demand, in the name of the common cause of the South, direction and assistance on our way. We thus acquired much information, and were never once suspected. It is my deliberate opinion that we could have travelled from Richmond to New Orleans in the same manner at that period of the war.

A little way out ·from our camp Dorsey met a man who seemed to be a Southern spy, and on the strength of this suspicion was strongly tempted to shoot him to prevent the irreparable harm he might do us. A little watching, however, partly dispelled first impressions. The same man afterwards offered Wilson a liberal reward to pilot him over the mountains, and actually claimed to be a Confederate spy. Wilson kept with him for a time and watched him narrowly, but became convinced that he had not the least suspicion of our expedition. He allowed him, therefore, to go on his way in peace. It is possible that he was not what he pretended, any more than we ourselves were Kentucky citizens. This man was met once more in Chattanooga, but then disappeared.

As we were mounting the first spurs of the Cumberland Mountains we encountered a Confederate soldier from the East, who was then at home on a furlough. He had been in many battles, among them the battle of Bull Run, which he described minutely. Little did he think that I, too, had been there, as we laughed together at the wild panic of the fugitive Yankees. He was greatly delighted to see so many Kentuckians coming out on the right side in the great struggle, and contrasted our conduct with that of some mean-spirited persons in his own neighborhood who were so foolish and depraved as to still sympathize with the abolitionists.

When we parted he grasped my hand with tears in his eyes, and said he hoped " the time would soon come when we would be comrades, fighting side by side in one glorious cause!" My heart revolted from the hypocrisy I was compelled to use, but having begun there was no possibility of turning back. We clambered up the mountain till the top was reached; then across the level summit for six miles; then down again by an unfrequented road over steep rocks, yawning chasms, and great gullies cut out by recent rains. This rough jaunt led us down into Battle Creek, which is a picturesque valley opening out into the Tennessee, and hemmed in by projecting ranges of lofty mountains. As we descended the slopes, a countryman we had overtaken told me how the valley had obtained its name. The legend is very romantic, and probably truthful.

There was an Indian war between two neighboring tribes in early times. One of them made a plundering expedition into the territory of the other, and after securing their booty retreated homeward. They were promptly pursued, and traced to this valley. The pursuers believed them to be concealed within its rocky limits, and to make their capture sure divided their force into two bands, each of which crept along the steep opposite sides towards the head of the valley. It was early in the morning, and as they worked their way cautiously along the mountain mist rolled downward as we had seen it do that morning, and enveloped each of the parties in its folds. Determined not to be foiled, they kept on, and meeting at the head of the valley, each supposed the other to be the foe. They poured in their fire, and a deadly conflict ensued. Not

till the greater number of their braves had fallen did
the survivors discover their sad mistake; then they
slowly and sorrowfully retreated to their wigwams.
The plunderers, who had listened to their conflict in
safety, being higher up the mountain, were left to bear
off their booty in triumph.

But we had little leisure for legendary tales. We
rested for the night with a wealthy secessionist, whom
our soldier friend on the mountains had designated as
" the right kind of a man." He received us with open
arms, and shared the best his house afforded. We
spent the evening in denouncing the policy of the Federal government and in exchanging views as to the
prospects of the war. Among other topics I happened
to mention an expatriation law which, as I had learned
from a newspaper paragraph, had been passed by the
Kentucky Legislature a few weeks before. This law
only made the reasonable provision that all persons
going South to join the rebel army should lose their
rights of State citizenship. The old man thought this
to be an act of unparalleled oppression; and in the
morning, before we were out of bed, he came into our
room and requested some of us to write down that infamous law that he might be able to give his Union
neighbors a convincing proof of Yankee wickedness!
We complied, and all signed our names as witnesses.
No doubt that document was long the theme of angry
discussion in many a mountain cabin.

So thoroughly did we maintain our assumed character
in this instance, that three days after, when the culmi-
nation of our enterprise came to the Confederates like
a clap of thunder out of a clear sky, it was impossible
to make our host believe that his guests were among
the adventurers. This we learned from a Union man
to whom he had shown a copy of the terrible expatriation law!

We were still more than forty miles distant from
Chattanooga on this Wednesday evening, and were due

at that place by five o'clock the next day. On each of the two preceding days we had measured about thirty miles,—a good rate of speed, but not sufficient. We had formed the resolution of taking a night journey of ten or fifteen miles, but before starting after supper, another squad arrived and managed to tell us that they had seen Andrews and been informed that the grand enterprise was postponed one day. This was a great relief, for it was hard to tear away from our comfortable quarters; but this delay was a serious mistake. In all combined movements in war, time is of prime importance. On the appointed Friday success would have been easy; on Saturday—but we must not anticipate.

Andrews had also caused the advice to be passed along the line that it would be better to attempt to cross the Tennessee at some point far west of Chattanooga, and taking passage on the Memphis and Charleston Railroad, endeavor to pass through Chattanooga by rail. He had heard of stringent orders being issued against any one crossing the river near this town without a pass. Farther down the stream these orders might not apply, or, in case of necessity, a raft might be constructed among the wooded mountains, and a passage obtained by that means.

About noon of the next day we came to Jasper, and spent a short time in the principal grocery of the place talking over the state of the country. We informed the idlers that there would soon be a mighty uprising of Kentuckians in favor of the Southern cause, but professed ignorance of the movements of Mitchel's army. In return we received the first vague reports of the battle of Pittsburg Landing. It was the impression that the Union army was totally destroyed, thousands of men being slain, and innumerable cannon captured. One countryman assured me that five hundred Yankee gunboats had been sunk! I ventured to suggest a doubt as to the Yankees having so many, but was not able to shake his faith.

The same night we reached the banks of the Tennessee, directly south of Jasper, and lodged at the house of a Mrs. Hall. A flat-boat owned by one of the neighbors was used as a ferry-boat, and arrangements were made for setting us on the other side of the stream early in the morning. The evening spent here was very enjoyable. Others of our party came in, and among them Andrews himself. After a good supper, we were all assigned to the best room, which had a roaring wood-fire in an open chimney, and two large beds in the corners. We met without any outward sign of recognition, but rapidly became acquainted. Each acted according to his own nature. The bountiful supper and the cheerful fire greatly refreshed us after the labor of the day. My companion, Shadrach, was soon acknowledged as the wit of the party, and received perpetual applause for his mirthful sallies. Andrews was silent, but appeared to greatly enjoy the fun. Dorsey, who had great forethought and prudence, and had decided that it was good policy, even among his comrades, to appear as ignorant as possible, felt highly complimented when told that his group had been described to some of the others who followed as " a party of country Jakes." Wilson gave us all the information wanted on every possible subject. Songs were sung, stories were told, and as the family formed part of the fireside company, many of the incidents may not have been quite authentic. Late at night this social evening's entertainment closed. It was the more highly appreciated as it was the first opportunity most of us had enjoyed of becoming acquainted with our leader and with each other.

In the morning Andrews started up the river on horseback. The flat-boat was bailed out, and we were just entering it, when a mounted man appeared and handed the ferryman an order forbidding him to allow any one to cross the river at his ferry for three days. We tried to get an exception made in our favor, as we had contracted with him the evening before, but he was unwilling to assume the risk. The messenger gave us the reason for the order, and a most interesting piece of news it was. General Mitchel was moving rapidly southward for some unknown object, and it was desirable on that account to stop all intercourse with the country beyond the river. The messenger volunteered the comforting assurance that " these brave Kentuckians will no doubt find a warm welcome at Chattanooga," and gave us the best directions in his power for reaching that point. We concealed our disappointment, and as soon as we were alone debated as to the best course to be taken. Two alternatives only were open. One was to build or seize a raft or boat and cross in defiance of the order. This was easy enough in the night, but in daytime it would be very hazardous, and that day, until five o'clock in the afternoon, was the only time at our disposal. We therefore took the only remaining course, and dispersing, hurried over the mountains towards Chattanooga.

Our journey was far from pleasant, as the rocky mountain-spurs here sweep directly down to the bank of this very crooked river. Several times we lost our way in the entanglements of the woods, but at length reached a valley that ran down to the Tennessee directly opposite Chattanooga. The road was now more frequented, and we talked freely with travellers, for all fear of being detected by those we chanced to meet had long since been dissipated.

One countryman related a very interesting item of news from the war in the East. It was to the effect that the Confederate iron-clad " Merrimac" had one day steamed out into the harbor of Fortress Monroe, and after engaging the Union " Monitor" for some hours, with no decisive result, had run alongside of her opponent, and throwing grappling-irons on board, had towed her ashore, where she, of course, fell an easy prey. This may serve as a specimen of the kind of news we perpetually heard while in the Confederate States.

Quite a number of persons—many of them of our own party—were waiting on the banks of the Tennessee River. The assemblage of so many of us on that side of the river was very unfortunate, as it materially increased the risk of discovery; but a very high wind was blowing, and the ferryman feared to risk his little shackly "horse-boat" on the turbulent stream. Our time was nearly exhausted, and we could not afford to wait very long. We urged the boatman very strenuously to set us over at once, but he wished to delay until the wind fell. Nothing as yet had been said to us about passes, but this was explained mentally by the conjecture that there was a guard on the other side, whose inspection we would be obliged to pass,—a more formidable ordeal than we had yet encountered. When requests for a speedy passage failed to move the ferryman, we changed our tactics, and talked in his hearing of the cowardice of Tennessee boatmen as contrasted with Kentuckians, or even the Ohio Yankees. When twelve or sixteen men deliberately attempt to make one man angry, they can generally succeed. The boatman soon tired of our raillery, and, entering his boat, told us to come on and show what we could do by lending him a hand, adding that he would put us over or drown us, he did not care much which. The invitation was promptly accepted, and by pushing with poles and pulling on the limbs of overhanging trees we moved up the stream to a point judged most favorable, and swung out into the waves. The ride was short and not without danger, but the peril on the other side was so much greater that we had little thought to give to the passage. "How should we meet and deceive the guard?" This was the important question. Our surprise was almost equal to our delight when we landed and found no one to bar our progress. The explanation was perfectly simple. The guard had not been placed that afternoon because it was not believed that any one would attempt to cross in the storm. Wondering at our good fortune, we hurried to the cars, and were in time to procure tickets for Marietta before the departure of the train, which was crowded with passengers, many of them Confederate soldiers. In such a crowd it was easy to avoid notice.

Every seat in the cars was filled, and we had to be contented with standing room. The fumes of whiskey and tobacco were very strong. Talking was loud and incessant, and turned mostly upon the great battle of Shiloh, the accounts of which were by no means so extravagant as at first, though a great victory was still claimed. We took part in the conversation freely, judging this to be the best way of maintaining our assumed disguise. No general system of passports had been brought into use, at least in this part of the South, and railway travel was entirely unrestricted.

The sun was about an hour high when we glided out of the depot, and it soon sank to rest behind the hills of Georgia. The time for our perilous attempt drew near. There was some diversity of opinion among the members of the party, as revealed by conversations both before and after, as to the prospects of success. The most of us felt some solicitude, but were far more hopeful than when we left camp. So many incidents had occurred substantially as they had been planned, that trust in the foresight of our leader, with the assurance that all would come out right, was greatly strengthened. The first feeling of strangeness which followed our plunge into the enemy's country had given way to confidence in the impenetrability of our mental disguise. For my own part I scarcely felt a doubt of success. It seemed to me that a dozen modes of escape were open in the improbable event of failure. I saw the dangers surrounding us clearly, but none of them now appeared more formidable than when I first asked Colonel Harris the privilege of joining the expedition. There were

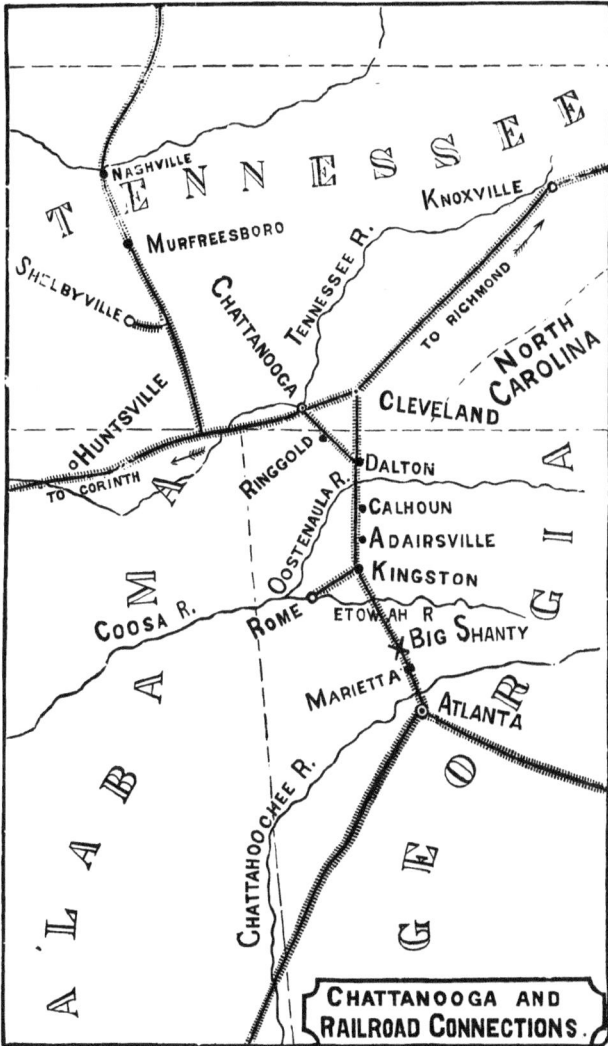

Map showing:

TENNESSEE
- Nashville
- Murfreesboro
- Shelbyville
- Knoxville
- Chattanooga
- Tennessee R.
- TO RICHMOND

NORTH CAROLINA

ALABAMA
- Huntsville
- TO CORINTH
- Coosa R.

GEORGIA
- Cleveland
- Dalton
- Calhoun
- Adairsville
- Kingston
- Ringgold
- Oostenaula R.
- Rome
- Etowah R.
- Big Shanty
- Marietta
- Atlanta
- Chattahoochee R.

CHATTANOOGA AND RAILROAD CONNECTIONS.

many bridges on the road we passed over, and we could not help picturing our return on the morrow and the vengeance we proposed wreaking on them. Darkness closed in, and on we went amid the oaths and laughter of the rebels, many of whom were very much intoxicated. I procured a seat on the coal-box and gave myself up to the thoughts suggested by the hour. There was now no need of trying to keep up conversation with those around. Visions of former days and friends—dear friends, both around the camp-fires and the hearths of home, whom I might never see again—floated before me. I also heard much talk of the merits of different States and regiments in the contest, and many discussions of the conscript law, which was just now coming into force. The opinion of the greater number of the soldiers seemed to be that while the provisions of the law were right in compelling all to take a part in the burdens of the conflict, yet that it would be of but little service, as the unwilling soldiers, who were thus forced into the ranks, would be no match for volunteers. Little did they imagine that in this terrible law their rulers had found a weapon which would enable them to repulse the Northern armies at every point, and protract the war for three years longer!

At this time the Union cause seemed most hopeful. All appearances indicated a speedy termination of the war and a complete re-establishment of the old government. Few great battles had taken place, but the preponderance of fortune as well as force seemed everywhere on the loyal side. In the West, our armies had during the last three months penetrated almost half-way to the Gulf; McClellan was preparing to move with overwhelming force towards Richmond; Burnside was dealing hard blows on the North Carolina coast; the force which captured New Orleans was already on the way; and at no point were the rebel forces a fair match for their opponents. Volunteering had almost stopped in the South, while recruits were pouring as a steady stream into the Northern armies, and continued to do so for a year longer. A rebellion almost isolated and placed everywhere on the defensive could not hope for long life unless new resources were discovered. The rebel leaders well knew this, and therefore passed the conscription law.

It is scarcely an exaggeration to say that there were two wars waged between the North and the South. The first was between the two people by means of volunteers, and the second between the two governments. For the first year the soldiers fought on both sides with scarcely a thought of pay or bounty, and without a hint of compulsion. But the South had reached the end of this period, and her volunteers were beaten and exhausted. This was not from any want of bravery on their part, but because of inferior numbers, and because, having less at stake than the volunteers of the North, they could less willingly support adverse fortune. Now the new law was enacted at the South which put all the able-bodied population at the service of the State. The advantages were immediate and obvious. All the volunteers who had enlisted for a limited time were retained. The depleted organizations were filled up to their full strength, instead of waiting for the recruiting of new regiments, and the conscripts thus became, in a few days, the equals of old soldiers. The second year of the war, in which the Northern volunteers fought the whole force the Southern States could bring into the field, was, on the whole, the most unfavorable of any period to the loyal arms. It became clear that the supremacy of the Union could not be restored unless the same potent weapon could be employed on her behalf. From the hour that the possibility of this was demonstrated, and a draft successfully enforced by the Union government, the issue was virtually decided. Despair might protract the contest, but the utter exhaustion of Southern resources was only a question of time. Was it necessary to permit the war

to pass from the first into the second stage? Might
not the victory of the Union volunteers have been
pushed so rapidly as to have prevented the South from
enforcing the conscription law over any considerable
portion of her territory, and thus have ended the contest at once? These were questions of tremendous importance, which could only be answered in the months
of April and May, 1862. Then was a golden opportunity which once lost could only be regained by years
of desperate fighting. A half-dozen great victories in
midsummer would be of less real value than a vigorous advance in the spring, which should at once dis-
courage the enemy, while at the lowest point of his
fortunes, and prevent the recruiting of his armies by
conscription. It has often been said that the North did
not win any decisive advantage until the abolition of
slavery. This is true, but it does not in the least con-
tradict the view just advanced. That great measure
committed the North absolutely to the conquest of the
South, and thus led to exertions adequate to the end
sought. Yet we must conclude, reasoning from a military point of view only, that if *the same* exertions had
been put forth earlier, they would have been even more
speedily effective.

These considerations, which were but dimly, if at
all, realized as we glided along in the darkness through
the heart of the rebel country, will render more intelli
gible the vast importance attributed by competent military authorities to the expedition in which we were
engaged. If we burned the bridges on the morrow,
General Mitchel would certainly capture Chattanooga
within three or four days, and spread his power over
East Tennessee and all the adjoining loyal distiicts.
The people of this section, now thoroughly alarmed and
enraged by the conscription, would enlist under his
banner by tens of thousands. Seven regiments had
already been formed by East Tennesseeans, who, under
circumstances of the greatest difficulty, had run away

6

into Kentucky. The communications of the Eastern and the Western rebel armies would be cut; and to destroy those armies in detail would only require the vigorous advance of the forces already opposed to them. This was a brilliant prospect to set before an expedition composed of only twenty-four men; but there is in it nothing beyond the realm of probability. and as I thought of the mere possibility of such achievements I felt that we might afford to despise all personal danger. To deliver a territory occupied by nearly a million citizens from conscription; to place an army in the most important strategical position in the rebel territory, for such Chattanooga was; to give the command of the great continental system of railways into the hands of our own troops, and to paralyze the plans of the enemy; these were, indeed, almost incredible results to flow from such a cause; but we believed then that such would be the meaning of our success. The reader who will study attentively the military situation as it was in 1862, with the railroads then existing, and add the fact that the Southern armies were then depleted to the lowest point reached during the struggle, will not be disposed to smile at such possibilities. It is certain that in the first hour of panic, caused by our attempt, the Confederates themselves acknowledged, not in words only, but in the most significant actions, the deadly peril to which they had been exposed.

With such thoughts the hours passed not unpleasantly. I noticed that we were making very slow time, and afterwards learned that this was general on Southern roads. The absorption in warlike affairs and the scarcity of iron and all other material, as well as of money, had caused the managers of the railroads to let them fall into bad repair, and this necessitated a low rate of speed. The fastest train on this road did not get beyond eighteen miles an hour. This was a decidedly unfavorable element in the problem we were to solve. Some of the adventurers were even less favorably impressed with our prospects than I was. The immense business of the road, which had become one of the most important in the whole South, rendered the running of a train when we captured it much more difficult. We saw many freight trains lying at the stations, and everything indicated that the capacity of this line of rail was being pressed to the utmost. Sergeant Ross and Alfred Wilson took the most gloomy view of our prospects of success, and even sought an opportunity, soon after, to dissuade Andrews from going any further in it. The latter thus explains his own feelings,—

" After getting seated, and there being no further cause of concern for the time being, I began to carefully study over the situation with all the thought I could, and to calculate our chances of success or failure. The result of my deliberations was by no means encouraging. We were one day behind the time appointed. I knew, too, or felt sure, that General Mitchel would not fail to march upon and take Huntsville, according to the arrangement made when we started. I also felt that if he did so there would be little room to hope for our success. It would cause the roads to be crowded with trains flying from danger, and it would be difficult to pass them all in safety. But it was too late now to change the programme. We must make the effort, come what might. I said nothing, however, to any one but Andrews; but on listening to my opinion on the situation, he encouraged me by saying there was yet a good chance to succeed. Indeed, he expressed himself in so sanguine a manner that I made no further argument; but I still thought my course of reasoning correct, whether the event should accord with it or not."

From the soldiers and others in the train we received a rumor which was full of startling interest to us,— nothing less than the reported capture of Huntsville by General Mitchel. Much incredulity was expressed, and details were wanting. His force was reported at twenty-five or thirty thousand men,—an extravagant but not unnatural over-estimate. We had no doubt of the truth of the report, though it would have better suited us if he also had been detained for one day, or even more.

It was near nine o'clock when the train reached the supper station. After all our fatigue we were well prepared to do justice to the bountiful meal that was spread. But there was such a rush for the table that several of our party were unable to get near it, and had therefore to continue their fast. The writer was more fortunate. Buffum, who was crowded back on account of his small size, managed to stoop down and slip up under the arm of a rebel officer just as the latter was rising from the table, and thus took his place while a half-dozen hungry travellers rushed for it. There was some laughing, and Buffum was applauded for his "Yankee trick," more than he would have been had it been known that he was actually a native of Massachusetts, and then engaged in the Federal service.

The train rushed on after we left the supper station, and as I had managed to get a good meal and also a comfortable seat in the changing, all reflections and dangers were soon forgotten in a sound sleep, from which I only awakened when the conductor shouted "Marietta!" It was then almost midnight, and the goal was reached. This was, for the present, the utmost boundary of our journey. We were now in the centre of the Confederacy, and before we departed had a blow to strike that would either make all rebeldom vibrate from centre to circumference or leave us at the mercy of the merciless. But the first thing to be done was to snatch a short repose preparatory to the hard work of the morrow.

CHAPTER IV.

A LOCOMOTIVE AND TRAIN CAPTURED.

THE greater number of us arranged to pass the night at a small hotel adjoining the Marietta depot. Before retiring we left orders with the hotel clerk to rouse us in time for the northward bound train, due not long after daylight. Notwithstanding our novel situation, I never slept more soundly. Good health, extreme fatigue, and the feeling that the die was now cast and further thought useless, made me sink into slumber almost as soon as I touched the bed. Others equally brave and determined were affected in a different way. Alfred Wilson says,—

"No man knows what a day may bring forth, and the very uncertainty of what that day's sun would bring forth in our particular cases was the reason that some of us, myself at least of the number, did not sleep very much. Our doom might be fixed before the setting of another sun. We might be hanging to the limbs of some of the trees along the railroad, with an enraged populace jeering and shouting vengeance because we had no more lives to give up ; or we might leave a trail of fire and destruction behind us, and come triumphantly rolling into Chattanooga and Huntsville, within the Federal lines, to receive the welcome plaudits of comrades left behind, and the thanks of our general, and the praises of a grateful people. Such thoughts as these passed in swift review, and were not calculated to make one sleep soundly."

As the hotel was much crowded, we obtained a few rooms in close proximity, and crowded them to their utmost capacity. Andrews noted our rooms before retiring, that he might, if necessary, seek any one of us out for consultation before we rose. Porter and Hawkins were unfortunately overlooked ; they had arrived on an earlier train and obtained lodging at some distance from the depot. The clerk failed to have them called in time for the morning train, as they had ordered, and, greatly to their regret and chagrin, they were left behind. This was a serious loss, as they were both cool, brave men, and Hawkins was the most experienced railway engineer of our company. W. F. Brown, who took his place in this work, was, however, fully competent, though possibly somewhat less cautious.

Long before the train was due, Andrews, who had slept little, if at all, that night, glided from room to room silently as a ghost, the doors being purposely left unfastened, and aroused the slumberers. It seemed to some of us scarcely a moment from the time of retiring until he came thus to the bedside of each sleeper in turn, and cautiously wakening him, asked his name, to prevent the possibility of mistake, and then told each one exactly the part he was expected to take in the enterprise of the day. There was hasty dressing, and afterwards an informal meeting held in Andrews' room, at which nearly one-half of the whole number were present, and plans were more fully discussed. Then Marion A. Ross, one of the most determined of the whole number, took the bold step of advising and even urging the abandonment, for the present, of the whole enterprise. He reasoned with great force that under present circumstances, with the rebel vigilance fully aroused by Mitchel's rapid advance, with guards stationed around the train we were to capture, as we had learned would be the case at Big Shanty, and with the road itself obstructed by numerous trains, the enterprise was sure to fail, and would cost the life of every man engaged in it. Andrews very gently answered his arguments and strove to show that the objections urged really weighed in favor of the original plan. No such attempt as we purposed had ever been made, and consequently would not be guarded against; the presence of a line of sentinels and of so many troops at Big Shanty would only tend to relax vigilance still further; and the great amount of business done on the road, with the running of many unscheduled trains, would screen us from too close inquiry when we ran our train ahead of time. This reasoning was not altogether satisfactory, and some of the others joined Ross in a respectful but firm protest against persisting in such a hopeless undertaking. But Andrews, speaking very low, as was his wont when thoroughly in earnest, declared that he had once before postponed the attempt, and returned to camp disgraced. "Now," he continued, "I will accomplish my purpose or leave my bones to bleach in Dixie. But I do not wish to control any one against his own judgment. If any of you think it too hazardous, you are perfectly at liberty to take the train in the opposite direction and work your way back to camp as you can."

This inflexible determination closed the discussion, and as no man was willing to desert his leader, we all assured him of our willingness to obey his orders to the death. I had taken no part in the discussion, as I was not in possession of sufficient facts to judge of the chance of success, and I wished the responsibility to rest upon the leader, where it properly belonged.

The train was now nearly due, and we proceeded to the station for the purchase of tickets. By the time they had been procured—not all for one place, as we wished to lessen the risk of suspicion—the train swept up to the platform. Hastily glancing at it in the early morning light, and seeing only that it was very long and apparently well filled, the twenty adventurers entered by different doors, but finally took their places in one car.

From Marietta to Big Shanty the railroad sweeps in a long bend of eight miles around the foot of Kenesaw Mountain, which lies directly between the two stations. This elevation is now scarred all over with rebel intrenchments, and was the scene of one of the severest contests of the war. This, however, as well as the whole of the three months' struggle from Chattanooga to Atlanta, came a year and a half later. At this time the nearest Federal soldiers were more than two hundred miles away.

When the train moved on and the conductor came to take our tickets we observed him carefully, as we knew not how closely his fate and ours might be linked together in the approaching struggle. The most vivid anticipation fell far short of the reality. Upon the qualities of that one man our success or failure hinged. He was quite young—not more than twenty-three or four, —and looked like a man of resolution and energy. We noticed that he was also scrutinizing us and the other passengers very closely, and naturally feared that he had in some manner been put on his guard. In fact, as we learned long afterwards, he had been warned that some of the new conscripts who were reluctant to fight for the Confederacy were contemplating an escape, and might try to get a ride on the cars. His orders were to watch for all such and arrest them at once. But he did not think that any of the men who got on at Marietta looked in the least like conscripts or deserters.

The train ran slowly, stopping at several intervening points, and did not reach Big Shanty until it was fully daylight. This station had been selected for the seizure, because the train breakfasted there, and it was probable that many of the employés and passengers would leave it for their meal, thus diminishing the opposition we might expect. Another most important reason for the selection was the absence of any telegraph office. But, on the other hand, Camp McDonald had been lately located here, and a large body of soldiers—some accounts said as many as ten thousand men—were already assembled. Their camp included the station within the guard-line. When Andrews and the first party had been at Atlanta, three weeks earlier, few troops had yet arrived at this point. The capture of a train in the midst of a camp of the enemy was not a part of the original plan, but subsequently became necessary. It was certainly a great additional element of danger, but it was not now possible to substitute any other point.

The decisive hour had arrived. It is scarcely boastful to say that the annals of history record few enterprises more bold and novel than that witnessed by the rising sun of Saturday morning, April 12, 1862. Here was a train, with several hundred passengers, with a full complement of hands, lying inside a line of sentinels, who were distinctly seen pacing back and forth in close proximity, to be seized by a mere score of men, and to be carried away before the track could be obstructed, or the intruding engineer shot down at his post. Only the most careful calculation and prompt execution, concentrating the power of the whole band into a single lightning-like stroke, could afford the slightest prospect of success. In the bedroom conference every action was predetermined with the nicest accuracy. Our engineer and his assistant knew the signal at which to start; the brakesmen had their work assigned; the man who was to uncouple the cars knew just the place at which to make the separation; the remainder of the number constituted a guard, in two divisions, who were to stand with ready revolvers abreast of the cars to be seized, and shoot down without hesitation any one who attempted to interfere with the work. Andrews was to command the whole, and do any part of the work not otherwise provided for. Should there be any unexpected hindrance, we were to fight until we either overcame all opposition and captured the train or perished in a body. If we failed to carry off our prize we were inevitably lost; if any man failed to be on board when the signal was given, his fate also was sealed. A delay of thirty seconds after our designs became clearly known would have resulted in the slaughter of the whole party.

When our train rolled up to the platform the usual

announcement was shouted, " Big Shanty; twenty minutes for breakfast!" Most fortunately for us, the conductor, engineer, firemen, and train-hands generally, with many of the passengers, poured out, and hurried to the long, low eating-room which gave its name to the station. The engine was utterly unguarded. This uncommon carelessness was the result of perfect security, and greatly favored our design. Yet it was a thrilling moment! Victory or death hung on the next minute! There was no chance for drawing back, and I do not think any of us had the disposition. A little while before, a sense of shrinking came over the writer like that preceding a plunge into ice-water; but with the next breath it passed away, and left me as calm and quiet as if no enemy had been within a hundred miles. Still, for a moment, we kept our seats. Andrews went forward to examine the track and see if there was any hindrance to a rapid rush ahead. Almost immediately he returned, and said, very quietly, " All right, boys; let us go now." There was nothing in this to attract special observation; but whether it did or not was now a matter of indifference. The time of concealment was past. We rose, left the cars, and walked briskly to the head of the train. With the precision of machinery, every man took his appointed place. Three cars back from the tender the coupling-pin was drawn out, as the load of passenger-cars would only have been an incumbrance. Wilson W. Brown, who acted as engineer, William Knight as assistant, Alfred Wilson as fireman, together with Andrews, mounted the engine, Knight grasping the lever, and waiting the word for starting. The appointed brakesmen threw themselves flat on the top of the cars. At a signal from Andrews, the remainder of the band, who had kept watch, climbed with surprising quickness into a box-car which stood open. All was well! Knight, at Andrews' orders, jerked open the steam-valve, and we were off! Before the camp-guards or the bystanders could do more than

CAPTURE OF A TRAIN.

Page 71.

turn a curious eye upon our proceedings, the train was under way, and we were safe from interruption.

The writer was stationed in the box-car, and as soon as all were in, we pulled the door shut to guard against any stray musket-balls. For a moment of most intense suspense after we were thus shut in all was still. In that moment a thousand conflicting thoughts swept through our minds. Then came a pull, a jar, a clang, and we were flying away on our perilous journey. Those who were on the engine caught a glimpse of the excited crowd, soldiers and citizens, swarming and running about in the wildest confusion. It has been said that a number of shots were fired after us, but those in the box-car knew nothing of it, and it is certain that no one was injured. A widely-circulated picture represented us as waving our hats and shouting in triumph. Nothing so melodramatic took place. The moment was too deep and earnest, and we had too many perils still to encounter for any such childish demonstration.

Yet it was a grand triumph, and having nothing of a more practical character for the moment to do, I realized it to the fullest extent. There are times in life when whole years of enjoyment are condensed into a single experience. It was so with me then. I could comprehend the emotion of Columbus when he first beheld through the dim dawn the long-dreamed-of shores of America, or the less innocent but no less fervent joy of Cortez when he planted the Cross of Spain on the halls of Montezuma. My breast throbbed fast with emotions of joy and gladness that words labor in vain to express. A sense of ethereal lightness ran through my veins, and I seemed ascending higher, higher, with each pulsation of the engine. Remember, I was but twenty-two then, full of hope and ambition. Not a dream of failure shadowed my rapture. We had always been told that the greatest difficulty was to reach and take possession of the engine, after which

success was certain.   But for unforeseen contingencies
it would have been.

Away we rush, scouring past field and village and
woodland.   At each leap of the engine our hearts rose
higher, and we talked merrily of the welcome that
would greet us when we dashed into Huntsville a few
hours later, our enterprise done, and the brightest laurels
of the war eclipsed !

We found the railroad, however, to be of the roughest
and most difficult character.   The grades were very
heavy and the curves numerous and sharp.   We
seemed to be running towards every point of the compass.   The deep valleys and steep hills of this part of
the country had rendered the building of the road difficult and costly.   There were numerous high embank-
ments where an accident would be of deadly character.
The track was also uneven and in generally bad condition, for the war had rendered railroad iron scarce
and high-priced, besides diverting all attention and resources into other channels.   This unfavorable character of the road very greatly increased the difficulty
experienced by an engineer unfamiliar with the route
in making rapid time, or in avoiding the varied difficulties incident to our progress.   But we trusted implicitly that the far-sighted plans of Andrews, the skill
of our engineers, and our own willing efforts would
overcome all hindrances.

Our first run was short.   There was a sudden checking of speed and a halt.   When those of us who were in
the box-car pushed open our door and asked the reason
for stopping so soon, we were told that the fire was low
and the steam exhausted.   This was startling intelligence, and caused a moment of consternation.   If our
" General"—the name of the locomotive we had captured—failed us at the beginning of the race, we too
well knew what the end would be.   For hundreds of
miles on every side of us were desperate and daring
foes.   A hundred times our number of horse and foot

could be gathered against us in a few hours. The most timid bird pursued by hounds feels safe, for its wings can bear it above their jaws. But if those wings should be broken! This engine gave us wings; but if it should be disabled no valor of ours could beat back the hosts about us, no skill elude their rage. But we found a less threatening explanation of our premature halt. The schedule time of our train was very slow,— only about sixteen miles an hour,—and the fires had been allowed to run down because of the expected stop of twenty minutes for breakfast at Big Shanty,—a stop that we had reduced to less than two minutes. Then the valve being thrown wide open, the little steam in the boiler was soon exhausted. But this difficulty was of short duration. A rest of three minutes, with plenty of wood thrown into the furnace, wrought a change, and we again glided rapidly forward.

But when viewed soberly, and in the light of all the facts since developed, what were the chances of success and escape possessed by the flying party? Was the whole attempt, as has been frequently asserted, rash and foolhardy? Or had it that character of practicability which is ever the stamp of true genius? Historical accuracy, as well as justice to the memory of a brave but unfortunate man, compels me to pronounce the scheme almost faultless. In this estimate I have the full concurrence of all who were engaged on the opposite side. It is hard to see how the plan could have been improved without allowing its projector to have had a knowledge of the precise condition of the enemy such as no commander at the beginning of an important enterprise ever has. No one of the plans by which Generals Grant and Sherman finally overthrew the Rebellion presented a clearer prospect of success.

These are the elements of the problem upon which Andrews based his hopes. Big Shanty is twenty-eight miles north of Atlanta and thirty-two south of Kingston. Short of these places he was convinced that no

engine could be obtained for pursuit. He could obstruct the road so that no train would reach Big Shanty
for hours. Pinch-bars and other instruments for lifting track might be found on the captured engine, or
obtained from some station or working-party. His
force of twenty men was counted ample to overcome
resistance at any switch or passing train. One irregular
train only was expected to be on the road, and that
would soon be met,—certainly at Kingston or before,—
after which it would be safe to run at the highest speed
to the first bridge, burn it, and pass on to the next,
which, with all other large bridges, could be served in
the same manner. Each bridge burnt would be an in-
superable barrier to pursuit by an engine beyond that
point. Thus every part of the scheme was fair and
promising. Only those critics who are wise after the
event can pronounce the attempt rash and hopeless.
The destruction of the telegraph would also be necessary; but this was not difficult. It seemed as if every
contingency was provided for, and then there was the
additional fighting power of twenty chosen men to
guard against any possible emergency. We were now
embarked on this most perilous but hopeful voyage.
Coolness, precision of work, and calm effort could
scarcely fail to sever the chief military communications
of the enemy before the setting of the sun, and con-
vince him that no enterprise was too audacious for the
Union arms.

CHAPTER V.

UNFORESEEN HINDRANCES.

AFTER the fire had been made to burn briskly Andrews jumped off the engine, ran back to the box-car,
about the door of which we were standing, and clasped
our hands in an ecstasy of congratulation. He declared
that all our really hard work was done and that our
difficulties were nearly passed; that we had the enemy
at such a disadvantage that he could not harm us; and
exhibited every sign of joy. Said he, "Only one train
to meet, and then we will put our engine to full speed,
burn the bridges that I have marked out, dash through
Chattanooga, and on to Mitchel at Huntsville. We've
got the upper hand of the rebels now, and they can't
help themselves!" How glad we all were! When,
three years later, the capture of Richmond set all the
bells of the North ringing out peals of triumph, the
sensation of joy was more diffused but less intense than
we then experienced. Almost everything mankind
values seemed within our grasp. Oh, if we had met
but one unscheduled train!

This reference of Andrews to one train which he
expected to meet before we began to burn bridges has
been quoted in many public sketches, and has led to
some misapprehension. He did expect to meet three
trains before reaching Chattanooga; but two of these
were regular trains, and being also farther up the road,
were not supposed to present any serious difficulty.
Their position at any given time could be definitely ascertained, and we could avoid collision with them, no
matter how far we ran ahead of time. But so long as
there were any irregular trains on the road before us,

our only safety was in keeping the regular time of the captured train. This was, unfortunately, very slow; but if we exceeded it we lost the right of way, and were liable to a collision at any moment. This risk was greatly increased by our inability to send ahead telegraphic notifications of our position. The order of southward-bound trains, according to the information we then had, was as follows : First, a way-freight, which was very uncertain as to time, but which we expected to meet early in the morning, and felt sure that it would be at Kingston or south of that point. This was the only real hindrance according to our programme, and it was to this train that Andrews referred. Behind this were the regular freight train, and still farther north the regular passenger train. As a matter of fact, we did meet these trains at Adairsville and Calhoun, the latter being somewhat behind time; but we might have met them farther north had it not been for unforeseen hindrances.

There is considerable discrepancy in the many published accounts of the following chase, which the writer has not in every case been able to perfectly reconcile. In the intense excitement and novel situations involved men were not likely to observe or remember every event accurately. But no pains have been spared to combine fulness and completeness in the following account. Using the best of my own recollections, consulting my comrades, reading carefully all published accounts, and especially going over the whole route years after, with Fuller and Murphy, two of the pursuing party, who kindly gave me all the information in their power, it is hoped that substantial accuracy has been obtained. Some of the incidents of the chase, such as the number of times the track was torn up, and whether we were fired upon by pursuing soldiers, allow some room for a conflict of memory. But the variations are not material.

Side by side with the road ran the telegraph-wires,

which were able, by the flashing of a single lightning message ahead, to arrest our progress and dissipate our fondest hopes. There was no telegraph station where we had captured the train, but we knew not how soon our enemies might reach one, or whether they might not have a portable battery at command. Therefore we ran but a short distance, after replenishing the furnace, before again stopping to cut the wire.

John Scott, an active young man of the Twenty-first Ohio, scrambled up the pole with the agility of a cat, and tried to break the wire by swinging upon it; but failing in this, he knocked off the insulating box at the top of the pole and swung with it down to the ground. Fortunately, a small saw was found on the engine, with which the wire was severed in two places, and the included portion, many yards in length, was taken away with us, in order that the ends might not be readily joined.

While one or two of the party were thus engaged others worked with equal diligence in taking up a rail from the track. No good track-raising instruments had been found on the train, and we had not yet procured them from any other source. A smooth iron bar, about four feet long, was the only instrument yet found, and with this some of the spikes were slowly and painfully battered out. After a few had thus been extracted, a lever was got under the rail and the remainder were pried loose. This occupied much more time than cutting the wire, and it required no prophet to foretell that if we did not procure better tools rail-lifting would have to be used very sparingly in our programme. In the present instance, however, the loss of time was no misfortune, as we were ahead of the schedule time, which we still felt bound to observe.

After another rapid but brief run, we paused long enough to chop down a telegraph-pole, cut the wire again, and place the pole, with many other obstructions, on the track. We did not here try to lift a rail; in-

7*

deed, we had little serious fear of any pursuit at this time, and merely threw on these obstructions because of having spare time to employ.

We thus continued—running a little ahead of time, then stopping to obstruct the track and cut the wire—until Cass Station was reached, where we took on a good supply of wood and water. At this place we also obtained a complete time schedule of the road. Andrews told the tank-tender that we were running a powder-train through to the army of General Beauregard at Corinth, which was almost out of ammunition, and that the greatest haste was necessary. He further claimed to be a Confederate officer of high rank, and said that he had impressed this train for the purpose in hand, and that Fuller, with the regular passenger train, would be along shortly. The whole story was none too plausible, as General Mitchel was now interposed between our present position and Beauregard, and we would never have been able to get a train to the army of the latter on this route; but the tender was not critical and gave us his schedule, adding that he would willingly send his shirt to Beauregard if that general needed it. When this man was afterwards asked if he did not suspect the character of the enemy he thus aided, he answered that he would as soon have suspected the President of the Confederacy himself as one who talked so coolly and confidently as Andrews did!

Keeping exactly on regular time, we proceeded without any striking adventures until Kingston was reached. This place—thirty-two miles from Big Shanty—we regarded as marking the first stage of our journey. Two hours had elapsed since the capture of the train, and hitherto we had been fairly prosperous. No track-lifting instruments had yet been obtained, notwithstanding inquiries for them at several stations. We had secured no inflammable materials for more readily firing the bridges, and the road was not yet clear before us. But,

on the other hand, no serious hindrance had yet occurred, and we believed ourselves far ahead of any
possible pursuit.

But at Kingston we had some grounds for appre-
hending difficulty. This little town is at the junction
with the road to Rome, Georgia. Cars and engines
were standing on the side track. Here we fully expected to meet our first train, and it would be necessary for us to get the switches properly adjusted before
we could pass it to go on our way. When we drew
up at the station there was handed to Andrews our
first and last communication from the management of
the road, in the shape of a telegram, ordering Fuller's
train—now ours—to wait at Kingston for the local
freight, which was considerably behind time. The
order was not very welcome, but we drew out on the
side track, and watched eagerly for the train. Many
persons gathered around Andrews, who here, as always,
personated the conductor of our train, and showered
upon him many curious and somewhat suspicious questions. Ours was an irregular train, but the engine was
recognized as Fuller's. The best answers possible were
given. A red flag had been placed on our engine, and
the announcement was made that Fuller, with another
engine, was but a short way behind. The powder story
was emphasized, and every means employed to avoid
suspicion. Andrews only, and the usual complement
of train-hands, were visible, the remainder of the party
being tightly shut up in the car, which was designated
as containing Beauregard's ammunition. The striking personal appearance of Andrews greatly aided him
in carrying through his deception, which was never
more difficult than at this station. His commanding
presence, and firm but graceful address, marked him
as a Southern gentleman,—a member of the class
from which a great proportion of the rebel officers
were drawn. His declarations and orders were therefore received with the greater respect on this account.

But all these resources were here strained to the utmost.

At length the anxiously-expected local freight train arrived, and took its place on another side track. We were about to start on our way, with the glad consciousness that our greatest obstacle was safely passed, when a red flag was noticed on the hindmost freight-car. This elicited immediate inquiry, and we were informed that another very long freight train was just behind, and that we would be obliged to wait its arrival also. This was most unfortunate, as we had been already detained at Kingston much longer than was pleasant. There were many disagreeable elements in the situation. A crowd of persons was rapidly assembling. The train from Rome was also nearly due, and though it only came to the station and returned on its own branch, yet it was not agreeable to notice the constant increase of force that our enemies were gaining. If any word from the southward arrived, or if our true character was revealed in any other way, the peril would be imminent. But we trusted that this second delay would be brief. Slowly the minutes passed by. To us, who were shut up in the box-car, it appeared as if they would never be gone. Our soldier comrades on the outside kept in the background as much as possible, remaining at their posts on the engine and the cars, while Andrews occupied attention by complaining of the delay, and declaring that the road ought to be kept clear of freight trains when so much needed for the transportation of army supplies, and when the fate of the whole army of the West might depend upon the celerity with which it received its ammunition. There was plausibility enough in his words to lull suspicion in all minds except that of the old switch-tender of the place, who grumbled out his conviction " that something was wrong with that stylish-looking fellow, who ordered everybody around as if the whole road belonged to him." But no one paid any attention to this man's complaints, and not many minutes after a distant whistle sounded from the northward, and we felt that the crisis had passed. As there was no more room on the side track, Andrews ordered the switch-tender to let this train run by on the main track. That worthy was still grumbling, but he reluctantly obeyed, and the long success on of cars soon glided by us.

This meant release from a suspense more intolerable than the most perilous action. To calmly wait where we could do nothing, while our destiny was being wrought out by forces operating in the darkness, was a terrible trial of nerve. But it was well borne. Brown, Knight, and Wilson, who were exposed to view, exhibited no more impatience than was to be expected of men in their assumed situation. Those of us in the box-car talked in whispers only, and examined the priming of our pistols. We understood that we were waiting for a delayed train, and well knew the fearful possibilities of an obstructed track, with the speedy detection, and fight against overwhelming odds that would follow, if the train for which we waited did not arrive sooner than pursuers from Big Shanty. When we recognized the whistle of the coming train it was almost as welcome as the boom of Mitchel's cannon, which we expected to hear that evening after all our work was done. As it rumbled by us we fully expected an instant start, a swift run of a few miles, and then the hard work but pleasant excitement of bridge-burning. Alas!

Swift and frequent are the mutations of war. Success can never be assured to any enterprise in advance. The train for which we had waited with so much anxiety had no sooner stopped than we beheld on it an emblem more terrible than any comet that ever frighted a superstitious continent. Another red flag! Another train close behind! This was terrible, but what could be done? With admirable presence of mind Andrews moderated his impatience, and asked the conductor of the newly-arrived train the meaning of such an unusual obstruction of the road. His tone was commanding, and without reserve the conductor gave the full explanation. To Andrews it had a thrilling interest. The commander at Chattanooga had received information that the Yankee General Mitchel was coming by forced marches and in full strength against that town; therefore all the rolling-stock of the road had been ordered to Atlanta. This train was the first instalment, but another and still longer section was behind. It was to start a few minutes after he did, and would probably not be more than ten or fifteen minutes behind. In turn, the conductor asked Andrews who he was, and received the information that he was an agent of General Beauregard, and that he had impressed a train into military service in Atlanta, which he was running through with powder, of which Beauregard was in extreme need. Under such circumstances he greatly regretted this unfortunate detention. The conductor did not suspect the falsity of these pretences, but told Andrews that it was very doubtful if he could get to Beauregard at Corinth by going through Chattanooga, as it was certain that Mitchel had captured Huntsville, directly on the line between them. Andrews replied that this made no difference, as he had his orders, and should press on until they were countermanded, adding that Mitchel was probably only paying a flying visit to Huntsville, and would have to be gone soon, or find Beauregard upon him. Andrews also ordered the conductor to run far enough down the main track to allow the next train to draw in behind him, and for both trains there to wait the coming of Fuller with the regular mail. His orders were implicitly obeyed; and then to our party recommenced the awful trial of quiet waiting. One of the men outside was directed to give notice to those in the box-car of the nature of the detention, and warn them to be ready for any emergency. Either

Brown or Knight, I think, executed this commission. Leaning against our car, but without turning his eyes towards it, and speaking in a low voice, he said, " We are waiting for one of the trains the rebels are running off from Mitchel. If we are detected before it comes, we will have to fight. Be ready." We *were* ready; and so intolerable is suspense that most of us would have felt as a welcome relief the command to throw open our door and spring into deadly conflict.

Slowly the leaden moments dragged themselves away. It seems scarcely creditable, but it is literally true, that for twenty-five minutes more we lay on that side track and waited,—waited with minds absorbed, pulses leaping, and ears strained for the faintest sound which might give a hint as to our destiny. One precious hour had we wasted at Kingston,—time enough to have burned every bridge between that place and Dalton! The whole margin of time on which we had allowed ourselves to count was two hours; now half of that was thrown away at one station, and nothing accomplished. We dared wait no longer. Andrews decided to rush ahead with the intention of meeting this extra train wherever it might be found, and forcing it to back before him to the next siding, where he could pass it. The resolution was in every way dangerous, but the danger would at least be of an active character. Just at this moment the long-expected whistle was heard, and soon the train came into plain view, bringing with it an almost interminable string of cars. The weight and length of its train had caused the long delay. Obedient to direction, it followed the first extra down the main track, and its locomotive was a long way removed from the depot when the last car cleared the upper end of the side track on which we lay. At length it had got far enough down, and it was possible for us to push on. Andrews instantly ordered the switch-tender to arrange the track so as to let us out.

But here a new difficulty presented itself. This man

had been in an ill humor from the first, and was now fully convinced that something was wrong. Possibly the tone in which he was addressed irritated him still more. He therefore responded to Andrews' order by a surly refusal, and hung up the keys in the station-house. When we in the box-car overheard his denial, we were sure that the time for fighting had come. There was no more reason for dreading the issue of a conflict at this station than at any other point, and we waited the signal with the confident expectation of victory.

But even a victory at that moment would have been most undesirable. We had no wish to shed blood unnecessarily. A telegraph office was at hand, and it was possible that before the wire could be cut a message might be flashed ahead. There were also engines in readiness for prompt pursuit, and while we might have overcome immediate opposition by the use of our fire-arms, our triumph would have been the signal for a close and terrible chase.

The daring coolness of Andrews removed all embarrassments. While men are hesitating and in doubt, boldness and promptness on the part of an opponent are almost sure to carry the day. Ceasing to address the switch-tender, Andrews walked hurriedly into the station, and with the truthful remark that he had no more time to waste, took down the key and began to unlock the switch. The tender cursed him terribly, and called for some to arrest him. The crowd around also disliked the action, and began to hoot and yell; but before any one had decided as to what ought to be done Andrews had unlocked and changed the switch, and waved his hand for the engineer to come on. It was an inexpressible relief when the cars moved forward and the sounds of strife died out. As soon as the locomotive passed to the main track, Andrews tossed the keys to the ruffled owner of them, saying, in his blandest manner, " Pardon me, sir, for being in such a hurry, but the Confederacy can't wait for every man's notions. You'll find it is all right," and stepped on board his engine. The excitement gradually ceased, and no thought of pursuit was entertained until startling intelligence was received a few moments later from Big Shanty.

Before describing the terrible struggle above Kingston, it will be well to narrate the operations of the persons whose train had been so unceremoniously snatched from them at Big Shanty. From printed accounts published contemporaneously by several of those engaged in the pursuit, as well as from personal responses to inquiries made regarding the most material points, the writer is confident that he can tell the strange story without essential error. It is a striking commentary on the promptness of the seizure, that the bystanders generally reported that only eight men, instead of twenty, had been observed to mount the train.

William A. Fuller, conductor, Anthony Murphy, manager of the State railroad shops at Atlanta, and Jefferson Cain, engineer, stepped off their locomotive, leaving it unguarded save by the surrounding sentinels, and in perfect confidence took their seats at the breakfast-table at Big Shanty. But before they had tasted a morsel of food the quick ear of Murphy, who was seated with his back towards the window, caught the sound of escaping steam, and he exclaimed, " Fuller, who's moving your train?" Almost simultaneously the latter, who was somewhat of a ladies' man, and was bestowing polite attentions upon two or three fair passengers, saw the same movement, and sprang up, shouting, "Somebody's running off with our train!" No breakfast was eaten then. Everybody rushed through the door to the platform. The train was then fully under way, just sweeping out of sight around the first curve. With quick decision Fuller shouted to Murphy and Cain, " Come on !" and started at a full run after the flying train ! This attempt to run down and catch a locomotive by a foot-race seemed so absurd that

8

as the three, at the top of their speed, passed around the same curve, they were greeted with loud laughter and ironical cheers by the excited multitude. To all appearances it was a foolish and hopeless chase.

Yet, paradoxical as the statement may seem, this chase on foot was the wisest course possible for Fuller and his companions. What else could they do? Had they remained quietly in camp, with no show of zeal, they would have been reproached with negligence in not guarding their train more carefully, even if they were not accused with being in league with its captors. As they ran, Fuller explained the situation and his purposes to his companions. They had neither electric battery nor engine. Had they obtained horses, they would necessarily have followed the common road, instead of the railroad, and if they thought of that expedient at all, it would be as distasteful to railroad men as abandoning their ship to sailors, and they preferred leaving that course for others. It would have been wise for those who could think of nothing else to do to ride as mounted couriers to the stations ahead; but whether this was done or not I have never learned. Certainly it was not done so promptly as to influence the fortunes of the day.

But the truth is that Fuller and Murphy were at first completely deceived as to the nature of the event which had taken place. They had been warned to guard against the escape of conscript deserters from that very camp; and although they would never have suspected an attempt on the part of the conscripts to escape by capturing their engine, yet when it was seen to dash off, the thought of this warning was naturally uppermost. Even then Fuller conjectured that they would use his engine only to get a mile or two beyond the guard line, and then abandon it. He was therefore anxious to follow closely in order to find the engine and return for his passengers at the earliest moment possible. Little did he anticipate the full

CAPTAIN WM. A. FULLER.
(Conductor of Pursuing Train.)   Page 87.

magnitude of the work and the danger before him.
That any Federal soldiers were within a hundred miles
of Big Shanty never entered his mind or that of any
other person.

For a mile or two the three footmen ran at the top
of their speed, straining their eyes forward for any
trace of the lost engine which they expected to see
halted and abandoned at almost any point on the road.
But they were soon partially undeceived as to the character of their enemies. About two miles from the
place of starting they found the telegraph wire severed and a portion of it carried away. The fugitives
were also reported as quietly oiling and inspecting their
engine. No mere deserters would be likely to think
of this. The two actions combined clearly indicated
the intention of making a long run, but who the men
were still remained a mystery. A few hundred yards
from this place a party of workmen with a hand-car
was found, and these most welcome reinforcements
were at once pressed into the service.

Fuller's plans now became more definite and determined. He had a good hand-car and abundance of
willing muscle to work it. By desperate exertions, by
running behind the car and pushing it up the steep
grades, and then mounting and driving it furiously
down-hill and on the levels, it was possible to make
seven or eight miles an hour; at the same time, Fuller
knew that the captive engine, if held back to run on
schedule time, as the reports of the workmen indicated,
would make but sixteen miles per hour. Fuller bent
all his thoughts and energies towards Kingston, thirty
miles distant. He had been informed of the extra
trains to be met at that point, and was justified in supposing that the adventurers would be greatly perplexed
and hindered by them, even if they were not totally
stopped. Had the seizure taken place on the preceding
day, as originally planned, he might well have despaired, for then the road would have been clear. Yet

he had one other resource, as will appear in due time, of which his enemies knew nothing.

Fuller did not pause to consider how he should defeat the fugitives when he had overtaken them, and he might have paid dearly for this rashness. But he could rely on help at any station, and when he had obtained the means of conveyance, as he would be sure to do at Kingston, he could easily find an overwhelming force to take with him. This Saturday was appointed as a general muster of volunteers, State militia, and conscripts, and armed soldiers were abundant in every village. But Fuller's dominant thought was that his property—the property with which he had been intrusted—was wrested from his grasp, and it was his duty to recover it, at whatever of personal hazard. That any serious harm was intended to the railroad itself he probably did not yet suspect.

Talking and wearying themselves with idle conjectures, but never ceasing to work, Fuller and his party pressed swiftly on. But suddenly there was a crash, a sense of falling, and when the shock allowed them to realize what had happened, they found themselves floundering in a ditch half filled with water, and their hand-car imbedded in the mud beside them! They had reached the place where the first rail had been torn from the track, and had suffered accordingly. But the bank was, fortunately for them, not very high at that spot, and a few bruises were all the damage they sustained. Their hand-car, which was also uninjured, was lifted on the track and driven on again. This incident increased both their caution and their respect for the men before them.

Without further mishap they reached Etowah Station, on the northern bank of the river of the same name. Here was a large bridge, which the Andrews party might have burned without loss of time had they foreseen the long detention at Kingston; but its destruction was not a part of their plan, and it was suf-

fered to stand. The mind of Fuller grew very anxious
as he approached this station. On what he should find
there depended, in all probability, his power to overtake the fugitives, whose intentions seemed more formidable with each report he received of their actions.
Andrews had firmly believed that no engine for pursuit could be found south of Kingston; but Fuller had
a different expectation.

Extensive iron-furnaces were located on the Etowah
River, about five miles above the station. These works
were connected with the railroad by a private track,
which was the property of Major Cooper, as well as the
works themselves. Murphy knew that Major Cooper
had also bought an engine called the " Yonah." It had
been built in the shop over which Murphy presided,
and was one of the best locomotives in the State. " But
where," Fuller and Murphy asked themselves, " is this
engine now ?" If it was in view of the adventurers as
they passed, they had doubtless destroyed it, ran it off the
track, or carried it away with them. They could not afford to neglect such an element in the terrible game they
were playing. But if it was now at the upper end of
the branch at the mines, as was most probable, it would
take the pursuers five miles out of their way to go for
it, and even then it might not be ready to start. This
diversion could not be afforded. Fuller and Murphy
had come nineteen miles, and had already consumed
two hours and three-quarters. The adventurers were
reported as passing each station on time, and if this
continued they must have reached Kingston forty-five
minutes before Fuller and his companions arrived at
Etowah, thirteen miles behind them. One hour and a
half more to Kingston,—this was the very best that could
be done with the hand-car. It was clear that if the
" Yonah" did not come to their assistance, they were as
effectually out of the race as if on the other side of the
ocean. Everything now hinged on the position of that
one engine.

Here we may pause to note how all coincidences, we might almost say providences, seemed to work against the bridge-burning enterprise. We were at Kingston three-quarters of an hour before our pursuers reached Etowah, thirteen miles distant. If there had been no extra trains, or if they had been sharply on time, so that we could have passed the three with a delay not exceeding fifteen or twenty minutes, which ought to have been an abundant allowance, every bridge above Kingston would have been in ashes before sundown! Or if the delay had been as great as it actually was, even then, if the locomotive "Yonah" had occupied any position excepting one, the same result would have followed.

But Fuller, Murphy, and Cain, with the several armed men they had picked up at the stations passed, could not repress shouts of exultation when they saw the old "Yonah" standing on the main track, ready fired up, and headed towards Kingston. It had just arrived from the mines, and in a short time would have returned again. Thus a new element of tremendous importance, which had been ignored in all our calculations, was introduced into the contest.

The pursuers seized their inestimable prize, called for all the volunteers who could snatch guns at a moment's notice, and were soon swiftly but cautiously rushing with the power of steam towards Kingston. The speed of nearly a mile a minute was in refreshing contrast to the slow and laborious progress of the hand-car, and they were naturally jubilant. But what lay before them at Kingston? The frequent obstructions of the track, the continued cutting of the telegraph, and especially the cool assumption of the leader of the adventurers in calling himself a Confederate officer of high rank in charge of an impressed powder train, all conspired to deepen their conviction that some desperate scheme was on foot. But they did not pause long to listen to reports. Their eyes and their thoughts were bent towards

Kingston. Had the adventurers been stopped there, or had they surprised and destroyed the trains met? The pursuers could scarcely form a conjecture as to what was before them; but the speed with which they were flying past station after station would soon end their suspense. Even the number of men on the flying train was a matter of uncertainty. At the stations passed observers reported that only four or five were seen; but the track-layers and others who had observed them at work were confident of a much larger number,—twenty-five or thirty at the least. Besides, it was by no means sure that they had not confederates in large numbers to co-operate with them at the various stations along the road. Fuller knew about how many persons had entered the train at Marietta; but it was not sure that these were all. A hundred more might be scattered along the way, at various points, ready to join in whatever strange plan was now being worked out. No conjecture of this kind that could be formed was a particle more improbable than the startling events that had already taken place. The cool courage of these pursuers, who determined to press forward and do their own duty at whatever risk, cannot be too highly rated. If they arrived at Kingston in time to unmask the pretension of the mysterious "Confederate officer," there would doubtless be a desperate fight; but the pursuers could count on assistance there and all along the line.

Fuller reached Kingston at least an hour earlier than would have been possible with the hand-car, and a single glance showed that the adventurers were gone, and his hopes of arresting them at that point were ended. They were, however, barely out of sight, and all their start had been reduced to minutes. But here again the pursuit was checked. The foresight of Andrews had blockaded the road as much as possible with the trains which had so long hindered his own movements. Two large and heavy trains stood on the main road; one of the two side tracks was occupied by the third freight, and the other by the engine of the Rome branch. There was no ready means for the passage of the " Yonah." Some precious time was employed in giving and receiving information, in telling of the seizure at Big Shanty, and hearing of the deportment of Andrews and his men at Kingston. Then a dispute arose as to the best means of continuing the pursuit, which threatened to disunite Fuller and Murphy. The latter wished to continue the chase with the " Yonah," which was a fine engine, with large wheels; but Fuller would not wait to get the freights out of the way, and, jumping on the Rome engine, he called on all who were willing to assist him to come on. A large, enthusiastic, and well-armed company instantly volunteered; the new engine, the " Shorter," pulled out, and Murphy had only time to save himself from the disgrace of being left behind by jumping on the hindmost car as it swept past. With all the time lost in making this transfer, and in mutual explanations, the pursuers left Kingston just twenty minutes behind the Federals.

What Fuller and his friends learned at Kingston left no doubt on their minds that some deliberate and far-reaching military movement was on foot. While its precise nature was yet concealed, the probability that the road itself, and possibly Confederate towns and stores, were to be destroyed, was freely conceded. All agreed that the one thing to be done was to follow their enemies closely, and thus compel them to turn and fight or abandon their enterprise. A large force—one or two hundred well-armed men—was taken on board, and instructions left that as soon as the track could be cleared another armed train was to follow for the purpose of rendering any needed assistance.

CHAPTER VI.

A TERRIBLE RAILROAD CHASE.

WE will now resume the direct narrative.

When Kingston was left behind, it was believed by our leader that, notwithstanding all our vexatious delays, we still had a margin of at least an hour's time. Our movements were arranged on that supposition. The next considerable station, Adairsville, was about ten miles distant, and the intervening country comparatively level. There were no considerable bridges in this space, and the most we could do was to run swiftly, and occasionally to obstruct the track. Our speed was increased to about forty miles an hour, and this swift running, after our long halt at Kingston, was exquisitely delightful. Looking out from the crevices of the box-car, we saw the hills and trees gliding swiftly by, and felt that each moment we were getting farther away from the foes who had so long surrounded us, and nearer safety and triumph. While we were actually under way our prospects did not yet seem very unfavorable. There were yet one freight and one passenger train to meet, which we would now encounter an hour farther south, because of our long hindrance; but we felt confident of our power to deceive or overpower them, and they did not embarrass our running because they were on the regular schedule. The freight was now almost due at Adairsville, and we expected the passenger train to overtake and go ahead of it from that point. If they were both on time we would also meet them there, and then have an absolutely open road to Chattanooga. It will show the tremendous risks that encompassed our enterprise, when we reflect that

so trifling a circumstance as the delay or the misplace-
ment of a train could introduce an "if" into our most
hopeful plans.

A short distance south of Adairsville we again
stopped, and Andrews called us to come forth and
work with a will. No exhortation was needed. John
Scott, as usual, climbed the telegraph-pole, and the
wire was soon severed. Two or three rails were slowly
and painfully battered loose with our iron bar, which
still constituted our only instrument for track-lifting.
These were loaded on the car to carry away with us.
There happened to be a large number of cross-ties
lying near, and these we also loaded up for future use.
When all was done we moved on, feeling that we had
provided for the delay or destruction of any train that
might pursue. It was also probable that the first train
which met us at Adairsville would be wrecked. This
was not our design, as we did not relish wanton mischief; but there was no safe way of giving warning,
and a wrecked train would have been a considerable
obstruction of the track.

We reached Adairsville before the expected freight,
but had only just taken our place on the side track
when its whistle was heard. When it came up, Andrews, who still personated a Confederate officer, and
exacted and received the obedience which in those days
of conscription and impressment was readily yielded to
military authority, ordered the train to be run past the
station and back again on the side track behind his
own, to wait for the expected passenger train. The
usual explanations about the powder train were repeated to credulous ears. Then came five minutes of
suspense and waiting. The train was behind time,—
a trifling matter in itself, but, in our situation, each
minute might turn the scale between death and life.
We could not afford to repeat the experience of Kingston. Not one bridge had yet been burned, and all we
could show for our hazard, beside our captured train,

were a few cross-ties and lifted rails. After a whispered word of consultation with his engineer, who was willing to assume the most deadly risks rather than to lie still, Andrews remarked to the bystanders that a government powder express must not be detained by any number of passenger trains, and then gave the word, " Go ahead!"

We started quite moderately, but, as soon as the station was out of sight, we noticed a wonderful acceleration of speed. The cars seemed almost to leap from the track, and we whirled from side to side at a bewildering rate. There was scarcely any slackening for curves or grades, and our whistle rang out with scarcely a moment's cessation. In the box-car we could retain no position for more than an instant, and were jostled over each other and against the sides of the car much oftener than was pleasant. No one of us had ever rode at such a rate before. Though we had no means of measuring the speed, none of us estimated it at less than a mile a minute. What was the meaning of such a break-neck pace? Had Andrews discovered that we were pursued, and was he making a desperate effort to escape from the enemy? Or was he simply hurrying to the bridges we were to burn? Such questions were easier asked than answered, for two cars and the tender intervened between us and the locomotive, on which our leader was. At any rate, the moments were rapidly carrying us towards our own lines, and a very few hours of such running would see us delivered from the series of perils which had so long environed us. We had learned that just beyond Calhoun, a station only ten miles from Adairsville, there was a large bridge, which we knew was marked for destruction. If that was passed without stopping, we would be convinced that an enemy was on our track, and that the race was simply for life. A few minutes would decide. But in the mean time, as an enemy might be following us, it occurred to the writer that it would be well to continue

obstructing the track. This was accomplished by
breaking open the hind end of the last box-car, and
shoving out one by one the ties previously loaded. A
part only of the ties on board were thus employed, as
we thought it possible that the remainder might be
more useful in other directions. Many of those sprin-
kled on the track showed a perverse disposition to
jump off, but we felt sure that enough remained to
make a pursuer cautious. Nothing more impressed us
with the fearful speed of our train than the manner in
which these ties seemed instantly to vanish when they
touched the ground.

By thus exerting the full speed of the engine Andrews hoped to reach Calhoun before the belated passenger train should arrive. The engineer stood with
his hand on the lever ready to reverse his engine the
moment an opposing train was sighted. The open
character of the country in this part of the route permitted a good outlook. The whistle was also kept
sounding that an opposite train might be warned and
checked. It was the intention of Andrews, in case of
meeting the expected train, to reverse his own engine
only long enough to escape the danger of collision,
and then to persuade or compel the other to back before him to the first siding. This lightning-like run
was bold and full of peril, but it was wise. Had the
same risk been promptly assumed at Kingston the whole
future of the enterprise would have been different. But
we reached Calhoun before any train was met. When
we slackened speed, just before arriving at the station,
we shoved out one more cross-tie, and then carefully
concealed the hole in the car by piling other ties across
it. As we drew nearer, great was the satisfaction of
Andrews and his engineer when they saw the belated
passenger train—our last obstacle—lying quietly at the
station. It had been just starting, but, on hearing our
whistle, it awaited our arrival. We ran down almost
against it, and, without getting off his locomotive, An-

drews shouted his orders to have the road cleared for
an impressed powder train. The news from the north
and west—the panic caused by the rumored approach
of General Mitchel—made this sudden demand seem
less unreasonable, and it was unhesitatingly obeyed.
The passenger train was switched out of the way, and
we glided smoothly by the last train we were to meet.
Thus, at length, we had reached the ground where
bridge-burning was to begin, and all obstacles were out
of the way; what could hinder full and decisive success?

Fuller and Murphy had not left Kingston many
minutes before they became conscious of the error they
had committed in exchanging the "Yonah" for the
"Shorter." The latter was a weak engine with small
wheels. It was now forced to the utmost, oil being
freely used with the wood in the furnace; but they
were unable to equal the tremendous speed with which
they had made the previous stage of their journey.
Though they had but two or three cars and the advantage of a level and unobstructed track, they could not
exceed forty miles an hour. They maintained a vigilant lookout, but ran with the steam-valve entirely
open, while Murphy and Cain both grasped the lever,
ready to use their combined weight and strength in
reversing the motion if any obstacle should be descried.
Their vigilance was soon approved. They observed
the point at which we had removed rails, and, by reversing, were able to arrest their motion just on the
edge of the break. But here they found themselves
confronted with a terrible obstacle. They had no rails
to replace those that had been carried off. Some instruments for track-laying were on board, and it was
suggested to tear up rails behind and place them in the
break. This double labor required too much time to
suit the ardent temper of Fuller and Murphy. At
once they repeated the old tactics which alone had given
them any hope of success. They abandoned their en

gine and ran ahead once more on foot. The remainder
of their company remained behind, and probably did,
after a time, succeed in lifting rails behind their engine
and laying them down before, as a contemporaneous
account asserts; but they had no further real part in
the chase.

Before the two footmen had gone far they encountered the regular freight train that we had met at
Adairsville. Thus their delay was reduced to a very
small amount. It seems that almost as soon as Andrews and his party had left Adairsville for their rapid
flight towards Calhoun, this train, guided either by the
decision of the conductor, or by a telegraphic message
from the management of the road, started southward,
and were met no more than a mile or two on their way
by the dauntless pursuers. Great was the amazement
of the men on the freight train to learn that the fine-
looking Confederate officer with whom they had been
talking five minutes before was probably a "Yankee"
engaged in the most daring exploit of the war. But
not much time was allowed for the indulgence of any
emotion. Fuller promptly took command of the train
and backed it with all possible speed to Adairsville.
Its engine, the "Texas," was known to Fuller as one of
the largest and best in the State. While backing and
pushing the whole train of nearly twenty cars it made
the most rapid speed that they had yet attained.

But still greater speed was necessary, and by throwing
all but one or two cars on the side track at Adairsville,
the noble engine was relieved and enabled to show all
its fine qualities. No turn-table being at hand, it had
still to be run backward; but that position does not materially lessen the power of an engine, though the risk
of accident is somewhat increased. This risk had been
taken, however, in so many instances by the desperate
pursuers, and with perfect safety, that they were willing to tempt fortune still further. The engineer of
the captured train had been left behind at the last

break, but his place was ably supplied by Peter
Bracken, of the " Texas." Starting from Adairsville
with a full head of steam, the distance of ten miles to
Calhoun was run in twelve minutes, and even this tremendous speed would have been exceeded but for the
slight delay caused by the ties dropped on the track.
When one of these obstructions was seen, Fuller, who
had stationed himself for that purpose on the end of
the tender which ran ahead, would jump off, remove
the tie, and be back to his place almost before the engine ceased to move. The uniform mode of stopping
to clear the track was by reversing the engine. Aside
from the time lost in these stops, the running must
have exceeded a mile per minute. This exceeding rapidity prevented any loss of distance in this stage of
the pursuit.

At Calhoun, Fuller scarcely made a full stop. He
told his tale in a few words and called for volunteers.
A number came just as he was moving on again; indeed, after the train was well under way, he secured a
still more valuable prize. The telegraph managers at
Chattanooga had found that the wires were broken, and
were endeavoring to discover the source of mischief.
By telegraphing to different stations and asking for re-
plies, they could easily make an approximate estimate.
But the difficulty was coming nearer: they discovered
that one station after another was being cut off from
communication with headquarters. South of Calhoun
they could get no reply at the time the passenger train
reached Dalton. They had, therefore, directed the
only operator at that station—a mere boy—to leave his
post and go to Calhoun for the purpose of discovering
and remedying the mischief. Fuller recognized him
on the platform, and reached out his hand, shouting,
" Come !" The boy took hold and was lifted on the
flying engine.

With no thought of our deadly peril we had stopped
a short distance above Calhoun to cut the telegraph

and oil the engine. Several of us were also engaged in battering out the spikes preparatory to lifting another rail. As we expected to spend ten or fifteen minutes in burning the large bridge which spanned the Oostenaula River, a little distance from us, Andrews thought it better that we should have a rail up in order to guard against the possibility of the train we had just passed being turned back after us in time to interrupt our work. It might have been better, as we were tempted to think afterwards, if we had begun on the bridge directly; but it was absolutely necessary to cut the wire, and the lifting of the rail would not take an additional minute.

The engine was inspected, and found to be still in perfect condition, though both wood and water were running low; the wire was severed; and eight of us had just taken hold of the loose end of a rail, out of which the spikes had been battered, and were trying to pull the other end loose also. But it was too firmly fixed, and we were about to release it, and wait the taking out of a few more spikes, when, away in the distance, we heard the whistle of an engine in pursuit! The effect was magical. With one convulsive effort the rail was broken asunder, and the whole party pitched in a heap over the low embankment. No one was hurt, and we were on our feet in a moment.

It did not require many moments to realize the situation. Our enemies were upon us at last! Their train was in plain sight. We could even see that they were well armed. There seemed to be no resource but flight.

But from whence came this train? The facts with which the reader is already familiar were all unknown to us, and the apparition of the pursuers all the more terrible on that account. We knew the difficulties against which we had struggled, and little thought that our pursuers had encountered nearly equal obstacles, over which they had so far been marvellously victorious.

Greater surprise would not have been created in our
ranks had the locomotive, to whose scream we unwill-
ingly listened, dropped from the sky! One plausible
conjecture only presented itself as to the presence of
this train, and, if this one was correct, it could be but
the earnest of speedy defeat and death. Possibly a
telegraphic message from the other side of Big Shanty
had traversed the wide circuit of more than two thousand miles past Atlanta, Richmond, Chattanooga, and
back again to Calhoun, reaching the latter place just
before the wire was cut, and inducing them to start
back the train we had just met at full speed after us.
All this was possible,—at least it seemed so to those of
us who were not in the secret of the wide-spread system
of military operations,—unless, indeed, the foresight of
our government had provided at this very time for the
severing of the telegraph on the Carolina coast, at which
place alone this circuit came within striking distance of
the Union lines.

But we had no time for idle conjectures. The fact
was patent that a train was bearing down upon us at
full speed. "Shall we stand and fight? Shall we
attack them now?" were questions eagerly asked.

But Andrews still hesitated to depart from the course
pursued so far. We had the rail broken which would
arrest the enemy, and probably give us time to fire the
bridge ahead. Then all might yet be well,—that is if
the stations ahead were not warned, and the track obstructed before us. Should that prove the case, then
to stand and sell our lives as dearly as possible, or,
abandoning our engine, to fly on foot across the country, were all the alternatives. The crisis of our fate
drew near, and our hardest and sharpest work lay just
ahead.

Influenced by such considerations, which were then
mainly confined to his own mind, Andrews, without a
moment's hesitation, gave the signal, which was as
quickly obeyed, for mounting the train. The en-

gineer threw the valve wide open, and, with a spring that threw us from our feet, the noble steed was once more careering forward. To his companions on the locomotive Andrews said, quietly, as he ever spoke in times of deepest excitement, "Push her, boys; let her do her best. We must lose no time in getting to the bridge above." Some of the engine oil was thrown into the furnace, and the already fiery pace sensibly quickened. The problem seemed perfectly simple. If we could reach the bridge, and get it well on fire in less time than our enemies could piece out the broken rail, we had still a chance of life and success. If not, more desperate means became necessary. The speed of the engine might save us a precious half-minute, and on such a narrow margin everything turned. Nobly did our good old locomotive respond to the call! Rocking, whirling, bounding,—it seemed a marvel that some of the box-cars were not hurled from the track. Inside these cars all was action. Though we could scarcely keep one position a moment, idleness could not now be indulged. We knew that the time for concealment had passed, and we wrought with flying fingers in preparation for our incendiary work. The forward end of our box-car, and both ends of the others, were knocked out by employing one of the heavy cross-ties as a battering-ram, and the greater part of the sides were loosened in the same manner, and torn into fragments for kindling. This destruction of barriers also opened a way of communication with the engine. Andrews approved what we had done, and told us frankly that our lives probably depended on the number of seconds we consumed in getting the bridge on fire. Just then an exclamation of wonder and dismay from our keen-sighted fireman, Alfred Wilson, drew attention. He declared positively that he saw the smoke of the pursuing engine still following us! It was scarcely credible, but he was so positive, and it was so important to know the truth, that our speed was slackened to ascertain. In a mo ment a whistle, clear and unmistakable, rang out from beyond a curve we had just passed. All doubt was at an end; but our surprise and consternation were as great as when the train was first discovered in pursuit. There had been no time to lay again the rail we had taken up, and the broken half of which we still had with us. It seemed a miracle wrought against us. But Andrews' resources were not yet exhausted. He ordered another effort, which might yet give us time to fire the bridge ahead, that he was most unwilling to pass without destroying. The locomotive was reversed, and our kindling-wood, with most of the ties, carried forward, and the moment we began to move backward the hindmost car was uncoupled. The pursuing locomotive was then in fearful proximity. We could see that it was running backward, and that a number of men were crowded on it. Almost at the same moment its machinery was reversed and ours turned forward. As we left them at lightning speed we could just see that their velocity was well checked before they touched our abandoned car.

But this was not yet sufficient. As we came to the next slight up-grade the same manœuvre was repeated, and our second car flung back at the enemy in like manner. The time lost in doing this brought them again near us, and we saw that they were pushing our first car before them.

But how had they passed the broken rail? For years I could get no satisfactory information on this subject. Some Confederate accounts spoke of a rail being taken up behind and laid down before the engine. But the time was too short to permit such an action. That a stop could be made, a rail taken up, spiked down again, and our engine, running faster than the wind, overtaken,—all of this well inside of five minutes,—was incredible. Very probably this course was adopted in the case of the next train which was pursuing not far behind. Other Confederate accounts say nothing about this rail, while a few assert that it was not broken at all, but only loosened and left in its place. But having personally helped in the desperate pull, having fallen down the bank with the party, and carried one end of the rail to put on our car, besides having my left hand long suffer from being clasped under the hand of William Campbell, the strongest man of our party, I naturally cannot accept this explanation. Conductor Fuller gave another solution of the mystery scarcely less strange, which I repeat as he gave it to me. He said that when he saw our engine start on from this point he could see no obstruction, and allowed the train to continue at high speed. A moment after he noticed a short blank in one of the rails. A terrible fear swept over him, for it was now too late to stop. But quick as a lightning-flash he noticed another fact,—that the place of the missing rail was on the *inside* of a sharp curve. He explained to me that a train at a very high rate of speed throws the most of its weight on the outside rail of a curve, which is always made a little higher than the other. Had an outside rail been broken the destruction of their train would have been inevitable, but the break was on the inside. With that rapid decision which the better class of railroad men learn to exercise, he signalled to the engineer, "Faster; faster yet!" There was a sharp jolt, and the locomotive and the cars attached were on the other side of the obstruction with their speed not even abated. The next train which followed was the passenger train that we had met at Calhoun, which had also been turned back after us. This train had track-layers and instruments on board, and did very quickly repair the damage; but if Fuller had waited even that long the bridge over the Oostenaula would have been wrapped in flames before his arrival.

Fuller saw the car we dropped, and by promptly having his engine reversed, reduced the collision to merely a smart shock. It was dextrously coupled fast

and driven forward at full speed. The second car we
dropped was treated in the same manner, and the
enemy's speed was scarcely diminished. The time lost
in dropping the cars was about as long as that lost in
coupling to them.

Thus in the short space between Calhoun and the
Oostenaula River three hindrances or perils, the greatness of which will be best appreciated by railroad men,
were overcome by the skill and daring of Fuller's
band, and in spite of them they attained a rate of running on this crooked and irregular road which would
have been most remarkable on a perfectly smooth and
unobstructed track.

Now the Oostenaula bridge was in sight, and we
slackened speed for a desperate attempt to burn it.
But before we could come to a full stop the pursuer
was close upon us, and very reluctantly we steamed
over the bridge and continued our flight. The prospect was rapidly darkening before us. It was certain
that one of the trains we had met at Adairsville or
Calhoun was turned back after us and driven with the
utmost determination. Of all conjectures to account
for this pursuit, that of a telegram by the way of Richmond was most probable and most portentous. If this
was really the case, our fate was sealed. With a re-
lentless pursuer hanging upon our heels, and the towns
ahead warned and ready to dispute our passage, human
bravery and foresight would avail nothing. I have
no doubt the mind of Andrews was weighed down and
perplexed by the uncertainty of our situation. Could
we have known even as much of the number and plans
of our foes as they knew of ours—above all, could we
have known whether the road was open before us—the
problem would have been simpler. Yet we had but
two hopes: to wreck the train behind us, a task of no
small difficulty now they were on their guard; or, failing in this, to distance them in running far enough to
lift some rails or burn one of the bridges still ahead.

If only one bridge could be burned, it would stop the pursuit for the time and leave us free to encounter the opposition before us.

Accordingly the jaded "General" was spurred to full speed. The load was now lighter, and as much of the kindling as we thought it prudent to spare was used in putting the furnace into a fiercer blaze. We also resumed the practice of dropping cross-ties from the rear of the car. These efforts had a marked effect in delaying the pursuers, for their smoke and whistle soon ceased to disturb us. But while running at this violent rate we had passed Resaca and thought it prudent to again cut the telegraph. While stopping for this purpose the writer took a rail which had been bent in lifting it, and placed it so that one end was held firmly under the track, and the other projected at a little elevation, towards the pursuing train. This was not more than accomplished when that train was heard again, and we mounted our engine and sped onward. As the rail was small and dark, the enemy ran right on it before it was observed, and Fuller afterwards declared that if it had been a little lower, it would have been sure to wreck them. But as it was, the end struck the edge of the car, and it was knocked harmlessly from the track.

Above Tilton we succeeded in getting a full supply of water from the tank. This was most welcome, as the water was nearly exhausted. The wood-station was at another place, and as our supply ran low we threw on fence-rails or any other available fuel whenever stopping to cut the wires.

Our condition was now widely different and more unfavorable than it was a short time before. With only one car, and that almost torn to pieces, even the magnificent coolness and self-possession of Andrews could scarcely avert suspicion at any station where we might be driven to halt. And with all our efforts we could never get much more than out of sight of our

pursuers. The time required for cutting wires and
spent in trying to take up track compensated almost
exactly for the time our pursuers spent in removing
the obstructions we continued to throw before them.
With all their efforts they could not get within easy
gunshot of us; neither could we distance them far
enough for the decisive operation of burning a bridge.
The relation of the two parties was peculiar and well
defined. Each party soon came to recognize the
strength and weakness which belonged to its own situation. With their better engine it would have been
comparatively easy for our pursuers to come near
enough to pick off man after man with their guns,
while entirely out of reach of our revolvers. But had
they come up so close, any obstruction we might have
placed on the track would have been terribly efficient.
As long as we possessed cross-ties or anything large
enough to wreck a train they were bound to keep a
respectful distance. The most favorable position for
them was just far enough in the rear to see when we
stopped or threw anything on the track, thus enabling
them to check up in time. They dared not come nearer
than this while we were in rapid motion, but they were
often farther behind.

Mile after mile the terrible chase continued. Station
after station was passed without the least lessening of
speed. The idlers about the platforms started back in
amazement and affright when they saw a train dash by
like a thunderbolt, closely followed by three others, the
latter screaming as loudly as their whistles were able.
To us, who were looking out from the baggage-car,
houses and villages, groves and hills, flashed by almost
too quickly for distinct vision. Then, in the hottest
speed, the whistle would sound "down brakes," and
the stop—usually made by reversing the engine—would
be so sudden that we needed to cling convulsively to
avoid being hurled from our places; then, in a moment,
we would spring to the ground and labor with the en-

ergy of despair at destroying the telegraph and the
track, or loading on ties, until the signal,—usually from
behind, given by the pursuing train,—when all would
rush on board, and the engine, putting its full strength
into the first leap, would dash on, jerking from their feet
all who were not braced for the shock. When under way
we could not sit down because of the terrible jolting of
the springless car. If we attempted to stand we fell
over or were thrown against the little that remained of
the sides of the car, and had to be very watchful not to
be thrown off altogether. Our actual position was a
rapid alternation of all possible attitudes, the favorite
being—judging from the frequency with which it was
assumed—that of bending over with the hands and
feet resting on the floor.

Those who were on the engine had a better opportunity of observing all that was passing. Alfred Wilson, who acted as our fireman, gives a vivid picture of
the race from that point of view. He says,—

"Our locomotive was under a full head of steam. The engineer stood with his hand on the lever with the valve wide open.
It was frightful to see how the powerful iron monster under us
would leap forward under the revolution of her great wheels.
Brown (the engineer) would scream to me ever and anon, ' Give
her more wood, Alf!' which command was promptly obeyed.
She rocked and reeled like a drunken man, while we reeled from
side to side like grains of pop-corn in a hot frying-pan. It was
bewildering to look at the ground or objects on the roadside. A
constant stream of fire ran from the rims of the great wheels,
and to this day I shudder when I reflect on that, my first and
last locomotive ride. We sped past stations, houses, and fields,
and were out of sight almost like a meteor, while the bystanders,
who barely caught a glimpse of us as we passed, looked on as if
in both fear and amazement. It has always been a wonder to
me that our locomotive and cars kept the track at all, or how
they could possibly stay on the track. At times the iron horse
seemed to literally fly over the course, the driving-wheels of one
side being lifted from the rails much of the distance over which
we now sped with a velocity fearful to contemplate."

But swift running alone could not save us. In a
more trial of speed between the two engines we were

sure in the end to be worsted. To wreck the pursuing
train was our great object, and to that end we employed
every expedient we could devise. By this time we had
a few more track-raising instruments, which Andrews
and Wilson had simultaneously taken from some switch-
tenders. Earlier in the race they would have been
worth their weight in gold, but it was now too late.
Even with their help we could take up a rail no quicker
than the Confederates, with ample supplies of rails, instruments, and trained workmen, could lay another
down. All the efforts we made in this direction were
a mere waste of time.

But the swiftness of pursuit was carrying both parties over long spaces. The next station of importance
that lay before us was Dalton, and this place, twenty-
two miles from Calhoun, was soon reached. This was
the largest town we had approached since starting in
the morning. It was the junction of another road
which led to Cleveland, on the main line to Richmond.
It had a further and terrible interest to us, in the
knowledge that there we would learn whether our
character had really been telegraphed ahead of us by
the way of the coast lines·and Richmond. But if it
had, we would learn it too late to make the knowledge
of any service. We would find a military force ready
to receive us at the depot, and our race would be run.
Yet we approached cautiously, ready, if there were any
suspicious indications, to reverse the engine at once and
run back towards the pursuing train, with the intention
of getting out of the town and trying to escape through
the fields. But we saw no more than the usual number
of persons about the depot, and Andrews at once leaped
from the engine, examined the switch, which was adjusted to throw a train on the Cleveland fork of the
road, had it changed, and answered all questions as
coolly and composedly as ever. The whole had to be
done very promptly, as the appearance of our poor
battered train was sadly against us, and we knew that

in a town the size of Dalton it would be easy to find
force enough for our arrest. Besides, it was sure that
in a few seconds Fuller and his tireless band would
appear on the scene. In no period of this eventful
day does the courage and self-control of Andrews shine
out more brightly than in the manner in which he here
caused the persons about the depot in a moment to obey
his orders and believe his story, even while thinking it
possible that they might have previous information of
his designs, and be only waiting the arrival of assistance to destroy him. The pursuing train was heard as
expected. Before our foes came near enough to reveal
our character everything was arranged, and taking the
left-hand road, that which led directly to Chattanooga,
we again darted forward.

This was, however, a decisive point in the race.
When we thus passed Dalton without having destroyed
our pursuers, we knew that all hope of passing through
Chattanooga with our engine must be abandoned. All
uneasiness on account of a possible telegram from Richmond was at an end, but there was a nearer danger,
which defined the limits beyond which we could no
longer hope to pass. There was a line of telegraph
along each of the diverging railroads. We could destroy but one of these, and it was certain that as soon
as Fuller and his friends arrived at Dalton and told
their story, warning would be sent ahead of us by the
other road. This will explain what some accounts
have left doubtful,—our neglect to cut the wire immediately after leaving Dalton. It made no practical difference to us whether the fatal message was sent directly
to Chattanooga and all intermediate stations, or whether
it went by the way of Cleveland and Chattanooga and
then back to the stations on our line. The distance was
twice as great in thus telegraphing around two sides of
a triangle, but this counted for nothing when lightning
was the messenger. Our only resource was in the fact
that we were now counting nearly as many miles as

minutes, and that we might be far on our way towards
Chattanooga, and possibly have some bridges burned,
before preparation could be made for stopping us. As
a last resource, we now fully expected to have to take
to the woods on foot.

Fuller well knew the decisive advantage he would
have at Dalton. As he neared that station he wrote
the following dispatch and gave it to the young operator
he had taken up at Calhoun, with instructions to put it
through to Chattanooga, both ways, with the least possible delay. It proves—if it were not afterwards written from memory and unconsciously modified—how
correctly he had already estimated the character of the
men he was chasing. This sagacity is scarcely less
wonderful than the daring with which he encountered
and overcame so many obstacles.

FULLER'S TELEGRAM.

" To GENERAL LEADBETTER, Commander at Chattanooga.

" My train was captured this A.M. at Big Shanty, evidently by
Federal soldiers in disguise. They are making rapidly for Chattanooga, possibly with the idea of burning the railroad bridges
in their rear. If I do not capture them in the mean time see that
they do not pass Chattanooga.

" WILLIAM A. FULLER."

Two miles above Dalton we stopped and obstructed
the track, and once more cut the telegraph wire. The
latter was of slight importance, but Wilson and others
urged it upon Andrews, and he did not wish to dis-
courage them by telling them that it was now useless.
But the removal of a rail might have been of more
value by giving us time for burning some of the bridges,
which are very numerous on this part of the road.
This stop was made in plain sight of a Confederate
regiment commanded by a Colonel Glen. The work to
be done, however, demanded too much speed for us to
apprehend their interference. But before the rail could
be more than loosened, the pursuers, who had halted at

Dalton for even a shorter time than we had, were upon
us again, and we once more mounted our engine and
sped onward. The telegram was sent ahead by this
line as well as the other a minute or two before the
wire was severed. It created a terrible excitement in
Chattanooga, but did us no real damage. Both the
pursuing trains were near us when we entered the great
tunnel north of Dalton. Our supply of cross-ties was
unfortunately exhausted, or they might have proved
very serviceable in the darkness. In fearful proximity
and with unabated speed the tunnel was passed. Murphy declares that he was quite relieved when he saw by
the gleam of light ahead that our engine was passing
on, for he had quite made up his mind that we would
attack them or drive our engine back upon them in the
darkness. But no such plan had entered our thoughts.
We would far have preferred a fight in open day.

We now resolved to play what had been reserved as
our last card. Running more slowly to economize fuel,
—though a high velocity was still maintained,—we tried
to light a fire in our only remaining car. It was already open at both ends, and now as much of the sides
and top as could possibly be obtained was also torn off
and prepared for fuel. The attempt to light these
splinters by matches did not succeed, for the wind
caused by the rapid motion blew them out. Fire was
then brought back from the engine, but this seemed to
smoulder rather than burn, for the rain, which fell in
torrents, blew through the unprotected car, and all the
boards were soaking wet. Never did kindling a fire
seem so difficult. When at length it fairly caught, and
began to burn briskly, our dampened hopes began to
brighten in sympathy with it. Might it not be that
our persistent struggle against ill-fortune was to win
the victory even yet? Just then a long covered bridge
was approached, which it was desirable on every account to burn. All of our party, whom the heat had
not already driven forward, were ordered into the nearly

empty tender, and the car was uncoupled in the middle of the bridge. We did not leave it hastily, but stopped near the farther end of the bridge to watch the result in breathless anxiety. We had scarcely halted when the black smoke of the nearest pursuer was seen, and he bore down upon us at full speed. We were very loth to leave our position. We could see that the flame was rising higher, but could also see that the enemy's train had a large number of men on board, some of whom had firearms. Oh, what would we not have given for a few of the muskets we had left in camp, to have held our position for even a few minutes, or even one minute! But our situation was too unfavorable to allow more than a momentary thought of resistance. At long range we were virtually unarmed. But we lingered still, until we saw the enemy pushing our blazing car before them over the bridge; then, being in reach of their firearms, and but poorly protected in our engine and tender, we again sought safety in flight. They pushed the blazing car before them to the first side track, which happened not to be far away, and then left it to burn at its leisure. Thus our forlorn hope expired.

But not all of the adventurers were willing to accept defeat even yet. A halt was made—the last—for the sake of again obstructing the track, and getting a few sticks of wood that lay near the track to replenish the waning fire of our engine. Some of the number, from the force of habit more than anything else, began to take up a rail. The writer then suggested to Andrews a simple plan, which, at this late hour, still offered a glimmering hope. Could we throw the pursuers off the track, we might burn a few bridges yet, though the most important had been left behind us, and we could no longer hope to run our engine through Chatta-nooga. This attempt would have been more full of peril than any other of the day, with the possible exception of the first seizure of the train; but its success

h 10*

would have turned the tables on our enemies over-
whelmingly. With sufficient promptness and desperation it might have succeeded, while its failure would
only have ended a hopeless struggle, exchanging certain
and immediate death for whatever faint chances of escape
might otherwise remain after the train was abandoned.
There had been many hints on the part of the soldiers
that we were running away from the enemy too many
times, and that it would be better to fight, but this was
the first definite proposal. The suggestion was to use
our remaining fuel in once more running out of sight
of the enemy, then, selecting a place for ambuscade in
the low, thick-set bushes that frequently came close to
the road, to obstruct the track in our usual manner.
When this was done, all of us, except one of the engineers, could hide, in such a position as to be abreast
of the enemy when he stopped to remove the obstructions. Our own engineer could wait until the pursuers
were in sight, and then start off as usual, but slowly,
so as to keep their attention fixed upon his train. We
had several times noticed how, in the case of an obstruction, the Confederates had checked their headlong
career, sprang to the ground even before the train had
stopped fully, and worked furiously at clearing the
track. This would be our opportunity for rushing
forth. We could shoot down all who were on the
engine or the ground, while one of our reserve engineers sprang on the engine and threw it back at full
speed, jumping off as it started. The result could
scarcely have failed to be a fatal collision with the
next pursuing train, which was never far behind.
Then we would have been free from pursuit, and left
only to reckon with the forces ahead. The place and
manner of leaving the train could then have been
selected at our leisure. We afterwards learned that
no preparation had been made to receive us farther
south than Boyce's Station, some three miles from
Chattanooga. There a strong military force had been

posted, the track torn up, and cannon planted. But we would never have ventured so near Chattanooga after knowing that a message had been sent ahead of us at Dalton. Our original hope had been to get so far ahead of all pursuit as to pass Chattanooga before the pursuers had reached Dalton. Then the junction of roads at the latter point would not have been an embarrassment to us, as will be made clear by a reference to the map.

Andrews said that the plan, of which a hint was given in a few rapid words, was good and worth trying. But the one great defect in his character as a leader came to the surface in this emergency. This was a disposition to turn everything carefully over in his mind before deciding. There was no time for reflection now. The Confederate whistle sounded, and our men, without waiting for the word of command, so accustomed had they become to this manœuvre, mounted the engine and sped away. Andrews bitterly regretted afterwards that this last expedient was not tried. With this exception, I do not know of anything more that could have been devised, beyond what we actually attempted.

One object only could now be attained by clinging longer to the train, the speedy abandonment of which was inevitable. Andrews wished to shorten the distance to our own lines as much as possible, so that the slender chance of escaping through the woods and mountains might be increased. It was far easier to travel on the engine than to run or skulk through the country on foot. It was better to continue this mode of locomotion as long as possible, or until we were carried as near Chattanooga as it was prudent to venture. The old lightning rate of running could not be maintained, but we were still moving swiftly. The engine was in a bad state, and really incapable of much further service. The fuel, too, was gone. For some time we had been reduced to the fragments that had been torn off the cars before they were dropped, and to

what we had gathered up along the roadside. Now all
that remained of a combustible character was crowded
into the fire-box for the last pull. Andrews had
always kept with him from the time we first met him
at the midnight consultation a mysterious and well-
filled pair of saddle-bags. These, of which he had been
very careful, and which were supposed to contain important and compromising documents, were now added
to the fire. It was a signal, if any were needed, that
the time had now come to prepare for the worst. Andrews and three others—Brown, Knight, and Alfred
Wilson—were now on the engine, and the remaining
sixteen were huddled together on the tender. At no
time since the writer had proposed attacking the pursuing train had he been in a position to urge the attempt on Andrews, and it was now too late. But another decision was arrived at on the engine against
which some of us on the tender would have protested
with all our energy had the opportunity been offered.
Alfred Wilson, whose opinion was directly opposite to
that of George D. Wilson and the writer, says,—

"A few minutes before we came to the final halt, Andrews,
Brown, Knight, and myself hastily discussed as to the best thing
to be done, and it was concluded that the best course was to separate and scatter in all directions."

This fatal decision arose from two causes. Andrews,
with all his courage, never rightly valued fighting men.
He preferred accomplishing his objects by stratagem
and in secrecy rather than by open force. It was simply
wonderful that in all the exigencies of this expedition
no one of his soldiers had been permitted to fire a single
shot, or even to draw a revolver upon the enemy. He
now considered that when scattered each one, as well as
himself, would be able to find concealment, or if captured, to evade detection by false stories. This was a
great mistake. The second reason for adopting this
fatal course was the belief that the scattering of the

party would also scatter pursuit, and make it less eager
in any one direction. Under ordinary circumstances
such would have been the result. But the terror and
the fierce resentment aroused by the daring character
of our enterprise caused the whole country to burst
into a blaze of excitement, and the pursuit to be
pushed with equal energy for scores of miles in every
direction.

An opposite course would have been far more hopeful. We were but twelve or fifteen miles from Chattanooga. Twenty miles of travel to the northwest
would have placed us on the opposite bank of the Tennessee River, among the loyal mountaineers of the district. If we had remained together we could have
traversed that broken and wooded country which lay
before us as rapidly as any pursuing soldiers. No
body of citizens not perfectly organized and armed
would have ventured to halt us. Cavalry pursuit away
from the main roads was impossible. Besides, one of
our party possessed a pocket-compass, and two others,
besides Andrews, were somewhat acquainted with the
country. The writer is convinced that we might have
left the cars in a body, and without even attempting
concealment, but only avoiding the public roads, have
hurried directly towards Mitchel's lines, and within
forty-eight hours have been safe in his camp.

But we can neither wonder at nor blame the mistake
made by our leader on this occasion, though it led to
months of wretchedness and the death of many of the
party. Andrews had met each new emergency with
heroic calmness and unfailing resources; but he was
now physically exhausted. He had been engaged in
the most intense and harassing labor for many days,
being without sleep for the past thirty hours and without food for twenty. An error in action was therefore
most natural and excusable, even if it disagreed with
the course which had been marked out in calmer moments. Wilson says,—

"Andrews now told us all that it was 'every man for himself;' that we must scatter and do the best we could to escape to
the Federal lines."

This, then, was the formal dissolution of the expedition by the order of its leader.   When we were
brought together again under widely different circumstances, we were simply a collection of soldiers, and
while we respected the judgment and advice of Andrews, we no longer considered that we owed him military obedience.

As Conductor Fuller now disappears from our story,
where he has been so conspicuous, and where his energy, skill, and daring shine in such brilliant colors, a
few words may be appropriately devoted to his work
and subsequent history.   All the evidence goes to show
that the Confederacy had no other available man who
could have saved the bridges on the Western and Atlantic Railroad that day.   With the exception of himself and his two companions, who were in a sense sub-
ordinate to him, though their services were of very
high value, no other person seemed capable of planning
or doing anything whatever.   With a conductor of less
energy in the place of this man, the probabilities are
that we would have had the whole day uninterruptedly
for the accomplishment of our task.   But for Fuller's
daring and perseverance the extra trains would have
but added to the number of wrecks along the line as
one after another ran upon the places where the track
had been torn up; while the burning of the bridges
and the loss of telegraphic communications would have
diffused a universal panic.

The Legislature of Georgia gave Fuller a vote of
thanks for his brilliant services, and instructed the governor to bestow upon him a gold medal; but, as he
laughingly said years after, "Gold was so scarce in the
South that it was hard to find enough for a medal.   It
was therefore postponed for a time, and then came the
final collapse of the Confederacy, and I got nothing."

The Confederate authorities gave him the rank of captain by brevet. Of course, the Federal government could not recognize services rendered against itself of however striking character. No one of the adventurers ever expressed any malice towards Conductor Fuller, believing that he simply did what he regarded as his duty. He retained his place as conductor until the whole road passed under the control of General Sherman, when he enlisted in the army. After seeing considerable military service, he was directed by the Confederate government to take charge of the rolling-stock of the Western and Atlantic Railroad, and keep it out of the hands of the Federals. He removed it to various parts of Georgia and South Carolina as the exigencies of the war and the narrowing territory of the Confederacy required. Finally, when the supremacy of the Union was restored, he brought it back to Atlanta and surrendered it to Federal authority. He afterwards resumed his place as conductor on the same road, and remained in that situation until 1875, when he located as a merchant in Atlanta. Here for many years he delighted in talking over this day of wild adventure.

Of his two companions, Cain continued for more than twenty years as an engineer on the same road, while Murphy built up a prosperous business as a lumberman in Atlanta.

CHAPTER VII.

A NIGHT IN THE WOODS.

MANY persons, on hearing an account of this unparalleled chase, have suggested one expedient by which they imagine the fugitive Federals might have destroyed their enemy and accomplished their own purpose. "Why did you not," they say, "reverse your own engine and then jump from it, thus allowing it to knock the pursuing train from the track?" There were good reasons against that course. Such critics might as well ask a man who has ascended half-way up out of a well in a bucket why he does not cut the rope over his head for the sake of crushing somebody at the bottom of the well. That engine was the basis of all our hopes, and we could not think of abandoning it until the direst extremity. At the last moment, however, this attempt to reverse the engine for the purpose of securing a collision was made. This final effort was unavailing. The steam power was so nearly exhausted that the locomotive moved backward very slowly, and accomplished nothing beyond delaying the pursuit on foot for a very few moments. The pursuing train had no difficulty in also reversing and running back a little way until the captured engine came to a dead standstill. Indeed, the hard service of the engine had very nearly destroyed it, even before we thus flung it back at the enemy. A Confederate account says, "Their rapid running and inattention to their engine had melted all the brass from their journals." Wilson is still more graphic,—

"I could liken her condition to nothing else than the last struggles of a faithful horse, whose heartless master has driven and lashed him until he is gasping for breath, and literally dying in the harness. The powerful machine had carried us safely for more than a hundred miles, some of the time at a rate of speed appalling to contemplate, but she was becoming helpless and useless in our service. She was shaken loose in every joint, at least she seemed so; the brass on her journals and boxes was melted by the heat; her great steel tires were almost red-hot, while she smoked and sizzled at every joint. Our race was almost run."

We are not able to give an account of the time occupied by us in the different parts of this long and fearful race. The general impression of a frightful rate of speed is, however, fully borne out by one fact, which rests on the authority of the engineer of the " Texas," and I am not sure that this simple statement is not more eloquent than the most vivid word-pictures of our chase. It is simply that he ran the distance of fifty and one-half miles, made all the stops at stations for explanations and reinforcements, as well as to remove obstructions and to switch off the cars we dropped, in the space of *sixty-five minutes.* This calm and definite statement, which I have never heard disputed, implies an average velocity, when in motion, of not less than a mile per minute ! That such a speed could be attained upon a crooked road, laid with old iron rails, and with the utmost efforts of an enemy in front to obstruct the track, seems little less than miraculous.

But to return to the direct story. When the final and fatal command to disperse was given, the soldiers, still obedient to orders, jumped off, one by one, and ran, either singly or in small groups, towards the shelter of the woods. The greater number fled in a western direction.

No time was lost by the enemy in organizing a most vigorous pursuit. This would have had little terrors if conducted only by the men on the pursuing trains. Some of these did join in it, but their part was insignificant. In an incredibly short space of time the whole country was aroused. The telegraph, no longer disabled, flashed alarm in every direction. Horsemen scoured at full speed along every highway, shouting their exaggerated stories to every passing traveller and to every house and village. The whole population for scores of miles on every side of Chattanooga seemed to have abandoned every other occupation, and devoted themselves exclusively to the work of hunting the fugitive Union soldiers. Each ferry and cross-road was picketed, while armed bands explored the sides of every mountain, and searched out every valley. The people, or at least the great part of those who thus engaged in this terrible man-hunt in the woods, were not novices in the work, and employed the most efficient agencies. The dark institution of slavery rendered the work of hunting down fugitive men very familiar. One of the points in which there is a strange conflict of testimony between Northern and Southern witnesses is in relation to the employment of blood-hounds in the pursuit of Union soldiers, especially when endeavoring to escape from prison. The writer wishes to be perfectly candid in this story, and can imagine one explanation of this discrepancy. Possibly the cause of the dispute is to be found in the use of the word "blood-hound." The pure-blooded Spanish blood-hound, a ferocious and terrible beast, is comparatively rare in the Southern States. But hounds, which were used for tracking men, and some of which were very large and fierce, were very common. To a poor man, whether white or black, flying for his life through some lonely wood, who hears, through the darkness of the night, the baying of a pack of hounds on his track, and knows that their fangs will soon be fixed in his flesh, it is little comfort to reflect that the deadly beasts are probably only mongrels and not of the pure Spanish breed! Hounds were freely employed in searching for the members of our party, and we felt our blood chill with horror as we listened to their baying. Escape by concealment for any considerable length of time was scarcely possible. Rapid flight over the roughest part of the country was the only alternative, and this was far from hopeful. The adventurers were so widely dispersed that no collective narrative of their perilous wanderings is practicable. Yet many circumstances were common to all the members of the party. The drenching rain, which continued to fall, added greatly to our discomfort, and was at once a help and a hindrance. It rendered the tracking dogs much less efficient, and frequently threw them off the track altogether, but prevented us from travelling by the sun and stars; and, as we had no other guide, the flight of the greater number became a mere aimless wandering through the woods,—sometimes even in a circle. The endurance of indescribable suffering from cold, hunger, and fatigue was also an experience common to all who eluded capture for any considerable period. The expectation of a violent death immediately on capture and detection was shared by all. The only mode of giving an adequate impression of this painful but deeply interesting part of the history will be to narrate with some detail the adventures of a few of those groups, which will best serve as specimens of all. I offer my own experience first; not that it is more interesting than others,—indeed, it is greatly surpassed in number and variety of adventures by the narratives of Dorsey and Wilson,—but because it is easier to tell my own experience,—that strange weird period of hunting in the woods and mountains of Georgia, in which I was the game,—a period which stands out alone in memory separated from all former and after life!

On leaving the train the writer was alone, and for a moment his heart sank within him. No one happened to strike off in the same direction, and, although some of the fugitives might have been overtaken or fallen in with, yet the wish was strong to accompany the same band who had been associated on the southward journey. In looking for these the opportunity of going with any of the other adventurers was lost. Indeed, I hardly wished to have any other companions, as the remainder were comparative strangers, and their trustworthiness had not yet been thoroughly approved. At that time I knew nothing of the locality in which I found myself,—whether it was fifteen or fifty miles from Chattanooga,—nor had I the most indefinite idea of the character of the country. I only knew that our army and territory lay north or northwest; but as the sun did not shine, I had no means of determining the points of the compass.

The train was still moving when I jumped off,—fast enough to make me perform several inconvenient gyrations on reaching the ground. As soon as I could stand firmly I looked about for a moment, and endeavored to grasp the situation and determine what to do. I had not anticipated that the train would be abandoned and we dispersed in the woods; but, on the contrary, had relied on being under the orders of a leader until we should succeed or perish. Now I was thrown entirely on my own resources, without even a conscious reliance on the protection of God. I cannot recall even breathing a prayer in this trying moment. Yet, in a dim way, I did feel that I was not utterly forsaken. One glance round the horizon—a swift balancing of the few elements of the problem that were within my reach—and then hurried flight was all time permitted. Most of my comrades were in advance of me. Three of them had taken the eastern side of the railroad, the remainder the opposite side. In my judgment the latter was best, and, following their example, I soon reached the cover of stunted pines that grew near. Feeling the necessity of getting some start before the enemy could arrange for pursuit, I continued to run at right angles away from the railroad. A little brook that ran parallel to the railroad was soon passed, and I pressed on up the long, steep, and open slope of a hill on its opposite side. Running up-hill was too severe to be maintained long, and I was obliged to drop into a walk in plain view of the enemy. Each step was fatiguing,

and my limbs seemed made of lead. This greatly aug-
mented my fears. It was more like trying to run
away from danger in a nightmare than any waking
sensation. I saw three of my comrades not far away
on the left, and, urging my failing strength to the
utmost, tried to overtake them, but in vain. This was
a great disappointment, for I dreaded solitude above all
things, and wanted the support of sympathy. I knew
that pursuit would be rapid and instantaneous, and
could hear shouts from the pursuing trains, which had
now reached the spot and were discharging a host of
enemies. Every breeze that sighed through the branches
of the naked forest sounded like the trampling of cavalry.

The country was rough and uneven. On the bottoms
and by the streams, as well as on the steep mountains,
were a few pines ; but on the slopes and tops of the
hills, which here are a low continuation of the Cumberland range, the timber is mostly of oak and other
varieties, which were not then in foliage. This was a
great disadvantage, because it left no hiding-place and
exposed us to the watchful eyes of our enemies.

As I struggled up the hill-side the sense of faintness
and exhaustion passed away, and with strength hope came
again. Nothing in this chase seems stranger than the
manner in which my strength ebbed and flowed. When
seemingly utterly powerless, without rest, food, or sleep,
vigor came back again on more than one occasion, and
the new supply would last for hours. My more rapid
pace soon carried me over the hill-top and down to the
bend of a little river, which I subsequently learned
was the Chickamauga,—the witness, afterwards, of one
of the most desperate battles of the war. It was then
swollen by the continuous rains, and for some time I
searched along its banks in vain for a crossing-place.
Believing that death was behind, I finally committed
myself to the turbulent stream, and succeeded in getting
over, but only to find that before me the bank rose in

an almost perpendicular precipice of shelving rock not less than one hundred feet in height. I dared not re-cross the stream, for I knew the enemy could not be far behind, and I therefore clambered up the precipice. Several times, when near the top, did I feel my grasp giving way, but as often some bush or projecting rock afforded me the means of saving myself. While thus swinging up the bare rocks, I could not help thinking what a fine mark I presented if any of the enemy, with guns, should happen to arrive on the opposite bank! At last, after imminent danger, I reached the top, again utterly exhausted, pulled myself out of sight, and sank down to breathe for a while.

I had been without breakfast or dinner, and had spent not only that day but many preceding ones in the most fatiguing exertion. Enemies were on every side. There was no guide even in the direction of home, for the sun still lingered behind an impenetrable veil.

While musing on this unenviable situation in which I found myself, a dreadful sound brought me to my feet and sent the blood leaping wildly through my veins. It was the distant baying of a blood-hound! A moment's reflection would have made it certain that in the existing state of Southern customs dogs would have been used to track fugitives in the woods. It was a mere every-day incident of slavery. But this consideration brought no comfort. Alone in the woods of Georgia, the horror of being hunted with dogs was in-describable.

A few moments' listening confirmed my worst fears. They were after us with their blood-hounds! not one pack alone, but all in the country, as the widening circle from which their dismal baying echoed revealed but too plainly. There was no longer safety in idle-ness. Yet the fearful sound was not without use in supplying a guide to flight, and I am now convinced that throughout the whole chase the dogs were of more real service to us than to our pursuers, as they rendered a surprise less probable. But none the less did they add to the repulsiveness and terror of our position.

Away across the hills and streams I sped, I know not how far,—I only know that the noise of the dogs grew fainter as the evening wore on. I had distanced them and began to breathe more freely. I even indulged the hope of being able to work my way ultimately to the Federal lines. Had the clouds permitted travelling by the sun and stars, this hope might have been realized.

As I descended the long slope of a wooded hill into a solitary valley, I saw a rude hut, with a man working in a cultivated patch beside it. Believing that he could not yet have heard of our adventure, I determined to risk something in order to get information. I also felt sure that one man could not arrest me. Approaching, I asked the road to Chattanooga, and the distance. He pointed the way, and told me that it was eight miles. Adding this information to the general knowledge I had of the geography of that district, it gave me some notion of my whereabouts. I did not wish to get any nearer the rebel town, as I rightly judged that in its vicinity pursuit would be most vigorous, but I continued my journey in that direction until out of sight, when I climbed the hill at right angles to my former course. This course was maintained for some hours, when an incident occurred which would have been amusing but for the fearful perils environing me.

I had often heard of lost persons travelling in a circle, but never gave much credit to such stories. Now, I had the proof of their credibility. I believe philosophers explain the phenomenon by saying that one side of the body has a little more vigor than the other, and that when we have no guide to direct us, the stronger side (usually the right), by its tendency to go ahead of the other side, gradually turns us in the opposite direction. In other words, the right foot outwalks the left, and thus, like a carriage-horse swifter than its mate in a driverless team, can only describe perpetual circles until the will-power again takes hold of the reins. But at this time I had never heard of such theories, and the following experiences presented themselves to my mind as an inexplicable and terrifying fatality.

I had crossed a road and left it for something like an hour, during which time I walked very fast, when to my surprise I came to the same place again. I was considerably annoyed thus to lose my labor, but struck over the hill in what I now supposed to be the right direction. Judge of my astonishment and alarm when, after an hour or more of hard walking, I found myself again at precisely the same spot! So much time had been lost that the barking of the dogs now sounded very loud and near. I was perplexed beyond meas- ure and seemingly hopelessly entangled. A few steps brought me to a stream that was recognized as having been crossed hours before. In sheer desperation I took the first road that appeared, and followed it almost regardless of where it led or who was met. Previously I had kept away from the roads, and sought the most secluded route. But the risk of meeting any tangible enemy was preferable to being the sport of that bewil- dering chance which seemed to be drifting me around in a remorseless whirlpool.

Thus I pressed forward till the rainy, dreary even- ing deepened into night. I recall no thoughts of prayer, no feeling of dependence upon an infinite mercy beyond the clouds. All the memory I have of mental processes is that there was a fixed, iron-like re- solve to use every power of body and mind to escape, and in perfect calmness to await the result. I intended to do all in my own power for safety and then perish, if it must be so, with the feeling that I was not re- sponsible for it. The reader, a little farther on, will find that this feeling was so powerful that I did not shrink from any sacrifice of truth, or even from enlist- ment in the rebel army. For me the stake was life or

death. I would win if my power could by any means
be stretched so far; if not, I would pay the forfeit
when I must.

It was not perfectly dark, for there was a moon beyond the clouds, and, as I heard a wagon approaching,
I stepped to the bushes beside the road and accosted
the driver. His voice assured me that he was a negro,
and I made bold to get from him as much information
as possible. Words cannot describe the flood of disappointment, vexation, and anger that swept over my
bosom when I found I was within four miles of Chattanooga,—that town which I regarded as the lion's
mouth! So far as I had a plan it was to leave this
place far to my right, and strike the Tennessee River
twelve or fifteen miles farther down-stream. I hoped
to do this, and to cross over the river by floating on
some dry branch of a tree before morning. If the stars
came out, so that I could travel a straight course, this
hope was not unreasonable. But near Chattanooga,
however, all the river would be watched and the country around strictly patrolled. But if discouraged by
the manner in which I seemed attracted towards the
rebel headquarters, despair was useless; so, learning the
direction both of Ringgold and Chattanooga from the
negro, who, like all of his color, was ready to do anything for fugitives, with whom he had a fellow-feeling
(though I did not make my true character known to
him), I pressed forward through the rain and mud.
As the road did not lead in the right direction, I again
travelled in the fields and woods.

For some time I felt sure of having the right course
in my head and hurried on. But when I had crossed
a large field of deadened timber I was completely lost.
Soon, however, I reached a road which seemed to lead
right, and followed it with renewed vigor for several
miles. At length I met three men on horseback. It
was too dark to tell whether they were negroes or white
men, but I ventured to ask them,—

i

" How far is it to Chattanooga ?"

"Three miles !"

" Is this the right road ?"

" Yes, sah, right ahead."

These, probably, were men sent out to search for the railroad adventurers, and they did not try to arrest me because I had accosted them so boldly and was going directly towards Chattanooga.

But it was evident I was again on the wrong road. Indeed, so hopelessly bewildered was I that it seemed impossible to travel any but the wrong road. As soon as the horsemen were out of sight I turned and followed them three or four miles, until I came to a large road running at right angles with my own, which terminated where it entered the other. I deliberated some time as to which end of this new road I should take. These mountain-roads are fearfully crooked, and the one I had been travelling bent too often to give me the direction even of the dreaded Chattanooga.

Many a time had I wished for a sight of the moon and stars. Long before the clash of arms had been heard in our peaceful land, before the thunder of battle had filled a nation with weeping, astronomy had been my favorite study, and I had often longed for the parting of the clouds, that, with my telescope, I might gaze on the wonders of the world above. But never did I bend so anxious an eye to the darkened firmament as in my solitary wanderings over the Georgia hills that memorable night. All in vain ! No North. Star appeared to point with beam of hope to the land of the free !

But at length I made choice, and, as usual, on this night chose wrong. After I had gone a long distance the moon did for a moment break through a rift in the clouds and pour her welcome light down on the dark forest through which I was passing. That one glance was enough to show me that I was heading towards the railroad I had left in the morning. Even then the light was a compensation for all the disappointment, but in a moment it withdrew and the rain fell again in torrents. Wearily I turned and retraced my tedious steps, hoping in vain for another glimpse of the moon.

One of my feet had been injured by an accident three months before, and now pained me exceedingly. Still I dragged myself along. My nerves had become ex· hausted by the long-continued tension they had endured, and now played me many fantastic tricks, which became more marked as the night wore on. I passed the place where the wrong choice of roads had been made, and still toiled ahead.

I was thinly clad, and as the wind, which had risen and was now blowing quite hard, drove the falling showers against me, my teeth chattered with the piercing cold. I passed many houses, and feared the barking of the dogs might betray me to watchers within; but my fears were groundless. The storm, which was then howling fearfully through the trees, served to keep most of those who would have sought my life within-doors. For a time I seemed to have the lonely, fearful, stormy night to myself.

At last all thoughts gave way to the imperative need of rest. I reeled to a large log not far from the road, on the edge of a small patch of woodland, and crawling close under the side of it, not so much for shelter from the driving rain as for concealment from my worse dreaded human foes, I slept in peace.

Up to the time of this profound and dreamless sleep the incidents of that terrible night are graven on my memory as with a pen of fire. But after waking I found a marvellous change, and the next experience of the night floats in memory with all the voluptuous splendor of an opium-dream. Had I been at all disposed to superstition, I would have had room enough to indulge it. A rational view of religion would have enabled me to recognize the manner in which a Merciful Father interposed to relieve my sufferings,—an interposition not less real or effective because, as I still believe, purely natural. But at that time I was indisposed to admit other than the material explanation. The want of sleep, fatigue, dampness, hunger, and intense mental tension were enough to cause a mild species of delirium. But the character of this was surely extraordinary, affecting as it did the senses and imagination only, and leaving the reason and will altogether untouched. I was as rational—as able to plan, and far more able to execute, during this singular psychological experience than before. But let me narrate facts and leave the reader to his own explanations.

I cannot tell how long sleep continued, but I wakened perfectly in an instant, and with a full realization of my position. But, in addition to this, I seemed to hear some person whisper, as plainly as ever I heard a human voice,—

"Shoot him! shoot him! Let us shoot him before he wakes!"

My first impression was that a party of rebels had discovered me in my hiding-place, and that my last moment on earth had come. But the next thought brought a new suspicion, and I cautiously opened my eyes to see if my senses were really playing me false.

Directly before me stood a bush or small tree. The first glance showed me a tree and nothing more. The next glance revealed a score of angels, all clad in lovely robes, that melted into the softest outlines, their heads nodding under feathery plumes above all beauty, and their wings, bordered with violet and pearl, slowly waving with indescribable grace. As my eye wandered farther, the whole grove was transformed into a radiant paradise, in which moved celestial beings of every order, all instinct with life and blushing with love. There were rose bowers, and ladies fairer than mortal, and little cherubs floating around on cloudlets of amber and gold. Indeed, all that I had ever seen, read, or imagined of beauty was comprised in that one gorgeous vision. It was very singular, and of this I can give no explanation, except the will of God, that no hideous, terrible, or even ugly image was seen. That there were not visions of blood-hounds, chains, and scaffolds, or other forms of terror, seemingly more appropriate to my condition, is unaccountable, so far as I know, on any theory save that of heavenly grace, and, personally, I wish for no better. It was also singular that though the brain and eye were thus impressed with ideal existences, I was perfectly calm and self-possessed, knowing the whole thing to be but a pleasing illusion. I had no fear of these figures of the brain, but, on the contrary, found them excellent company. They did not always personate the same characters. Occasionally they would change to the old feudal knights, arrayed in glittering armor. The finest landscapes would start up from the cold wet hills around, like mirages in the desert. Panoramas of the most vivid action passed before me, and the ear joined the eye in the work of pleasing illusion, for even language was not denied to my visitants, whose voices were inexpressibly melodious, and even very sweet music was occasionally heard.

Not less remarkable was the renewal of strength I felt. To walk or run was no longer a burden. To say that I was perfectly refreshed is altogether an inadequate expression. I seemed to have supernatural strength, and to be incapable of any weariness or disagreeable sensation whatever. Even the merciless pelting of the cold rain was pleasant and delightful! I was perfectly easy and peaceful in mind, feeling no fear, though perfectly conscious of my real situation and peril, and retaining the full force of the resolve to use every exertion for escape.

While night and darkness were thus changed into visions of beauty and joy around me, another faculty penetrated beyond these highly-colored illusions, and showed me, though in faint lines, the true face of the country and of events. Yet I had no hesitation in controlling my conduct with respect to the faint rather than the bright pictures, and was only once, for a few minutes, deceived, and then by supposing the real to be fictitious. The error very nearly involved me in a serious difficulty. At a cross-road, I saw from a distance what I supposed, at first, to be a group of my spectral friends standing around a fire, the ruddy blaze of which rendered them clearly visible. They were not so beautiful as former figures, but I advanced un-suspectingly towards them, and would probably have continued until too late for retreat had not my progress been arrested by a sound of all others least romantic,— the squealing of a pig! The men around the fire had caught the animal, and were killing it preparatory to roasting it in the fire! This immediately drove away the seraphs and the angels! I listened, and became convinced that they were a picket sent out to watch for just such travellers as myself. Some dogs were with them, but these were, fortunately, too much absorbed in the dying agonies of the pig to give attention to me.

I crawled cautiously away, and made a long circuit through the fields. A dog from a farm-house made himself exceedingly annoying by following and bark-ing after me. I did not apprehend danger from him, for I had managed to keep my trusty revolver dry all this time, but I feared he would attract the attention of the picket.

When he left me I returned to the road, but came to three horses hobbled down, which, no doubt, belonged to the picket behind, and had to make another circuit to avoid driving them before me. Then I pressed on, hoping that some good chance, if not providence, might bring me to the steep banks of the Tennessee. Yet I was not sanguine, for the country was more open and level than I expected to find in the vicinity of the river. Very many miles—possibly a score, or even more, for my pace was rapid—were passed in this manner, but at last my visions began to fade. I was ьorry to see them go, for they seemed like a good omen, and they had been cheerful companions. When the last form of beauty disappeared the chill horror of my situation froze into my veins; my strange strength also passed gradually away. I would find myself staggering along almost asleep,—would wander a short distance from the road to a secluded spot, throw myself on the flooded ground, and be instantly asleep,—then, in a few moments, awaken, almost drowned by the pitiless rain, and so weary, cold, and benumbed that I could scarcely rise and plod onward.

Thus the latter part of that dreary night wore on. It seemed an age of horror, and places a shuddering gulf between my present life and the past. At length the cold gray dawn of a clouded morning broke through the weeping sky. Day brought no relief. I had not yet any guide, and had not stumbled on the Tennessee. I feared to make inquiries. Every one I saw seemed a foe. Still, I did not avoid them, or leave the road for any great distance. Slowly a new plan formed itself in my mind, for, if the rain and clouds continued, I despaired of working my way to our lines. What this plan was will appear in due time. It will be enough to say here that I did not now think a capture would be fatal, if once far enough away from the place where the train was abandoned, to plausibly deny all knowledge of that raid. I hardly thought it possible that I could endure another day and night alone in the woods. To prepare for all emergencies, I carefully washed all traces of that terrible night from my clothes. The wet would not matter, for the falling rain accounted perfectly for that.

It was Sabbath morning, but it came not to me with the blessed calmness and peace that accompany it in my own far-off Ohio. I realized how sweet those Sabbath hours and Sabbath privileges had been, which I had never valued before. I saw the people going to church, and longed to go with them. Of course this was impossible, but with the thought came more of a feeling of worship and of desire for God's protection than I had ever known before. In that hour I believe His blessed Spirit was calling me; but I soon turned my mind in another direction, preferring to plan for my own deliverance, and to arrange the stories I would tell if arrested, or if I ventured to any house for food, as would soon be necessary.

CHAPTER VIII.

IN THE ENEMY'S POWER.

But I will dwell no longer on the miseries of this dreary morning. Its hours went tediously by, marked by no special incidents till about noon. Just beyond Lafayette, Georgia, I was observed by some one on the watch for strangers. A party of pursuit numbering twenty or thirty was at once organized. I knew nothing of my danger till they were within fifty yards, when I heard them calling for me to stop.

A single glance showed my helplessness. I laid my hand instinctively on my revolver, but knew that fight was useless. Neither was flight possible. The country was open and I was too weary to run, even if some of the party had not been mounted and others armed with rifles and shot-guns. It was time to see what could be made of my plans carefully contrived for just such an emergency. Therefore, making a virtue of necessity, I turned round and demanded what they wanted, though I knew only too well. They said courteously enough that they wanted to talk with me awhile. Soon they came up, and a brisk little man who had the epaulets of a lieutenant, but whom they called "Major," began to ask questions. He was very bland, and apologized

profusely for interrupting me, but said if I was a patriotic man (as he had no doubt I was) I would willingly
undergo a slight inconvenience for the good of the
Confederacy. I endeavored to emulate his politeness,
begging him to proceed in the performance of his duty,
and assuring him that he would find nothing wrong.
He searched me very closely for papers, and examined
my money and pistol, but found no ground for suspicion.

He next asked me who I was, where I came from,
and where I was going. I expected all these questions
in about that order, and answered them categorically.
I told him I was a citizen of Kentucky, of Fleming
County, who had become disgusted with the tyranny
of the Lincoln government, and was ready to fight
against it; that I came to Chattanooga, but would not
enlist there because most of the troops were conscripts,
and the few volunteers very poorly armed. I told him
where I had lodged in Chattanooga, and many things
about the troops there, using all the knowledge I had
acquired of that character while riding on the cars to
Marietta the preceding Friday. I had also heard many
words of praise spoken of the First Georgia Regiment,
and now told the major that I wished to join that
noble organization. This flattered his State pride, but
he asked me one question more,—why I had not gone
directly to Corinth, where the First Georgia was, without coming to Lafayette, which was far out of the way.
The question conveyed much information, as I did not
before know that I was near Lafayette, or out of the
road from Chattanooga to Corinth. I answered as well
as I could by alleging that General Mitchel was said to
be at Huntsville, and that I was making a circuit around
to avoid the danger of falling into his hands.

This seemed to be perfectly satisfactory to the little
man, and, turning to the attentive crowd, he said,—

"We may as well let this fellow go on, for he seems
to be all right."

12*

I was greatly rejoiced at these words, and cast about in my own mind to see if I could not gain something more before passing on the way. But my joy was premature. A dark-complexioned man on horseback, with his hat drawn over his brows, looked slowly up and drawled out,—

"Well, y-e-s! Perhaps we'd as well take him back to town, and if it's all right, maybe we can help him on to Corinth."

This was rather more help than I wanted, but there was no help for it. Besides, I reasoned that if I could keep on good terms with this party, I could get information and aid that would be invaluable towards my final escape. Nothing could really suit me much better than actually to be forwarded to Corinth and enlisted in the First Georgia. I knew the ordeal of questioning before that course was determined on would be very trying, but did not despair. If I could only have had some food and a few hours' rest!

They conducted me to the largest hotel of the place, where I was received with much ceremony, but they neglected to order dinner. I could have had drink enough, but was too prudent to touch it, even if I had not always been a teetotaler. Soon all the lawyers came in,—Lafayette is a county-seat,—and they all had liberty to question me. For four mortal hours, as I could see by a clock in the room, I conversed with them and answered questions. We talked of everything, and their questions grew more and more pointed. I answered as well as I could, and never let an opportunity pass to put in a question in turn, for it was much easier and less perilous to ask than answer. When I told them I was from Kentucky, they wished to know the county. I told them Fleming. They asked after the county-seat. This also I could give. But when they asked after adjoining counties I was sorely perplexed. One of them said it was singular a man could not bound his own county. I asked how many of them

could bound the county we then were in. This question had a double purpose,—to gain time and information. They mentioned several and fell into a dispute,
to settle which a map had to be produced. I got a
look at it also,—a mere glance, for it was soon out of
reach of my eager gaze; but I had seen much. Then
they requested a narrative of my journey all the way
from Kentucky. This I gave very easily and in great
detail as long as it was on ground not accessible to my
inquisitors. I told the truth as far as that would not
be compromising, and then pieced out with inventions.
The time I had spent on the train and in the woods
were hardest to arrange for. I had to *invent* families
with whom I had lodged; tell the number of children
and servants at each place, with all kinds of particulars.
I knew not how many of my auditors might be familiar
with the country I was thus fancifully populating, and
was careful not to know too much. I plead forgetfulness as often as that plea was plausible, but it would not
do to use it too often. I might have refused to answer
any question, but this would have been a tacit admis-
sion of some kind of guilt,—at least as good as a *mob*
would have required. I might safely use any retorts
and sharpness in conversation,— and I did talk with
perfect freedom,—but I had the feeling that silence
would have brought me in danger of the lash and the
rope. Can the reader conceive of any situation more
critical and perilous: starving and almost fainting from
weariness, in the midst of a growing tavern crowd,
questioned by acute lawyers, and obliged to keep every
faculty on the alert, feeling that an incautious answer
would probably lead to an instant and frightful death,
and compelled under such pressure to tell falsehood
after falsehood in unending succession?

But I had an increasing hope if my endurance continued to the end. At supper-time I meant to boldly
demand food, and I felt sure of getting it. Besides,
although they were clear that I was a suspicious char-

acter, they did not seem in any way to connect me with the great railroad expedition,—the only identification I feared. The very fact that I was so far away from the point where the train was abandoned was in my favor. Temporary confinement, enlistment in the army, anything they were likely to do was without terror as long as I was not connected with the daring adventure which had culminated the day before. They were somewhat perplexed by the assurance with which I spoke, and held numerous private consultations, only agreeing that the case needed further investigation.

Matters were in this position when a man, riding a horse covered with foam, dashed up to the door. He came from Ringgold and brought the news—of deeper interest to me than to any one else—that several of the bridge-burners had been taken near the place where they abandoned the train. When first apprehended they claimed to be CITIZENS OF KENTUCKY, FROM FLEMING COUNTY; but on finding that this did not procure their release, they confessed being Ohio soldiers, sent by General Mitchel to burn the bridges on the Georgia State Railroad!

I have no reason to believe that any of those who were captured described their companions, or gave any information leading intentionally to their discovery. This was not needed. The unfortunate telling of the same fictitious story and the subsequent revelation of their true character on the part of some of the number who were captured close to the abandoned train, unmasked the others as well. After the first captures, which were made Saturday afternoon, whenever a fugitive was arrested who hailed from *Fleming County, Kentucky*, and was not able to prove his innocence, he was at once set down as a member of the railroad party.

The message from Ringgold ended all uncertainty in my own case. I was at once conducted, under strict guard, to the county jail.

The little major was my escort. He took advantage
of his position to purloin my money, and then turned
me over to the county jailer. That personage took my
penknife and other little articles of property, then led
me up-stairs, unfastened a door to the right, which led
into a large room with barred windows, and having a
cage, made of crossing iron bars, in the centre. He
unlocked the small but heavy iron door of the cage
and bade me enter. For the first time in my life I was
to be locked in jail! My reflections could not have
been more gloomy if the celebrated inscription had
been written over the cage that Dante placed above the
gate of hell, " All hope abandon, ye who enter here."
     There did seem absolutely no hope for me. I was
there as a criminal, and I knew that life was held too
cheaply in the South for my captors to be fastidious
about disposing of an unknown stranger. I had heard
the message from Ringgold, and at once comprehended
its bearing against me. Nothing save a confession of
my true character as a soldier and my real business in
the South would be credited. The probability was that
even this would only make my doom the more speedy.
     In that hour my most distressing thoughts were of
the friends at home, and especially of my mother,—
thinking what would be their sorrow when they heard
of my ignominious fate,— if, indeed, they ever heard,
for I had given " John Thompson" instead of my own
name. That all my young hopes and ambitions, my
fond dreams of being useful, should perish, as I then
had no doubt they would, on a Southern scaffold,
seemed utterly unbearable. But one moment only did
these thoughts sweep over me; the next they were rejected by a strong effort of the will as worse than useless, and were followed by a sense of unutterable
relief, for I could now rest. I had found a refuge even
in prison, and needed no longer to keep every failing
faculty at the utmost tension. The sweetness of rest
for the moment overcame every other feeling save

hunger, and that, too, was soon satisfied. The jailer brought some coarse food, which was devoured with exceeding relish. There was another prisoner in the same cage,—probably a detective, put in for the purpose of gaining my confidence and leading me to a confession. His first step was to plead ill health as an excuse for not eating his share of the prison food. I excused him, and ate his allowance as well as my own without difficulty.

He then wished to talk, and asked me some questions, but I was in no mood for further conversation. Being cold I borrowed his prison blankets, of which he had a plentiful supply, and, wrapping myself up in them, soon sank into a deep sleep—profound and dreamless—such as only extreme fatigue can produce. The quaint advice contained in the last words of my companion, however, lingered in my memory. Said he,—

" If you are innocent of the charge they make against you, there is no hope for you. You are much worse off than if you are guilty, for they will hang you on suspicion, while, if you are a soldier, you can tell what regiment you belong to, and claim protection as a United States prisoner of war."

My sleep lasted until long after dawn of the next morning. This repose, with the breakfast which followed, completely restored my strength, and with the elasticity of youth I began to revolve my situation and plan for the future. I was not long left in loneliness. The people of the village and surrounding country came in throngs to see a man who was supposed to belong to the daring band of engine thieves,—one of the most common names by which our party was recognized during our imprisonment. They were very free in their criticisms of my appearance, and some were very insulting in their remarks. But I would not allow myself to be drawn into conversation with them, for I had a momentous question to decide in my own mind.

The more I thought of the advice of my fellow-prisoner the more weighty did it appear. I did not value it because it was his opinion, but because it seemed reasonable. I also longed to assume my true name once more and my position as a soldier. The thought of perishing obscurely and in disguise was most revolting. Besides, I felt that a soldier had more chances of life than a suspected wanderer. Our government might put forth energetic efforts to save those who were in such deadly peril. I remembered, with increasing hope, that the Federals, at this very time, held a number of rebel prisoners in Missouri, who had been captured while disguised in Federal uniform inside of our lines, engaged in an attempt very similar to our own,—the burning of some railroad bridges. Why might not these be held as hostages to assure our safety, or even exchanged for us? To entitle me to any help from our government I must be William Pittenger, of the Second Ohio Volunteer Infantry, and not John Thompson, of Kentucky. My mind was soon made up,—the more readily that I heard my citizen visitors talking about the capture of several others of our party, who had all admitted that they were United States soldiers. They were influenced, no doubt, by the same course of reasoning that I have indicated. I believe this decision ultimately saved my life.

But there was room for choice as to the manner of making my confession. I told the jailer that I had an important communication for the authorities, and he reported the matter to some person of influence, who summoned a vigilance committee, and ordered me before it.

I found them prepared to renew the examination of the previous day. They had the same lawyers in waiting, and, indeed, all the principal men of the town. When their preliminaries were over, they asked the nature of the communication I wished to make, and hoped that I could throw some light on the mysterious capture of the railroad train. I said,—

"Gentlemen, the statements I made yesterday were intended to deceive." ("So we suspected," said one of the lawyers, *sotto voce.*) "I will now tell you the truth."

The clerk got his pen ready to take down the information, and the roomful of people assumed an attitude of deepest attention.

"Go on, sir; go on," said the president.

"I am ready," said I, "to give my true name, and the division and regiment of the United States army to which I belong, and to tell why I came so far into your country."

"Just what we want to know, sir. Go on," said they.

"But," I returned, "I will make no statement whatever until taken before the regular military authority of this department."

Their disappointment and surprise at this announcement were almost amusing. Curiosity was raised to the highest pitch, and did not like to postpone its gratification. They employed every threat and argument in their power to make me change my decision,—some of them saying that I should be hanged to the nearest tree if I did not. But I knew my ground. I told them that though an enemy I was a soldier, possessed of important military information, and, if they were loyal to their cause, it was their duty to take me at once before some regular military authority. The leading men admitted the justice of this view, and when they found that I would reveal nothing there, they made arrangements to take me to Chattanooga. This was distant about twenty miles from Lafayette. Ringgold, near which we abandoned the train, was about the same distance to the east. In that long and terrible night of wandering I had travelled twenty miles in a straight line, and, with my meanderings, must have walked more than fifty.

My reason for postponing my confession until reaching Chattanooga was that I wanted to get out of the hands of the mob as soon as possible. There was no body of soldiers or responsible authority in Lafayette. If I had perished there no one, in any contingency, could have been called to account for it. Where a department commander was stationed I would have to reckon with him alone, which was far preferable, and I counted on the curiosity of the mob to preserve me as long as my secret was not revealed.

I was remanded to the jail to wait for the preparation of a suitable escort. After dinner about a dozen men entered my room, and guarded me out to the public square. There a carriage was waiting, in which I was placed, and then commenced the complicated process of tying and chaining.

By this time a great mob had gathered, completely filling the square, and in the most angry and excited condition. Some persons questioned me in loud and imperious tones, demanding why I came down there to fight them, and adding every possible word of insult. I heard many significant hints about getting ropes, and the folly of taking me to Chattanooga when I could be hanged just as well there.

For a little time I made no answer to any question, and paid as little attention as possible to what was said. But the tumult increased, and the mob grew so violent in its denunciations that I feared a passive policy would no longer serve. Though I was being very effectually bound, my tongue was still at liberty. I had no experience in managing mobs, but I felt, by a kind of instinct, that mobs and dogs are very similar,—neither likes to attack a person who quietly and good-humoredly faces them. I had proved this with savage dogs several times for mere sport, but this was a more serious matter. I was not much in the humor of talking, but it was better to be led by policy than by inclination. Selecting, therefore, some of the nearest persons, I spoke to them. They answered with curses, but in the very act of cursing they grew milder and more willing to converse. I answered their innuendoes cheerfully, jesting, whenever opportunity offered, about the manner I was being secured, the bracelets they were giving me, the care they had for a "Yankee," as they persisted in calling me, and tried to look and speak as if the whole matter were a mere comedy. I soon got some of the laughers on my side, and before long had the satisfaction of hearing one man say, regretfully, " Pity he is a Yankee, for he seems to be a good fellow," and another agree to the sentiment. Yet I was not sorry to hear the driver announce that we were now ready to start.

The manner in which I was tied indicated that my captors intended to "make assurance doubly sure, and take a bond of fate." One end of a heavy chain was put around my neck, and fastened there with a padlock; the other end was passed behind the carriage-seat, and hitched to my foot in the same manner, the chain being extended to its full length while I was in a sitting position, thus rendering it impossible for me to rise. My hands were tied together, my elbows were pinioned to my sides by ropes, and, to crown all, I was firmly bound to the carriage-seat, while two horsemen, armed with pistols and carbines, followed the carriage at a short distance, and my evil genius, the little major, took the seat beside me, likewise armed to the teeth. I ought to have felt secure, but did not. The same exaggerated caution was often noticed afterwards.

As we left Lafayette behind, the sky, which had been clouded for days, suddenly cleared. The sun shone in beauty, and smiled on the first faint dawnings of spring that lay in tender green on the surrounding hills. What would I not have given for such a day forty-eight hours earlier! But even then it was very welcome, and my spirit grew more light as I breathed the fresh air and listened to the singing of the birds.

My companions were quite talkative, and I responded

as well as I could. They even tried to make me think
that the extraordinary manner in which I was tied and
guarded—with which I reproached them—was a compliment, showing that they had formed a high opinion
of my daring character! Their conversation was pleasant and courteous enough, except that when they passed
houses they would cry out, " We've got a live Yankee
here !" Then men, women, and children would rush
to the door, staring as if they saw some great monster,
and asking,—

" Whar did you ketch him? Goin' to hang him
when you get him to Chattanooga?" and similar expressions without number.

I cared little for this at first, but its perpetual recurrence was not without its effect in making me think
that they really would hang me. In fact, my prospects were far from encouraging; yet I considered it
my duty to keep up my spirits and hold despair at
arm's length while any possible ground for hope remained. The afternoon wore slowly away as we journeyed amid grand and romantic scenery that in any
other circumstances would have been enthusiastically
enjoyed. But now my thoughts were otherwise engaged.

I was not so much afraid of death in itself as of the
manner in which it was likely to come. Death amid
the smoke and excitement and glory of battle never had
seemed half so terrible as it now did when it stood, an
awful spectre, beside the gallows ! And even sadder
it was to think of friends who would count the weary
months, waiting and longing for my return, till hope
became torturing suspense, and suspense deepened into
despair. These and kindred thoughts were almost too
much for my fortitude; yet, setting my teeth hard, I
resolved to endure patiently to the end.

The sun went down, and night came on,—deep,
calm, and clear. One by one the stars twinkled into
light. I gazed upon their beauty with new feelings,

as I wondered whether a few more suns might not set
me free from the short story of earthly things and make
me a dweller beyond the sky.   A spirit of prayer
and the faint beginnings of trust stirred within me.
Hitherto I had been looking at passing events alone,
and refusing to contemplate the great new experiences
death would open.   But now my thoughts took a new
direction.   God was helping me, and inclining my
heart upward.   I was to pass through many more terrible scenes and taste bitter sorrows before I could recognize His voice and fully repose on His love.   I was
not then a member of church nor a professor of religion.   I believed the doctrines of Christianity, and
purposed some day to give them practical attention.   It
had been easy to postpone this purpose, and, latterly,
the confusion and bustle of camp-life had almost driven
the subject out of my mind.   But now God appeared
very near, and, even amid foes and dangers, I seemed
to have hold of some hand, firm but kind, beyond the
reach of vision.   What influence was most powerful in
turning my thoughts upward I cannot tell,—whether
it was the familiar outlines of the grand constellations,
the quiet and stillness all around, so congenial to exhausted nature after the excitement of the last few days,
or a yet more direct message from the Highest,—I
only know that the memory of that evening, when I
was carried, chained, down the long hill to the valley
in which Chattanooga lies, there to meet an unknown
fate, is one of the sweetest of my life.   My babbling
guards had subsided into silence, and, as we wended
along through the gathering darkness, high and noble
thoughts of the destiny of man filled my breast, and
death appeared only a mere incident of existence,—the
gate out of one department of being into another.   I
was nerved for any fate.

  It may be thought strange that in these moments of
reflection and spiritual yearning I had no feeling of remorse for any of the deceptions of which I had been

guilty. But I had not. It did not even occur to me
to consider them as sins at all. If necessary or expedient I would then have added to them the sanction
of an oath with equal recklessness. Some sophistry—
felt rather than reasoned out—about the lawfulness of
deceiving or injuring public enemies or rebels in any
possible way—a conviction that they had forfeited
everything, even their right to be told truth—must
have controlled me. Before starting on this expedition
I had placed the highest value on truth, and would
have regarded a wilful lie with scorn and loathing.
But I accepted deception as one of the incidents of the
enterprise, and all sense of its wrongfulness passed
away, and did not return until long afterwards.

We arrived at Chattanooga while a feeble glow of
the soft spring twilight lingered in the air. The headquarters of General Leadbetter, then district commander, was in one of the principal hotels of the town,
and we at once drove there. I was left in the carriage
while the major ascended to inform him of the arrival.

The town had already been informed. The curiosity
to see one of the men who had captured the train and
frightened the women and children of Chattanooga
into the woods only two days before was intense, and a
very large crowd soon assembled. They behaved as
such assemblages usually did, jeering and hooting, and
calling me by every epithet of reproach the language
afforded,—wanting to know why I came down there to
burn their property and murder them and their children
as well as free their negroes. To these multitudinous
questions and assertions I made no answer. I was
much amused (afterward!) by their criticisms of my
appearance. One would say that "it was a pity so
young and clever-looking a man should be caught in
such a scrape." Another, of more penetrating cast,
"could tell that he was a rogue by his looks,—probably
came out of prison in his own country." Another was
surprised that I could hold up my head and look around

on honest men, arguing that such brazen effrontery in one so young was a proof of enormous depravity of heart. I gave no opinion on the subject. Indeed, I was not asked.

There was one man I noticed in particular. He was tall and venerable-looking; had gray hair, gray beard, a magnificent forehead, and, altogether, a commanding and intellectual expression. He was treated with marked deference by the throng, and as they parted and allowed him to come up to my carriage, the thought arose, "Surely I will receive some sympathy from that kind and noble-looking man."

His first question confirmed my hope. Said he,—
"How old are you?"

I answered, "Twenty-two, sir."

Gradually his lip wreathed itself into a curl of unutterable scorn, and, gazing steadily on me, he slowly uttered,—

"Poor young fool! And I suppose you were a school-teacher or something of that kind in your own land! And you thought you would come down here and rob us, and burn our houses, and murder us, did you? Now let me give you a little advice: if you ever get home again, (but you never will!) do try, for God's sake, and have a little better sense and stay there." Then he turned contemptuously on his heel and strode away. The rabble rewarded him with a cheer. I could never find out who he was; but after that I looked for no more sympathy in that crowd.

My conductor now returned and escorted me into the presence of General Leadbetter. I was glad of the change, though there was little about this man to inspire confidence. They said he was from the North originally,—a native of Maine, I believe. His habits were so intemperate that a Confederate captain afterwards informed me that he always lived in one of two states,—either dead drunk or gentlemanly drunk. His record was, even this early in the war, of a very ill

character, for he had been the principal agent in hanging a considerable number of East Tennessee Union
men under circumstances of great barbarity. To this,
it was said, he owed his present position. Such was
the man in whose hands my fate now rested.

All the facts concerning him I learned afterwards,
except one that was apparent when I entered the room.
He was considerably under the influence of liquor,
though not to an extent which interfered with the
transaction of business. He began to question me, and
without any regard for truth I gave him the story that
I supposed would be best for my own interest. I told
him I was a United States soldier, giving my name,
company, and regiment correctly ; but told him I was
sent on this expedition without my previous consent,
and was ignorant of where I was going or what I was
to do, which I only learned as fast as it was to be executed. He next inquired who was our engineer, but
I refused to tell. I afterwards found that they were
exceedingly anxious to discover the name of the person
who ran our train, imagining him to be some official
connected with the Georgia State Railroad. He then
asked after the purpose of the expedition. I pleaded
ignorance as far as any positive information went ; but
as this did not satisfy him, I gave him my inferences.
There was no betrayal of Union interests in this, for
all I told him was what any thoughtful person, map
in hand, would have supposed,—the destruction of
bridges and the capture of Chattanooga and the occupation of East Tennessee. He was very attentive, and
said,—

"But has Mitchel men enough for all that? My
spies report that he has not more than ten thousand
infantry and three regiments of cavalry."

This was so near the truth that I did not wish to
confirm it. So I took another departure from accuracy,
and said,—

"That must refer only to his advance-guard, and

leaves out of account that part of his command which has not yet left Nashville."

"What!" he returned, "is there a reserve army?"

I assured him there was, and that with the regiments on their way from the West and Northwest, sixty or seventy thousand men would be at Nashville for Mitchel's disposal in three or four weeks!

Leadbetter then asked, "What do you soldiers think is going to be done with such a large army?"

"We are confident," I answered, "that Chattanooga will first be captured, then Atlanta, and afterwards Mitchel may probably strike for some point on the coast, so as to cut the Confederacy in halves."

The general rubbed his forehead for a moment, then exclaimed,—

"It's a grand plan. They can do it if they have men enough. But I had no idea that Mitchel had such backing."

How I did wish that he had! but I knew better.

Then wheeling his chair directly in front, and fixing his eye steadily on me, he continued,—

"I am much obliged to you for this information. Now, sir, I want you to tell me just how many men you had on that train, and to describe each one so that I may know them when I get hold of them."

This was too much! I answered, "General, I have freely told you whatever concerns only myself, because I thought you ought to know that I am a soldier under the protection of the United States government. But I am not base enough to describe my comrades."

"Oh!" sneered he, "I don't know that I ought to have asked you that."

"I think not, sir," I replied.

"Well," retorted he, "you need not be so particular. I know all about it. Your leader's name is Andrews. What kind of a man is he?"

I was thunderstruck! How should he have Andrews' name, and know him to be our leader? I never imagined what I afterwards found to be the true cause,—that Andrews had been captured, with documents in his possession which implicated him so completely that he acknowledged his name and the fact of his leadership. I had every confidence that *he*, at least, would escape and devise some means for our relief. So I answered boldly,—

"I can tell you only one thing about him, and that is, he is a man you will never catch."

As I said this I thought I noticed a peculiar smile on the general's face, but he only replied,—

"That will do for you;" and turning to a captain who stood by, continued: "Take him to the hole,—you know where that is."

With a military salute, the captain took me out of the room. There was an explanation of the general's smile! Before the door, heavily ironed, stood Andrews, waiting for an audience, and with him Marion Ross and John Wollam. I did not think it prudent to recognize them, nor they to recognize me, so we passed each other as strangers.

CHAPTER IX.

OTHER CAPTURES.

As all the members of our party were ultimately assembled at Chattanooga, so that from that time our stories flow together. it is now well to bring the separated threads of narration down to that point. One of the shortest and most lamentable was that of Jacob Parrot and Samuel Robinson, both of the Thirty-third Ohio Regiment. When they left the train in company they reached the woods, but on the wrong side of the road. After being concealed for a short time they came back to the railroad, but in attempting to cross it were observed by four citizens and captured. They were immediately conducted to Ringgold, where a company of Confederate soldiers was stationed. A course of questioning here began, but Parrot refused to tell anything. He was but little over eighteen years of age, very boyish-looking, and entirely destitute of education. So they seem to have thought him a favorable subject for receiving the treatment applied to those fugitive slaves who hesitate in answering questions. He was taken out of the room by an officer and four men, who stripped him and, holding him down over a large stone, administered over one hundred lashes on his bare back, leaving scars which the writer has often seen, and which he will carry to his grave. Three times the whipping was suspended, the poor boy let up and asked if he was ready to confess, and on his refusal he was thrown down again, and the torture continued. They wished to force from him the name of the engineer and the particulars of the expedition. But all their efforts were in vain. The crowd procured a rope and were about to hang him, but an officer of higher rank came up and prevented this final barbarity.

The wonderful fortitude of the poor boy was of no avail. He and his comrade were caught so near the place where they left the disabled engine, and they were so utterly unable to give any account of the manner in which they came to be there, that both would no doubt have perished if Robinson had not—after first trying the Fleming County, Kentucky, story, and being falsely informed that Parrot had confessed everything—finally given his name and regiment, with the general outline of the expedition. After this confession they were imprisoned for a time in Ringgold, and afterwards brought to Chattanooga.

D. A. Dorsey furnishes me an account of his adventures, which were in some respects peculiar. My own special friend, George D. Wilson, was with him, as well as William Bensinger and Robert Buffum. I use Dorsey's own graphic language,—

" We fled from our broken down iron-horse in a northeasterly direction towards the adjacent hills. These were sparsely studded with timber, but almost entirely destitute of undergrowth, and, of course, afforded but little opportunity to hide from our pursuers. The latter were following upon our trail, well armed and very numerous. Here occurred the first of many an amusing scene, such as often light up the most horrible situation. Buffum had worn a peculiar long gray coat, reaching nearly to his feet, of which he had been very proud. Now he found it a sore impediment to his precipitate flight, and unbuttoning it, ran right out of it, leaving it spread out on the old dry weeds behind him, —not even stopping to get the bottle out of the pocket, in which he and I had been deeply interested for the past twenty-four hours.

" On we went, or rather flew, until we had distanced our pursuers, and found ourselves in a denser forest. It was very cloudy. The sun was completely hidden, and we could not tell which was north, south, east, or west. We wandered on until near midnight, when we came to a log hut in a small opening, surrounded by a dilapidated rail-fence. The light of a blazing fire shone through the cracks in the wall, and we walked to the door and knocked repeatedly. Getting no answer, Wilson pulled the latch-string and walked in. There a tall Georgian lay stretched at full length on the floor, with his bare feet to the fire, almost undressed, and suffering all the agonies of colic. Over him bent his better half, busily engaged in administering hot-ash poultices. Of course, under such circumstances, our application for food availed nothing, and we were obliged to plod on through the darkness, mud, and rain. Before morning we came to another cabin, which we did not enter, but borrowed a pail of milk from the porch, and taking it to the woods, speedily devoured it. Then we wandered on, hoping for clear sky, but the clouds were unbroken, and our wandering at random continued all the morning.

" About ten o'clock, in the forenoon, we saw some persons on horseback, who were evidently hunting for us. We managed to elude them, and getting back to ground they had passed over, concealed ourselves by lying down. Several other parties were seen, but by shifting our position we avoided them for some hours. The increasing number of our pursuers, however, convinced us that we were in the most deadly peril.

> " ' Oh, ye woods, spread your branches apace !
> To your deepest recesses I fly ;
> I would hide with the beasts of the chase,
> I would vanish from every eye

> " ' And hark ! and hark ! the deep-mouthed bark
> Comes nigher still and nigher.
> Burst on the path a dark blood-hound,
> His tawny muzzle tracked the ground,
> And his red eye shot fire.'

"These words of the poet were fully echoed by my feelings. The much-dreaded blood-hound was upon our trail. We discovered three of them descending a hill over which we had recently passed, right on our track, and four men behind them. As soon as the latter discovered us, one of their number hallooed, and was answered by shouts in every direction. This demonstrated that we were surrounded. We advanced and boldly met the first four, and endeavored to deceive them as to our real character. Our denials of being the men who captured the train the day before were all to no purpose. Soon we were surrounded by at least fifty men, armed with shot-guns, rifles, and pistols. One man carried a long *rope*. To say they were furious would be a mild description. They demanded, in all kinds of profane and vindictive language, our immediate surrender. We were separated into two squads. Buffum and Bensinger stood together, and did what they could to prove that they were victims of a case of mistaken identity. Wilson and I were a few yards distant, and, as he was the better talker, I left it all to him. He protested that we were not the men they wanted, but citizens of Virginia hunting for fugitive slaves. He told a very nice and plausible story,—I thought it ought to have convinced any reasonable man,—but it was in vain."

[This was the only case, except one, so far as I know, where the Kentucky story was varied from, and even then Buffum and Bensinger were using it. Had Wilson and Dorsey been alone they might have succeeded better. Dorsey continues :]

"We had to surrender or fight. The latter course would have been madness. We handed over our revolvers and pocket-knives on demand, and then commenced the most terrible threats of vengeance. A young blood, who appeared not more than sixteen, put a pistol at Wilson's head, and would, no doubt, have shot him had he not been prevented by one they called ' major.' A rough fellow they called ' Black Billy' presented a double-barreled shot-gun to my breast, swore he had sixteen buckshot in each barrel, and unless I made a ' clean breast' of it he would blow them all through me. This roused my indignation, and considering my life worth nothing if I confessed, while a confession might implicate others, I said, ' Gentlemen, we have surrendered, and you have our arms. We are in your power. If you want to shoot, just shoot !'"

LIEUTENANT D. A. DORSEY.

(One of the Adventurers.)   Page 156.

"Throwing my breast forward, in full expectation of receiving the shot, I was surprised to see him drop the butt of his gun to the ground and make arrangements for tying our hands. Having thus secured us, they conducted us to a house about a mile away, and gave us a pretty good dinner.

"Here we learned that a reward of one hundred dollars had been offered for each of the 'engine thieves.' We also learned that we were only nine miles from Ringgold, which convinced us that much of our travelling the night before must have been on the *back track*. We were certainly not as far from Ringgold when captured as we had been when the previous night set in.

"After dinner we were taken to Ringgold on foot, and *put into jail*,—the first one into which I had ever set my foot. It was Sunday, April 13, 1862. This same evening we were all removed by rail to Marietta, Georgia, where we arrived about midnight, and were there placed in a literal dungeon of the worst character,—dark, dreary, damp, and swarming with rats and smaller vermin. From this point we had started northward for the capture of the train two days before with high hopes. What adventures since that time!

"We hoped when day dawned that there would be some light in this filthy hole, but we were disappointed, for, although we could distinguish the difference between day and night, yet not enough light entered this dismal place to enable us to recognize our most intimate friend!

"A heavy guard of six hundred cadets was placed around us for the purpose of keeping down the mob. We were told that a whole company of rebel soldiers had left camp at Big Shanty to come to Marietta to lynch us, but were overtaken by their officers wnen about half-way to Marietta and dissuaded from so rash an act, the officers arguing that we were soldiers, and it would not do for them to thus violate the rules of war, and also assuring them that we would be properly dealt with, and, in due time, executed. They thus succeeded in turning them back to camp.

"We remained here a whole day and two nights. On Tuesday we heard a strange noise,—a horrible clanking and rattling of chains, while a footstep was heard mounting the outside staircase, which was the only one. Into the hall the jailer came (for it was he), and, opening the trap-door, ran a ladder down into our dungeon. Then he called Wilson up into the hall, and put one end of a new trace-chain round his neck, and locked it with a padlock, while he also placed a pair of handcuffs on his hands. I was then called, the other end of the trace-chain put around my neck, and my hands secured in the same manner. We were thus coupled together by the neck, as well as handcuffed. Bensinger and Buffum were used in the same way. Then Hawkins and Porter, of whose presence we had no previous knowledge, were called out, chained and ironed in the same manner. We were then conducted to a box-car, which had in it some bales of cotton, and started northward. The sergeant in charge of us stopped the party at Dalton, and awaited the arrival of the officer in command, who was to come on the next train. It was night, and, although our guard was as kind as they well could be under the circumstances, they had no means of feeding us. A mob surrounded the depot and threatened to hang us, but the guards managed, not without serious difficulty, to keep them off. Here we had a most grateful surprise,—one of the few really pleasant incidents which mitigated the horrors of our experience. A few Dalton ladies, with their servants, came into the waiting-room, and supplied us with a first-class supper. We relished it hugely, for we had been altogether without dinner, and our breakfast was of the scantiest character. This was the first meal we had ever eaten with chains and irons upon us, and, as the reader may judge. we felt and acted very awkwardly with these useless appendages. The ladies who had been so bountiful, requested some of our party to stand up that they might have a good look at them. They complied, in pairs at a time, and, when the other four had passed inspection and resumed their seats, their little servant-boy came with the same request to Wilson and myself. Wilson very politely declined, instructing the boy to 'tell the ladies that we are not here on exhibition, but, if they will come over this way, we will be glad to see and talk with them.' The offer was accepted, and two, a matron and young lady, apparently mother and daughter, came to our side of the room, and we had a conversation long to be remembered. They sympathized with us, and wept freely. With us the wound was too deep for tears. The ladies returned to the other part of the room when the conversation was ended, but took seats, and remained until the expected train arrived and we started for Chattanooga. All this time the mob was howling and cursing and threatening outside, and we flatter ourselves that the ladies stayed to exert a restraining influence, and hinder them from proceeding to extremities. Before we left, the younger lady referred to sent the little boy to me *with a pink rose*, with one row of leaves around it, and her name.

"The presentation of that rose seemed to exasperate those of the mob who saw it, and I am free to confess that I regretted the action, for at one time it seemed as if they would break in and seize us. But the firmness of the sergeant kept them back. I regret that I was so unchivalrous as to soon forget the name given, but in our circumstances who would try to remember a name, even that of a beautiful lady? The only encouragement as to our prospects we had yet received was that our fate would be a warning to our comrades in arms, none of whom would venture to engage in such another foolhardy expedition. The flower served more to recall home and friends than to awaken hope of any availing friendship and help in that part of the country. It was twisted round and round between my closely-cuffed hands—for the cuffs I wore had no connecting links, and fitted very tight—until one by **one** the leaves **all fell off, and** when the last **was** gone I got Wilson to put the **stem in my** pocket, and kept it a long time.

"We arrived at Chattanooga next morning. There was again **the inevitable** crowd to welcome us. 'Will those hounds hunt?' **bawled out** a coarse-voiced individual, as they led us by our neck-chains through the crowded street.

"The landlord of the hotel to which we were taken to await orders was a Union man, whom I have met since under very different circumstances. At his own expense, and on his own responsibility, he ordered his servants to bring us a good breakfast. We had by this time got on good terms with the clever guards who brought us from Marietta, and parted from them with real regret. They requested to have our names written in the little diaries many of them carried. Putting the book in one cuffed hand and the pencil in the other, they were amazed to see how well we could write under such circumstances.

"The next scene in our strange history was a terrible contrast to the peaceful occupation of eating a good breakfast and writing our names in diaries. We **were** marched to what our new conductor called 'the hole.' From the upper **room of a** prison a ladder was put down through a trap-door, and we **were** ordered **to descend into** what I can only call *hell*, for it was that **to** us. The **ladder drawn up**, the trap-door again fallen, and now in the murky **gloom came** whispered recognitions from our comrades, the warm **clasp of friendly** but ironed **hands. Andrews** and all his men **except two—Mark W**ood **and Alfred** Wilson—were now gathered **together."**

It will be remembered that J. R. Porter and M. J. Hawkins were not on the captured train at all, but joined Dorsey and his comrades at Marietta. We abridge the account of their mishaps given by Porter:

"Through some mistake or negligence of the hotel waiter **we** were not called in time for the train" (on the morning of the capture), "though we got to the depot in time to see it pass out of sight. I cannot describe my feelings at that moment. . . . We could hardly make up our minds how to meet the emergency.

"Then we leisurely strolled about the town, expecting every moment to hear of the capture of the train. Nor did we have to wait long, for the news soon reached town that a train had been captured at Big Shanty while the passengers and crew were at breakfast, and that it was done so quickly and easily that they could not imagine who did the deed or what it meant. Soon **everything was wild with excitement and the town was** thronged **with excited rebels, waiting to hear further developments. . . .** Hawkins and I concluded to 'skip out' for a time. After reaching a piece of woods we came together and congratulated ourselves on our success thus far, but what to do next we hardly knew. . . . After much hesitation we determined to go to Big Shanty, or Camp McDonald, as it was a rebel camp of instruction, and join the rebel army."

This was to put their heads into the lion's mouth. Their best course would have been to have leisurely worked their way southward instead of going where the excitement was highest. But it is always easy to be wise after the event.

" We came in sight of the camp late in the day, and marched into camp and reported at headquarters. Here we found several rebel officers, one of whom, who bore the marks of a colonel, turned his attention to us. After a short interview, which seemed plausible to him, he ordered us to report to the commanding officer of the Ninth Georgia Battalion for enlistment. One of the companies not being full was called into line, and took a vote whether or not we should be received into the company. The vote was unanimous in our favor, and we, after giving fictitious names, were assigned to a certain mess for our suppers. After supper we made the acquaintance of several of our new messmates, relating dismal stories of our treatment by the ' Yankee' hirelings in Kentucky, which made a good impression on our comrades as to our loyalty to the Confederacy.

"Everything went right with us until in some manner it leaked out among the rebels that the Yankee raiders, by mistake or accident, had left two of their party at Marietta. How this information got out I never learned, but it could not be otherwise than that some of our party had indiscreetly told more than he ought when captured. Who the man was we never learned."

Then followed the usual questionings, ending in the acknowledgment by these two of their share in the enterprise and their position as soldiers. It is not necessary to suppose, as Porter does, that one of the two captured on Saturday—it could have been no others, for Porter and Hawkins themselves were arrested Sunday morning—gave information of two of our number being left behind. Porter and Hawkins told the same Kentucky story,—even enlarged upon it to their rebel messmates, and this was enough to direct suspicion towards them. Then when examined separately by the rebels it was impossible that they could avoid becoming entangled in their stories. After examination these two were committed to the Marietta jail, where they met Dorsey and his comrades, as narrated above.

The last one of these narratives that our space will permit us to insert is the most eventful of all. Alfred Wilson and Mark Wood were the last of the whole party to be captured. The story is told in the most graphic manner by Wilson in his published account of the expedition. I would gladly give it in his own words but for its great length, and for the further fact that he gives literally many of his conversations with the rebels, in which both parties indulge in no small amount of profanity.

As Wilson ran from the abandoned engine, of which he had been the fireman, he heard his name called, and, halting a moment, was joined by Wood, the only native Englishman of the party, and from that time the two became inseparable companions. They gained an open field on a long slope in front of them, but did not feel safe in trying to cross it, especially as they were out of breath and the enemy not far away. They fortunately saw where a tree had been cut down, probably the preceding summer, and the brush lay scattered around with the dead leaves still clinging to it. Wilson adroitly covered Wood with some of the brush, making the heap so that it would not attract attention, and then crawled under beside him. There they waited with revolvers drawn, expecting to be discovered, and determined, in that event, to fight to the death. The rebels came very near, so that in some instances they might have been touched by the hidden fugitives. Their peril was extreme, but the pursuers were watching the men at a distance rather than looking for those at their feet. Much of the rebel conversation could be overheard. One of two stalwart pursuers, armed with muskets, while just by the brush-heap, cried out,—

"There goes two of them! Come on; let's go for them!"

"Let's get more help," responded the other.

"But you see they have no guns," urged the first, and they rushed out of hearing.

These two poor men remained in that one place a long while before they dared venture forth. Their escape from detection was little less than miraculous. So many persons had trampled over the ground where they left the train that the dogs could do nothing at tracking them, or their refuge would soon have been discovered. The incessant rain added very much to their discomfort, as it did in the case of all the fugitives, but helped to throw the dogs from the track.

After dark, however, they crawled out from the brush-heap, and could scarcely walk. After looking about, they decided to take an opposite course from what they had seen their comrades take, which was in the main westward from Chattanooga. They wished to pass far to the eastward of that town, and knew that they must carefully avoid it.

The remainder of that night they travelled rapidly, and about daybreak found an old barn and hid themselves in a mow of corn-fodder, where they slept comfortably until about one o'clock, when they were discovered by two women who were hunting eggs. The latter were greatly frightened, and ran to the house which stood near, but Wilson and Wood followed, said they had been in pursuit of the train-robbers, and preferred sleeping in the barn to disturbing anybody at the house. Dinner was over, but some corn-bread and buttermilk was furnished. This was the first food since leaving the train, and it was most acceptable. They paid for it, and went on their way greatly refreshed.

But they did not think it prudent to go far before seeking concealment in a dense thicket to await the approach of night. A squad of mounted soldiers went by on the road they had just left, apparently searching for some one. At nightfall they shaped their course, as nearly as they could, towards the Tennessee

River, east of Chattanooga. They avoided the roads,
but narrowly escaped running into a picket. At dawn
the foot of the mountains was reached, and the wan-
derers breathed freer than in the open country. They
witnessed the rising of the sun, and were greatly cheered
by its genial warmth. Sleep and weariness claimed
them until nearly night, and with darkness they started
on again. It was hard work, feeling the way over
rocks, climbing precipitous places, and descending the
steep inclines through bushes and briers.

On Wednesday morning mountains were on all sides,
with no sign of human life or habitation. They took
a nap in the warm sun, but hunger soon roused them.
That one meal of corn-bread and buttermilk was all
the food they had eaten since their start on Saturday.

Thus pressed by hunger, they resolved to travel day
as well as night, as in that lonely region it was not
likely they would be molested. In the afternoon they
reached the brow of a high mountain, overlooking a
lovely and peopled valley. Almost perishing with
hunger, they concluded to venture down and apply for
food at a hut a little separated from the rest. A young
woman appeared at the door, and, after hearing their
story, proceeded to get them a meal. Wilson asked the
way to the next town, the name of which he pretended
he could not just speak, but she helped him out by
mentioning—" Cleveland ?" They feasted on ham,
eggs, and rye coffee, and went on their way rejoicing.

Wilson determined to have a map of the country.
So leaving Wood outside well hidden, he ventured into
Cleveland, and bought " Mitchell's Geography and
Atlas," the work, as he thought, of his commanding
general ! He returned to Wood, tore out such portions
of the map as they needed, and threw the rest away.
They were now able to form an intelligible plan, though
the one selected was full of peril. Wilson seems to
have been fond of the water, and certainly managed
well upon it. He wished to reach the Tennessee River.

procure a boat of some kind, and float down the river past Chattanooga to some point within the Federal lines.

By evening the travellers had reached the limits of that mountain ridge, and came down again into the valley. Another secluded log house induced them to apply for food without waiting till they were on the verge of starvation. Here they were very fortunate. Only a noble-looking lady was at home at first. She heard their story, but made up her mind that they were Union men, and in that belief gave them the best fare she had, and would accept no pay for it. She and her husband, who afterwards came in, gave them all the information in their power as to the best way of avoiding the rebel cavalry in the neighborhood, and asked no confidence in return.

But misfortunes were before them. They now passed through a thickly-peopled valley, observing the greatest caution. Notwithstanding their vigilance they were suddenly halted by Colonel Snow's cavalry,—a company of rebel home-guards, whose principal business it was to keep down the Union men of the vicinity. By shrewd diplomacy they succeeded in making the captain believe that they belonged to the neighboring town of Harrison. While accepting this statement he insisted that they were trying to run away to the Union army, but agreed that they might return to their homes if they would first take the oath of allegiance to the Confederacy, and then be ready to join his company when he called for their services. The oath was a bitter pill, but they swallowed it, and were set at liberty.

They might now have taken a very safe course up the line of the Cumberland Mountains into Kentucky, but Wilson's mind was fixed upon getting a boat and going down the Tennessee, which was almost in the opposite direction. Their thoughts recurred to the Union family where they had been fed the evening before, and they resolved to return thither, and, revealing their true character, try to get help in crossing the valley to the river.

As was safest, they came up to the hut in the night. The man admitted Wilson, while the woman stood with a rifle cocked, to kill him if he proved to be an enemy. Wood had been left at some little distance outside, so as to excite less alarm. Having been sworn themselves that day they were in the mood for continuing that business, and therefore swore the man to be true to them. He kept his oath far better than they did theirs. He told them they must not be seen about his house, and led them to an abandoned hut, which stood in a secluded spot on a remote part of his farm. He then furnished them with a bundle of quilts, and told them to stay in the cellar and be perfectly quiet, assuring them that they would be safe until he could get a chance to pilot them out of the neighborhood. He and his wife supplied them with provisions while they remained here, which was for several days. Two or three reasons led to this delay. Rest was sorely needed after the fatigue endured in mountain travel, Snow's cavalry were still in the neighborhood, and they waited also for a dark night and a trusty guide to take them to the river.

The latter was found in the brother of the loyal woman whose guests they were. This man took them without difficulty, by a circuitous route, in the nighttime, to a tributary of the Tennessee, by following which they could not fail to reach the main stream.

The reason Wilson gives for his strong desire to travel by water is quite cogent. In the uneven mountainous country it was next to impossible to keep a direct course in night travel, even if they knew the general direction, while the stream would always keep them in the right way. Had they asked for guidance by their Union friends in the direction of Kentucky, however, they would have received it.

They soon saw a boat on the other side of the river, but, as the creek was swollen and encumbered with driftwood, they could not swim across. Wilson, who always took the lead, left his companion to conceal himself, and, going boldly to the bank, hallocd until a man answered, who, at his request, ferried him across. As the ferryman could not change a five-dollar note, Wilson promised to return that way in the evening—it was then morning—and make it right. He hid during the day, and came back after dark, and, in the absence of the owner, "borrowed" the boat, took Wood aboard, and was soon far away towards the Tennessee. The theft of the boat stands on the same grounds as to justification with the numerous falsehoods told by all the adventurers,—a military necessity.

At the mouth of the creek they found a patrol-boat anchored nearly across the stream, but, as it was pitch-dark and raining, they were not discovered, and, gliding close under her stern, were soon afloat on the swift current of the Tennessee. They rejoiced in this, but found that their perils were not yet over. The incessant rain was very chilling, and blinded their eyes, the wind blew almost a gale, and the current whirled them on with dangerous speed. They were in constant apprehension, for they could see but a little way before them, and scarcely knew where they were going. Many times they very narrowly escaped wreck. Few things in the whole history of the railroad adventure are more romantic than the picture of these two men piloting a frail, stolen skiff down the mountain river during a night of rain and storm.

Their motion was so rapid that they feared dawn might find them in the vicinity of Chattanooga, by which town it was necessary for them to pass. Therefore they began, in good time, to cast about for a safe landing and hiding-place. After many ineffectual attempts, they found a small island, hugged close to the shore, and reached the lower end, where they were out of the current, pulled themselves under the overhanging branches, and drew the boat on shore.

Their position was still one of extreme discomfort. The rain had changed to sleet and hail, and all effort to get warm or dry was in vain. Daylight revealed a small cabin on the shore near by, from which the smoke curled up invitingly. Their suffering was unendurable, and they decided to seek shelter.

They launched and crossed. Poor Wood, who afterwards died of consumption, brought on by exposure, and who was now almost frozen, said, "Alf, you will have to make up some lie to tell them. They will ask us a thousand questions."

Wilson answered, "I don't know what I can tell them. I am too cold to speak the truth, though."

The usual Kentucky story was modified to suit their surroundings. They asked for boats, and professed to be sent out to destroy all on the river, except where they were in the hands of trustworthy men, with the object of preventing Union men running away from the conscription. This was plausible, and they were warmed, dried, and fed.

They now ran down a short distance in the daytime, tied up, and hid in a field. A man and boy saw their boat, and were about to take it, when the adventurers, unwilling to be done by as they had done, and confident in their story, came out and stopped the proceeding. They asserted that it was a government boat, and that they belonged to a regiment in Chattanooga, which place they learned was only five miles away. The man invited them to his house to wait the lulling of the storm. They accepted, and after nightfall pushed off again, passing Chattanooga, which they had so long dreaded, in safety. They were now almost jubilant, but soon found that everything was not smooth sailing. I presume the storm, which had been so disagreeable, had also been a shelter, and that without it they might not have got by the rebel headquarters so easily.

There is a deep gorge a few miles below the city, where the mountains rise abruptly from the water in frowning grandeur. The river is greatly narrowed, and, suddenly bending to the left, dashes its furious current against a wall of rock, and forms a foaming eddy. Our two navigators "perceived even in the darkness that there was danger ahead. The great roar and noise caused by the dashing of the angry waters against the rocks warned us. We hugged the left hand with our little boat as closely as possible. As we passed the angry whirlpool, into which we seemed to be drifting, our boat was struck a tremendous blow by a floating log. We thought we were all dashed to pieces. The blow hoisted us away, however, several yards to the left, and we went flying down the gorge like the wind. We were afterwards told that a number of adventurous persons had, at different times, lost their lives in trying to run down this place by getting swamped in this great torrent or whirlpool, and it was no doubt owing to the blow we received from the floating log, by which our boat was knocked just beyond the reach of danger, that we escaped as fortunately as we did. It was a providential blow for us, though it had wellnigh crushed our boat. We pulled at our paddles with might and main to keep the water from swamping our boat, which sank pretty low in the current and was now going at railroad speed. We soon reached smoother water, and again felt ourselves safe."

A man on the bank warned them not to try to run through the "suck," a worse place than that which they had just passed. With much urging, and the promise of three dollars reward, they got him to agree to pilot them through. He was a skilful boatman, and took them in safety, though their boat was nearly filled with water.

Because of these dangers they had been running in daylight. They were soon hailed by a squad of rebel cavalry, but, being well over on the opposite side, rowed on without seeming to notice them. They were now coming to the most dangerous part of their journey,— that near the Federal lines, where the vigilance of the enemy was most constantly exercised. They therefore

resolved to travel only at night, hiding themselves and
their precious boat by day. That night they passed
Bridgeport, where they expected to meet Mitchel, but
found he had not yet arrived.

When they sought a solitary cabin to get food the
next day they heard great news,—that the Yankees
were in the town of Stevenson. This was confirmed
by numerous fugitives who were seeking safety from
the dreaded enemy. They got back to their canoe,
rowed down the river until they judged themselves
opposite Stevenson, and then started across the country
to find their friends. The good news elated them so
much that they made the fatal mistake of not waiting
for nightfall. Consequently they found themselves in
the town sooner than they expected, and then to their
dismay discovered that the streets were swarming with
rebel soldiers! The story of the frightened fugitives
had entrapped them.

But they put the best possible face on the matter.
Buying a few articles in a store, they attempted to
stroll leisurely out, but were stopped by an officer on
guard and questioned. They answered plausibly,—
probably with the Kentucky story, as they were now
away from the river,—and were about to be released,
when a man brought a *false* accusation. He recognized
Wilson as being one of the Federal cavalry that charged
into the town the previous night, and dared him to
deny it! He did deny it, but in vain, and having
been believed so often when telling falsehoods, it was
only a fair compensation that he now told the truth to
unbelieving ears.

Wilson and Wood were put on a hand-car and run
back to Bridgeport. At this place an excited member
of the crowd that gathered around them declared that
he knew them both,—that he had seen them on the
train with Andrews! Wilson always thought this
man as much mistaken as his last accuser, but denial
was no more availing than in that case. They were

H   15

taken before General Leadbetter, questioned separately, as usual in the captures, Wood " perspiring like a man in a July harvest," and both virtually convicted, although Wilson answered the questions addressed to him in the most undaunted manner. They were taken to Chattanooga, fastened together with a chain around their necks, and handcuffed, as the others had been, and ordered to the hole. When they descended the ladder and joined our miserable company there assembled, they heard some plaintive voice say in the darkness, to which their eyes had not yet become accustomed, " Wilson and Wood !   They have got every one of us !" It was true.   Every one of the bold band had been captured and were gathered into one of the vilest dungeons ever used by man to torture his fellow-man!

CHAPTER X.

A HORRIBLE PRISON.

A PLAIN picture of the Chattanooga prison into which the members of the railroad party were thrust cannot be given in all its detail without shocking the sensitive reader.   Even when the coarser features are omitted enough will remain to task credulity.   The book and newspaper accounts published by the survivors are not, however, the only evidence upon which the extraordinary story rests.   In the Appendix the official report is given, based upon sworn testimony, and to this any one who may be disposed to doubt this narrative is referred.

Yet I would not hold the Southern people or even the Confederate government wholly responsible for the barbarous and outrageous treatment experienced at this place.   The system of slavery is primarily responsible,

for it provided such dens as the negro prison at Chattanooga. An intemperate man of Northern birth—
General Leadbetter—found that the fortunes of war
had placed a score of men, one after another, in his
hands, and, feeling that they deserved severe treatment
for the daring character of their enterprise, he reck-
lessly ordered them, as fast as they were brought before
him, to be committed to "the hole" without stopping
to consider what accommodations it afforded. His
subordinates, afraid of being themselves suspected of
disloyalty if they showed sympathy with the prisoners,
offered no remonstrance, and the result was suffering
almost too fearful for belief.

The captain, to whose charge I had been committed
by General Leadbetter at the close of my examination,
called a guard of eight men and conducted me through
the streets to the northern part of the town. We
halted before a little brick building surrounded by a
high board fence,—the negro prison of Chattanooga,
known as "the hole." A portion of the building was
occupied by the jailer. The prison part consisted of
two rooms, one directly under the other, and also partly
underground. The upper room was accessible only by
an outside staircase, and the lower had no entrance except from a trap-door directly overhead.

The jailer, whose name was Swims, met us at the
outer gate. He was a poor, ignorant creature,—a bad
specimen of the "poor white" of the South, and had
all his life been engaged in the lowest employments.
He was old,—perhaps sixty,—and had abundant hair,
which was very white, while his face was dry and
withered. His voice was always keyed on a whining
tone, except when some great cause, such as a request
of prisoners for an extra bucket of water, excited him,
and then it rose to a hoarse scream. Avarice was his
predominant characteristic. He seemed to think that
his accommodations were vastly too good for negroes
and Yankees, and that when they were admitted to his

precincts, they should be thankful and give as little trouble as possible. Such a man was able to greatly aggravate the hard lot of the unfortunate prisoners in his care. It should also be stated that he was very fond of a dram, and frequently became sufficiently intoxicated to reveal many important matters that would otherwise have been concealed.

Swims bustled up to the gate, growling about being troubled so much, unlocked it, and, admitting us, led the way up the outside stairway into the outer room. I then thought I understood why the general called the place " the hole." This room was only thirteen feet square, and entirely destitute of chairs, beds, or any conveniences whatever. Five or six old, miserable-looking men were in it, who appeared not to have been washed for months. I shuddered at the thought of taking up my abode in such a den. But I was not to be allowed that luxury.

Said the jailer to the captain, " Where shall I put him ?"

" Below, of course," replied the captain.

The jailer advanced to the middle of the room, and, taking a large key from his pocket, knelt down and unlocked two rusty locks; then, with a great effort, raised a ponderous trap-door just at my feet. The hot air and the stifling stench that rushed up from below drove me back a few steps; but the bayonets of the guards were just behind, and I was compelled to move forward again. A long ladder was thrust down through the trap-door, and the warning given those below to stand from under. A mingled volley of cries, oaths, and remonstrances ascended, but the ladder was secured, and I was ordered to descend, ironed as I was. The long chain and the ropes had been taken off, but the handcuffs remained. I did not like to go down that ladder into the gloom below, but there was no alternative. The darkness hid every object from view, but I clambered down step by step to a depth of fully thir-

A TERRIBLE DESCENT.

teen feet,—for the place, as I afterwards learned when
I had more leisure for observation, was of cubic form,
just thirteen feet in length, breadth, and height. I
stepped off the ladder, treading on human beings I
could not discern, and crowded in as best I could.

The heat was so great that the perspiration started
from every pore. The fetid air made me, for a time,
deadly sick, and I wondered if it could be possible that
they would leave human beings in this fearful place to
perish. The thought of the Black Hole of Calcutta
rose instantly before me. I did not think life could be
sustained in such a place for many hours. But I was
yet to learn the wonderful possibilities of human endurance.

My breath came thick and heavy, and I expected
suffocation. The ladder was drawn up, and with a dull
and heavy thud that seemed to strike my heart the
trap-door fell. It was like being closed alive in the
grave! I wedged and forced my way through the
throng to the window. The one I reached was just
beneath the wooden, outside stairway, and even at noon
gave very little light. The only other window was at
the opposite side of the room and below the level of
the ground. They were only holes in the thick walls,
a foot square, and filled with a triple row of thick-set
iron bars that almost excluded every current of air. I
got my face near the bars and breathed the purest air I
could get, until the horrible sense of suffocation diminished as I became partially accustomed to these fearful
surroundings, and then turned to ascertain the condition of my prison companions. It was wretched beyond description. They were ragged, dirty, and crawling with vermin. Most of them were nearly naked;
but the air was so stiflingly warm that those who had
clothing had removed all they could. I soon found
it necessary myself to disrobe, as far as my handcuffs
permitted, and even then the perspiration was most
profuse. It was an atmosphere of death.

I was the first one of the " engine thieves" put into this horrible place, though several had been captured earlier. When I entered there were fourteen other white prisoners and one negro—sixteen in all—crowded into a room thirteen feet square. My dungeon partners were East Tennessee Union men. In how many other prisons these hapless victims to their own loyalty were immured I cannot tell; I found some of them in every prison of which I became an inmate, in Virginia and Georgia as well as Tennessee. The negro had been arrested on suspicion of being a fugitive, and treated in the manner usual in such cases. No trial was granted. A suspected fugitive was simply arrested and severely flogged. This usually brought some kind of a confession, true or false, as the only way to stop the torture. He was then committed to prison and advertised in accordance with his confession. If no answer came in a specified time, he was taken out and flogged into a new confession and re-advertised. Thus whipping and advertising continued until the close of the year, when he was sold at auction to pay jail and whipping fees. If he was a slave, his master could take him out earlier; but a free negro had no prospect but the year of torture and afterwards perpetual bondage! Can we too often thank God that the whole awful system of slavery has been swept away? Poor Aleck had been in this horrible prison seven months, with no prospect but that of remaining five more and then being sold. He was so kind and accommodating that he became a general favorite, and when he was taken out to be whipped we could not help feeling the deepest sympathy.

Every society has its aristocracy, and I soon found that here the highest rank was accorded to those who were charged with having done most against the Confederacy. There was one blind man, charged with being a spy, and he was considered much above the ordinary Union men. The rebels thought he was counterfeiting blindness, but I believe it was real. I was charged with the greatest offence of any yet confined in that dungeon, and was, of course, treated with becoming deference.

About an hour later the trap-door again opened, causing a stream of comparatively cool air from above to rush down. It was an inconceivable relief,—a *luxury* that none could appreciate who had not, like us, been deprived of God's greatest physical blessing—pure air.

We wondered who was coming next, as the feeble glimmering of a candle above revealed several forms descending. The Tennesseeans cried out, "Don't put any more down here! We're full! We'll die if more are put down here!" But these remonstrances, reasonable as they were, produced no effect. Down they came, and I, stationing myself at the foot of the ladder, spoke something indifferently to them, and heard my own name called in return. There was a warm clasp of ironed hands, and I knew that I had true comrades in our common misery. It was Andrews, Wollam, and Ross. Strangely mingled feelings swept over my bosom. I was sorry that they had come to this terrible place, yet glad of their companionship. We got into a corner by ourselves, for we did not know but a spy might be waiting to catch our words, and cautiously spoke of our past adventures, and strove to form some plans for the future. The trap-door was soon closed, and the free air, which had seemed to flow to us in sympathy, was once more shut out.

Others of our band were brought, I do not remember whether the same evening or the next morning, and we wondered what had become of those who were still absent. But they continued to arrive by twos and threes until all had met in this doleful place of assemblage. The whole number was twenty-two, and as fast as they came the Tennesseeans with us were removed into the room above, and we had the foul den all to ourselves. This allowed the advantage of talking freely without fear of betrayal.

We had great difficulty in arranging ourselves for sleep on account of the smallness of the room. An easy calculation will show how closely we were packed. A small corner was necessarily reserved for the water- and slop-buckets. Then two rows, with ten in each row, left two over, who had to be disposed of somehow. We did the best we could. Some sat against the wall, while others leaned against the breasts of those who were thus supported. Every motion caused the most dismal clanking of chains, for the chains were not re- moved even in such a dungeon. After we had been packed away for the night, if any one wanted to move his position, or go for a drink, he was sure to tread on some of his neighbors, and, tempers being naturally very short here, some warm altercations took place, which contributed still more to disturb our slumbers. A fight in the darkness with manacled hands was sev- eral times prevented with great difficulty by those of us who were more pacifically disposed.

A few of us, who were more fortunate, had no chains around our necks, but only wore handcuffs. I was *strongly attached* to William Reddick, one of a pair of handcuffs being placed on my left hand and the other on his right. In two instances three persons were fas- tened by one chain, which passed around the necks of each. William Campbell, a man of immense strength, was a member of one trio. I have seen him several times take hold of the chain near his own neck, and saying, " Come here, you Yanks," parade his two chain- comrades, in spite of all their resistance, back and forth over the room.

In this wretched situation we slept much. The great quantity of carbonic acid our breathing produced acted as an opiate, and served in some measure to stupefy us and deaden the sense of pain. In the morning we slept or dozed, for we had no motive to rouse up until about nine o'clock. The next morning after my arrival I was awakened—early, as I supposed—by the opening of the

trap-door and the delicious shower of cool air that fell
upon us. As I looked up, there was the white head of
our old jailer bending over and saying, in drawling
tones, " Boys, here's your breakfast," and he lowered a
bucket by a rope, with a very small piece of corn bread
and a tiny morsel of meat for each of us. It was seized
and devoured almost instantly. I had eaten nothing
since the day before, and this pitiful supply only served
to whet my appetite. But there was no more. I learned
that we were to get our meals only twice a day, and then
only a starvation allowance. The quality was that which

> " —— captives' tears
> Have moisten'd many a thousand years,
> Since man first pent his fellow-men
> Like brutes within an iron den."

I suppose our food in all our imprisonment was about
equal as to quantity and quality with that supplied at
Andersonville and other Southern prisons. But in the
chaining, and the close packing in dungeons, probably
no prisoners during the whole war fared so badly as we
did.

During the day that succeeded my arrival in this
place of horrors a few more of our party were brought
in, and among them was my especial friend, George D.
Wilson. I found that the same reason which had led
to the acknowledgment of my true character as a United
States soldier had induced them to make the same confession. Anxious and frequent were the consultations
we held as to the best course for us now to pursue. It
was too late for absolute denial of our participation in
the railroad adventure, even if that had ever been expedient. The only possible course which seemed to
offer any hope was to continue to claim the character
and protection of soldiers engaged in regular warfare,
and to this end answer all reasonable questions that
might be asked. But there were certain facts we
pledged ourselves in no case to reveal. Among these

m

was the name of our engineer, which they were specially anxious to ascertain. The fact of ignorance in
such a material matter would indicate that we were
merely following the orders of those higher in authority, and would preserve poor Brown, who had acted in
that capacity, from any special dangers. The fact of
a previous expedition having been sent down into Georgia upon the same errand as our own, was on no account to be divulged, as it was likely to stimulate our
captors to inflict sterner punishments by way of preventing similar attempts in future. We were not to
allow it to escape that William Campbell was a civilian
only and not an enlisted soldier, as this would have
made his position more perilous than our own. We
were also to conceal having given any expressions of
willingness to engage in such an expedition, claiming
to have been detailed without our own consent, and ordered to obey the directions of a man placed over us.
The most vital point was in relation to Andrews. He
had already admitted being the leader of the expedition. We could, therefore, do him no good by pretending not to know him, but he asked that we should
not admit having any knowledge of him before we
were put under his orders ; and, for our sake as well as
his, we resolved to "suppose" that he was some regularly commissioned officer of the Federal army. Most
of us knew him in his true character,—that of a secret
agent or spy. But to have admitted that fact would
have been fatal to any hopes he may have had, and
would have very seriously prejudiced our own case.
The position we, therefore, took, in all our statements,
was that of non-commissioned officers and soldiers belonging to three Ohio regiments, who had been detailed for an unknown service, and ordered to report to
an unknown officer, who had called himself Andrews,
and that we had faithfully and unquestioningly obeyed
such orders as had been given us. We agreed to urge
that a flag of truce should be sent to our lines to in-

quire if we were not what we claimed to be, well knowing that, while General Mitchel would boldly avow us,
and stretch his power to the utmost for our protection,
he would be very careful not to say anything to the
prejudice of our leader.

Our plans were carried out to the letter. No one of
our "reserved facts" was ever known to the enemy until
we were all beyond his power, and the flag of truce was
not sent only because the commanding officer said that
he was perfectly satisfied to accept all our representations as true. As others of our company were captured
and joined us, they gave our plans their cordial approval, and in the separate and formal examination of
each one, gave their names, companies, and regiments.
This could not fail to produce conviction of the truth
of our story, and gained us the sympathy of all whose
bosoms were not steeled against every kindly feeling.
To this plan, conceived in the dungeon and consistently
carried out, I attribute, more than to anything else, the
escape of any part of our number.

Though we did not now recognize Andrews formally
as our leader,—he having repeated his previous declaration that we were to rely on ourselves,—yet we communicated our plan to him, and he gave it his cordial
approval, saying that if we closely adhered to it we
would have some chance for our lives. No small
amount of effort was made by the rebel authorities to
induce us to tell more than we did. Their energies
were bent especially to finding out the engineer. They
would ask the question in the most casual manner, and
a number of times, when one man was taken out alone,
he would be offered safety and release if he would only
tell this one thing, and threatened with instant death
if he did not. But no one was moved. The opinion
seemed to be that the discovery of the engineer would
reveal the whole mystery of the enterprise. In this
they were mistaken, but the opinion was not unnatural.
They would also ask in many forms the question,

" How came it that you would consent to leave your camp in citizens' clothes for an enterprise you knew nothing about, and under the leadership of a person you had never seen, and whose rank and position you say you were ignorant of ?" The answer was always the same in substance : " We were told by our officers to follow this man, and we considered it a soldier's duty to obey." I had to pass a more protracted examination than any of the others, perhaps because I had told General Leadbetter so many of my inferences about war affairs when first taken before him. For two or three days I was even separated from my comrades and daily questioned. I thus gained a short relief from the horrors of the negro prison, and could easily have secured my own safety by dishonor; but although I talked freely, I did not go a single word beyond the line which Wilson and myself, with the approval of all the others, had marked out. At last I overheard the acute lawyer who acted as examiner on these occasions say to General Leadbetter, " It is no use. He is either ignorant or too sharp to tell anything." I felt greatly complimented, and was then taken back to the horrors of the old dungeon, where I was warmly welcomed by my comrades, most of whom had passed a similar though briefer ordeal. It was on this occasion that the officer of the guard happened to lay a newspaper he was reading near me. I was hungry for news, and in a moment seized and concealed it in my clothing. It was missed and a great search made, but as I was handcuffed and looked innocent, suspicion did not fall on me. It was a great prize, for it contained a complete account of our chase as given by our pursuers. Through all our subsequent adventures I carefully preserved it, and at the date of writing it is still in my possession. The estimate it gives of the military importance of our expedition, and of what we actually accomplished, goes beyond what has been sketched in the preceding pages. (See Appendix No. II.)

After these examinations were over, the misery of our dungeon-life closed about us again. Whether we would be left there to perish, or whether some kind of a trial would be given us with the alternatives of release or execution,—what was the position of the armies outside, or the progress of the war,—we could not tell. In dreams only we were free. I remember lying down one afternoon and dreaming of the most beautiful snow-capped mountains in East Tennessee, and awakening with a freshness and hopefulness which lasted for many hours. But even dreams were not all thus pleasant; too often they rivalled the prison itself in shapes of terror and pain.

One or two of our number managed to conceal a little money when searched, and, as our rations were very small, it was resolved to spend it for food. The jailer agreed to get us any provisions we wanted, so far as the money would go. There was an anxious discussion as to the most profitable mode of investment. Wheat bread and molasses—the latter being very cheap —were chosen, and the precious money tied to the rope, which was our only mode of communication with the upper world, and drawn up. It was at our evening meal. We knew Swims would not trouble himself to bring the provisions that evening, but we anticipated a bountiful breakfast, with the keenness that only starving men could feel. When the breakfast bucket dangled at the end of the rope the next morning, it was quickly seized, and lo! only the usual miserly allowance of " pone" and meat. " Mr. Swims, have you got the bread and molasses yet?" eagerly demanded a voice from below. In his most whining tones he drawled out, " B-o-y-s, I lost that money." Had he been on our level instead of thirteen feet above, he might have learned how desperate men can become when hungry. But there was no remedy. The captain of the guard, when appealed to, considered it a good joke !

16

CHAPTER XI.

LIGHTS AND SHADOWS OF PRISON.

SOME two weeks after our capture Andrews received
a very brief trial. The charges against him were two,
—that of being disloyal to the Confederacy and of
being a spy. On the first count the evidence against
him was strong. A Mr. Whiteman, from Nashville,
Tennessee, whom Andrews himself had directed to be
summoned, and who had once been a partner of his in
some business, testified that Andrews had repeatedly
visited the South as a blockade-runner, bringing to
Whiteman some ten thousand dollars' worth of goods in
that manner, and that he had always professed allegiance
to the Southern Confederacy, representing himself to be
a citizen of the same, and an enemy to the United States.
When captured, he had passes in his possession which
showed that he had also taken the oath of allegiance to
the Southern government. He had, at the same time,
admitted his part in the railroad adventure, which was
assuredly an act of hostility against the South. Indeed, several persons were produced who saw him on
the train, or directing its movements at some of the
various stations during the chase. So far as I could
learn, there was no direct evidence produced to show
that he was or ever had been a spy, although this might
be suspected from his passing back and forth across
the lines, and so soon after acting as an enemy. His
case was entirely different from that of the men he led,
and much more unfavorable. They claimed to have
been acting all the while as enemies, and now to be
prisoners of war. They declared, and were ready to
prove, their position in the Federal army. He gave no

account whatever of his position, or the authority under which he was acting, and allowed the court-martial to establish their case as best they might. He was very reticent, as was proper, even among our band, as to his plans and hopes, but it was whispered among us that he expected the liberal use of money from an outside source to influence the court, or aid in his escape if condemned. I never heard him, however, intimate anything of the kind, and he certainly received no such help in escaping. He employed two able lawyers, and they strove for delay, and at the last gave him reason to hope that some informalities in the proceedings would require the whole trial to be gone over again. No decision, however, was officially given, but he was put back in the same prison, and no more strictly guarded than the remainder of us, which was judged to be a favorable indication of the result.

One day our old jailer, being very drunk, told us that General Mitchel had advanced to Bridgeport, only twenty-eight miles distant, and there defeated the rebels, capturing some of the very same men who had been our guards but a day or two before. How we wished to have been with him ! and how we hoped for a further advance on his part ! To be captured with Chattanooga would be glorious ! The officers of the guard were obviously uneasy. They took the strictest precautions. There were twenty-six men constantly on guard,— surely enough to watch over twenty-two, confined and chained in a dungeon as we were.

Mitchel came nearer. We even heard the boom of cannon in the distance, and his advance probably saved our lives, by taking us for the time out of the clutches of Swims and Leadbetter, for a much longer confinement or rather suffocation there must have been fatal. The ladder was thrust down and we were ordered to come out. We would, then, have gladly remained in that vile den a little longer, in the hope of Mitchel's arrival, but we crawled up. Our fastenings were inspected, to see that none of us were in condition to make a sudden dash for liberty; we were formed into a column, with a line of rebel soldiers on each side, and then marched out through the gate towards the cars. Strangely the free air fanned our brows and strangely the wide sky bent above us. Very grateful was the sense of openness and room in the streets through which we passed, even although ironed, with a rebel soldier on either hand. For three whole weeks twenty-two men had been cooped up in a dark room much smaller than an ordinary parlor. No wonder the streets of the hostile town seemed like freedom by comparison. We were soon seated in the cars, and were carried in the evening back southward on the road we had rushed over under such thrilling circumstances three weeks before.

How beautiful all nature appeared! It was now May, and the time that we had spent in darkness had not been lost in the outside world. The landscape had been robed in richer verdure, the budding trees had swelled into leafy screens, the sky was of a softer blue, the birds warbled with new melody, and everything seemed to wear its holiday dress.

O the joy! the gladness! of being once more under the blue canopy of heaven, and of looking up to its unfathomable depths, with no envious bars to obstruct our view! Many a time have I looked on the most romantic scenery in the freshness of May, but never did I so deeply feel the pleasantness and beauty of the world as on that balmy evening, when the rays of the setting sun, glowing from the west, streamed over the grass and wheat-fields on their path, and poured in mellowed, yellow radiance through the car-windows. But I could not quite forget that I was chained to my companion and surrounded by guards with gleaming bayonets!

The wild excitement caused by our raid had not subsided, and as it became known that we were passing along the road, a mob greeted us at every station. It is not necessary to again describe these assemblages, for all were alike,—threatening, rude, loquacious, and insulting.

We also noticed that soldiers on guard were at every station, and that each bridge we passed was strongly guarded. There could be no doubt that all these precautions, so different from the careless security of less than a month previous, were among the tangible results of our enterprise. It was estimated that on the various roads of the South not less than three thousand troops had been diverted from the field and employed in securing communications in all parts of the rebel States. A general passport system, with all its vexations, had been introduced. Surely our enterprise, though unsuccessful in its immediate results, was far from fruitless.

We passed Big Shanty, passed Marietta, which had been the extreme point of our former journey southward, and went on to Atlanta. Here there was no jail room for us; but before going farther we had to wait all day in the cars for the evening train. Our arrival was soon noised abroad, and a larger mob than we had seen before gathered and proclaimed their intention of hanging us. The guard defended us manfully, and several persons were seriously injured. But while the disturbance was in progress, one man succeeded in reaching the window unnoticed and handed us a paper, using only the single, magical word, "a friend," and then disappeared in the throng. We read the paper by snatches, as we could do so secretly, and found it to contain glorious news,—*the capture of New Orleans!* Other items of news were adroitly wormed out of our guards, who could not be kept from talking with us, and we were full of hope that the darkening prospects of the Confederacy would brighten our own outlook, by rendering the advocates of a declining rebellion more cautious in their treatment of loyal soldiers. All information was prohibited to us; but from the common soldiers, the negroes, and often from the officers of the guard themselves, we managed to pick up items of intelligence, which gave us a general idea of the course of affairs.

In the evening we left Atlanta, and after a journey not marked by any notable event reached Madison, in the same State. This was then a flourishing village, and had a pleasing look as we entered it. Some six hundred imprisoned Union soldiers had been already gathered here, and we freely indulged the hope, which was encouraged by our guards, that we would be put with them and henceforth treated only as prisoners of war. But we soon found that the brand of criminality for our daring adventure was not so easily effaced. We were marched past the dilapidated cotton-factory, where our fellow-soldiers were confined, to the old county jail. It was then entirely unoccupied, as all the prisoners had been released to join the Confederate army. It was a gloomy stone building, with two rooms, but both were above-ground, and the lower was entered by an ordinary door. This lower room, in which about half of our party, including myself and Andrews, were placed, was very dark, and its heavy stone walls rendered it quite damp. But for our previous experience at Chattanooga it would have been thought a wretched place. It was so much better than that, however, that we almost enjoyed it. Indeed, we could not have endured such confinement as that at Chattanooga for many weeks longer. Several of our number could scarcely walk, and all were greatly injured in health by the three horrible weeks we had spent there. Now we were further from the pernicious influence of General Leadbetter, and, although we were still kept in irons by his explicit orders, yet the captain of the guard, in whose direct charge we were, showed us all the kindness in his power, easing the irons which pressed too heavily upon swollen limbs, and procuring us abundance of good water, as well as a better supply of the coarse food, which we ate in common with our guard.

The citizens of the town were freely admitted to see us, and ranged themselves—always in the presence of the guard—along one side of the room, and talked of all the exciting events of the day. We were now in our true character, and were not likely to be benefited by concealing our real sentiments. I used to greatly enjoy their surprise and horror when I avowed myself an abolitionist, and told them that I had always been one. They had been talking about abolitionists for years, but had never before seen a man who would admit the justice of the charge. The citizens expressed much admiration for us and for the daring of our expedition, contrasting the latter with what they were pleased to call the cowardice of the Northern armies in general. George D. Wilson one day earnestly assured them that we were the poorest men in Mitchel's division, and had only been sent on this expedition because he had no use for us!

Here occurred one of the romantic incidents of prison-life. We had been intensely anxious for some direct communication with our own army, but from our side there was no means of effecting it. One day, however, a man dressed in a rebel uniform came with the throng of visitors, and managed to talk quite a while, and, as I thought, in a very disconnected manner, with Andrews. I also thought I noticed an exchange of signs between them. As soon as he and the visitors had gone, and we were once more alone, Andrews told us that the man was a spy in the service of the United States, and that they had managed, even in the presence of the guard, and without exciting the least suspicion, to say all that was necessary, and that we might be assured that our friends on the other side of the lines would soon know all about us. I was a little incredulous, thinking that the great anxiety of our leader to communicate with some one who was a Federal spy, as he himself had been, had caused him to misunderstand this man, and supposed his signs recognized when they were not.

But when the captain of our guard brought us supper, he lingered a little in conversation, and remarked that a most singular thing had taken place that afternoon, and that after this we would receive no more visitors. Being pressed for explanations, he finally gave them. He said that the provost-marshal of Madison had received information that one of Lincoln's spies was in town, and had even been among our visitors, though, the captain said, he was glad that the spy had found no opportunity to reveal himself to us! The marshal at once despatched a squad to arrest him. They found the suspected stranger at the depot, just as the cars were coming in. He was boisterously indignant at his arrest, and told them that he had papers in his pocket which would prove his character anywhere. They let go their hold on him, so that he might produce his papers. He lectured them roundly while pretending to search in his pockets, until he noticed that the train, which was starting, had attained a good degree of headway, and then, just as the last car swung by, he suddenly flung the soldiers from him and jumped aboard. There was no telegraph station at Madison, and no other train that evening, so that an effective pursuit was out of the question.

The Confederates were very much enraged, and our confinement was rendered much more strict. But we felt ample compensation in the hope that our officers would now know just where we were, and be able to make all possible efforts for our safety. Whether the spy surmounted all other perils and got safely to our lines, we never heard.

Three days only did we remain at Madison,—days of comparative quiet and hope, during which we recovered some degree of our wasted strength, which was sadly needed for future trials. The rebel authorities, having become convinced that Chattanooga was not

in present danger from General Mitchel, ordered us
back to that place. Our destination was not known to
us, and the usual rumors circulated as to being now on
our way for exchange. To move from one prison to
another—an experience we had quite frequently—was
always a welcome relief, and served, in some measure,
to mitigate the excessive rigor of our confinement. We
went back over the same road we came, and had again
to run the gauntlet of insulting and jeering mobs. We
traveled in rude box-cars, wet and filthy, and were har-
assed by the fear of going back to our miserable prison
at Chattanooga. One circumstance rendered the journey
more endurable. Captain Laws, who commanded the
guard, and his soldiers also, had been in close association with us for several days, and had become really
interested in our welfare. While he did not relax any
of his vigilance, he strove to make the hardship of our
position more endurable, and showed a friendly spirit
on every occasion. His good will was especially valuable when we reached Chattanooga.

The remorseless order had been given for our return
to the negro prison. Captain Laws could not change
this, but by using his influence with Colonel Patrick
Cleiburne, a man of humanity, who occupied the position of provost-marshal of Chattanooga for a short
time, he got permission for us to remain in the upper
room instead of being forced into the dungeon below.
This was a great relief, for although we were equally
crowded, yet the upper room was above-ground, had
three windows instead of two, and these were of larger
size. We had, therefore, a much better supply of air
and light. We were very sorry for the fourteen poor
Tennesseeans who were put below.

Our enemies displayed a wonderful degree of caution
in the manner of guarding us. Even when we were
below, where a man, if left alone, could scarcely have
gotten out without assistance, they never raised the
trap-door unprotected by a strong guard. Old Swims

remonstrated against our being in the upper room, and seemed in perpetual terror. He fretted, and predicted that evil would come from showing the Yankees so much indulgence. Yet the precautions observed ought to have reassured him. Before our door was opened a strong guard was always brought up-stairs into the jailer's room, from which ours was entered, and arrayed in two lines with levelled bayonets. At the same time the stairway was guarded, and the whole jail surrounded by a strong force outside of the wall. We had not yet been relieved of our fetters,—at least, not by Confederate authority.

Colonel Cleiburne had asked permission to remove our irons, and this being refused, he gave us, on his own responsibility, an inexpressibly great indulgence. For an hour or two every fine afternoon he ordered the guards to bring us out into the jail-yard. This was something to look forward to all the day, and made our second confinement at Chattanooga far less irksome and prostrating than the first. To simply sit in the sunlight and watch the clouds drifting in the blue above, or to walk back and forth watching the lengthening shadows of the mountains, was intense enjoyment. We will never cease to be grateful to the brave Irish soldier who secured us these indulgences, which, simple as they were, had not been expected.

But we felt that the wearing of irons for so long a period was entirely unnecessary, and set our wits to work for the removal of such needless incumbrances. One of the party had managed to secrete a small knife in his sleeve while being searched, and with this he whittled out rude keys from the bones of the meat given us, which readily unlocked our handcuffs. The padlocks on the chains were served in a similar manner. We did not dare to let any one of the guards know of this expedient, or appear in public in our new liberty, lest more effectual means should be devised of securing us. To avoid detection while thus unchained we always kept some one on the watch. When a footstep was heard on the outside stairway the signal was given, and a quick rattling of chains accompanied the adjustment and relocking of our bonds. When the door opened we would appear all properly chained, but when alone we would soon be free again. This deception was continued as long as we were kept in irons.

We here took up the amusement of mock trials. Andrews had been tried, and the remainder of us expected to be, either in a body or singly. This may have suggested the diversion, which soon became very popular. One of the company would be charged with some offence, usually a trifling breach of our self-imposed prison rules. William Campbell, whose immense personal strength better enabled him to enforce his decisions, usually officiated as judge, until at last he got the name of "judge" firmly fixed upon him. We had ample time for this sport, and the opposing counsel would make very long and learned speeches. So interesting were these arguments, and so eloquent were our appeals, that no one of the auditors was ever known to leave the court-room while they were in progress ! The witnesses were very slippery, and it was often difficult to reconcile their testimony. Some friends of the prisoners nearly always attempted to resist the laws and prevent the infliction of penalties, but in such cases the *personal weight* of the judge decided the affair. This resistance would give rise to new arrests and trials, and thus the work became interminable.

Another and more refined source of enjoyment was found in music. There were several good singers in the party, and by practising together they soon acquired great proficiency. Most of the songs, under the leadership of Marion Ross, were of a tender and sentimental cast, such as " Nettie Moore," " Carrier Dove," " Twenty Years Ago," " Do they miss me at Home?" etc. The most frequent time for singing was when twilight began to fall. Then all other occupations would be laid aside, and in the gathering darkness the voice of song would roll out as full and sweet as if not strained through prison-bars. The guards were very fond of our singing, and frequently groups of citizens also would gather around the high jail-fence to listen. Words of sympathy and kindness for the "caged Yankees" became more common, and there were a good many tangible manifestations of the same feelings. The guards who came in contact with us,—a considerable number, as one squad replaced another,—together with many of their officers and many residents of Chattanooga, began to ask why we were not treated as other prisoners, and the shameful chains taken off. I do not know whether this produced any essential change in our fortune. Most likely it was the reason we were not brought to trial in a town where we would have been sure of so much sympathy, but were arraigned in a distant place, and before officers who were strangers to us.

Yet no friendliness on the part of our guards, or mitigation in the horrors of our treatment, put the thought of escape out of our minds, although it did divide our counsels and delay an attempt. With many others, I was convinced that we ought to make a bold push for liberty. The very strictness of the guard was a challenge to do our best to overcome it. If there were a few gleams of humanity in the present treatment, this was merely because our captors had discovered us to be human beings and not monsters; besides, there was enough still in the vile nature of our food and rigor of our confinement to justify the most desperate effort for freedom. If we tried and failed, we might lose our lives in the attempt; but this was a risk soldiers have to take in every enterprise; if recaptured, we would be no worse off than we were, for the charge of attempting to escape could be no more deadly than the old one of seizing the train. But those who did not wish to make the attempt, among whom George D.

Wilson was foremost, maintained that our enemies were growing daily kinder, and that we would soon be formally placed on the footing of prisoners of war; the commander of the guard, Captain Laws, had become even intimate with Wilson, and had assured him that our good conduct was producing a profound impression in our favor; to forfeit this now by a foolhardy attempt to escape might turn the scale against us. Ross agreed with Wilson. He was a Freemason, and some members of the fraternity visited him, and gave him assurances of friendship, together with some small sums of money, which he generously used to procure us all a little greatly-needed addition to our food. We no longer made our purchases through Swims, but through Captain Laws, who did not lose the money intrusted to him.

Finally the majority decided in favor of an attempt to escape. Two plans were proposed,—the first by the writer. When men who are not expecting danger are suddenly surprised, there is a moment when they are incapable of action, and may be at the mercy of a bold adversary. The same plan, in general outline, was carried out long afterwards with the most brilliant success. It was simply to have our irons off when the guards came to feed us in the evening, and then, as the door opened, to make a simultaneous rush upon the levelled bayonets outside, wrest the muskets from their holders, and pour down the stairs on the guards below. If we succeeded in reaching the ground before the guards fully realized what was going on, a few moments would suffice to disarm them, and then we could leave the prison-yard in a solid body, run with all our speed to the ferry-boat which lay on our side of the river, not far distant. Once over the river, armed with muskets and bayonets, we would have been comparatively safe.

But Andrews did not like this plan for the same reason that made him so unwilling to use our arms in

desperate fighting during the race on the train. He
proposed another plan, which, as he still had great influence with us, was adopted. His proposition was that
some one—John Wollam, I think, was selected for the
perilous attempt—should conceal himself under the bed
in the jailer's room as we passed through it on our return from the breathing-spell in the yard, and remain
there until all was quiet at night; then come out and
noiselessly unlock the door; after this we could rush
down, seize the guard, and proceed as in our first plan.
The time for this bold attempt was fixed for a moon-
less night not far distant.

There were two soldiers of the original twenty-four
detailed for our enterprise who failed to reach the designated rendezvous at Marietta. One was from the
Twenty-first, the other from the Second Ohio Regiment. They had been suspected and compelled to join
a rebel battery, representing themselves as brothers
from Kentucky. In the skirmish at Bridgeport the
member of the Twenty-first found an opportunity to
run across the railroad bridge and join Mitchel. This
caused suspicion to rest on his supposed brother, who
was arrested, brought to Chattanooga, and thrown into
the dungeon while we were there. There was some
suspicion that he might have belonged to our party,
but we refused to recognize him, and after confinement
for some time he was sent back to the battery again,
and from it, after many remarkable adventures, succeeded in making good his escape to the Union lines.

There was at this time a great talk of our exchange,
and our drooping hopes revived. A son of General
Mitchel's was captured, but the general held a large
number of rebel prisoners, and released one of them—
a lieutenant—on parole, to propose an exchange. This
man visited us and raised the most sanguine hopes
in our bosoms. The Confederate officers encouraged
those hopes, but said we must first go through a merely
formal trial to prove that we were really soldiers, after

which we would be included in the exchange which
would undoubtedly be made. We wanted them to
refer the question of our soldiership to General Mitchel,
but we have every reason to believe that they not only
never asked him anything about us, but used all the
means in their power to prevent him from obtaining
any knowledge of our situation. The exchange was
effected, but we were not included, and the lieutenant
was not permitted to return to the loyal camp.

These delusive hopes had served to delay a little
longer our projected escape, but at last we resolved to
end the suspense. The very day we had fixed upon
for the desperate enterprise an event occurred which
deranged the plan in the most unexpected manner by
dividing our party. George D. Wilson, who was very
sick, was taken down into the yard closely guarded.
While he was there Captain Laws came to him, and
said that he had received an order for twelve of our
number to be taken to Knoxville, to pass the formal
investigation which had been so long talked about, and
which was to fix the character of the whole party as
prisoners of war. Wilson asked who the twelve were
to be, and wished that he might be one. The captain
told him that this was easily arranged, as the order
called merely for twelve, without giving names. He
further offered Wilson the privilege of naming eleven
others beside himself to go, saying that he would do
well to select the ablest men,—those who could do
themselves most credit on examination. Whether this
was a mere incident, or whether it was a plan laid to
have Wilson select the most prominent men of the
party, that they might be tried and put to death, I
have never learned. In the light of the subsequent
history, this choice was a matter of profound importance, and my own opinion is that the names were purposely left blank, and Wilson induced to make the
choice, with the view of his leaving out the nine who
might best be reserved for the exercise of mercy after

the others were capitally punished. If this was the case, I cannot persuade myself that Captain Laws was in the secret. But poor Wilson was completely misled. He told me that he considered that those who went to Knoxville would probably be exchanged first, if any difference was to be made. So he put down his own name first, and mine next. Then followed the other two who belonged to our regiment,—the Second Ohio; then William Campbell, the muscular citizen of Kentucky, and the list was filled out by the names of Wilson's especial friends from the other regiments. As we twelve, who were to go to Knoxville, waited the hour of starting, a shade of gloom fell upon us. For nearly two months we had been companions in trials and privations such as fall to the lot of few men, and now our band was to be separated. There was no certainty of reunion; for, in spite of fair words, the fact remained that we were in the power of desperate and deadly foes, who would not hesitate a moment in taking our lives, if they saw it for their own advantage to do so.

The parting with Andrews, our noble leader, was especially affecting. We had been accustomed to ask his advice in all emergencies. He had been already tried by court-martial, and, although no sentence had been given, the long delay was not a favorable omen. We knew that he was the first mark for the vengeance of the foe. Officers and visitors, in bidding us hope, had no words of comfort for him. He bore this like a hero, as he was, and continued to hope for some deliverance. But now, after we had sung our songs together for the last time, and came to bid him farewell, we were all moved to weeping. I will never forget his last words, as he pressed our hands, with tears in his eyes, and said, in a low, sad voice that thrilled through my inmost being, " Boys, if I never see you here again, try to meet me on the other side of Jordan." Never did we look upon his noble face again !

CHAPTER XII.

THE FIRST TRAGEDY.

WE will first narrate the history of the nine soldiers and their leader, from whom we parted with so much sorrow and foreboding when the remainder of us were sent to Knoxville. Various reasons have been conjectured for this separation, one of which has been given in the preceding chapter. Another that has been entertained by many of the party, who have had the opportunity of reviewing the facts, is that the enemy was now ready to proceed in the work of vengeance, and wished to lessen any possible danger of escape on our part when we had been driven to desperation by the beginning of the bloody work. If this was their design, it was not without success, for the attempt to escape, fixed for the very day of our separation, was in consequence postponed for a time.

A week elapsed, during which nothing occurred to break the monotony of imprisonment. The plan of escape had been modified to be more easily within the reach of the diminished numbers of the prisoners. The jack-knife, which had made keys for unlocking the handcuffs, was again brought into use. The jail walls consisted of brick, and were lined inside with heavy plank, reaching to the top of the upper room and covering the ceiling. Three men leaned against the wall, while a fourth stood on their shoulders, and with the knife cut into the heavy plank overhead. It was no light task to cut out a hole large enough to admit the passage of a man's body into the attic. A small part of each day only could be devoted to the work, and the utmost vigilance was needed to prevent discovery. The

17*

"singing hour" was especially serviceable, as then the noise of the knife could not be heard. The cut, when so nearly completed as to require little more labor, was so filled up as not to attract notice from below, and attention given to other parts of the work. Just then an incident occurred which added the energy of desperation to the efforts for liberty.

Captain Laws entered the prison-yard one day, while our comrades were enjoying the shade of the prison in the afternoon breathing-spell, which had been procured by the kindness of Colonel Cleiburne and himself, and going up to Andrews, with averted face, handed him a paper. Andrews glanced at it, stood perfectly still a moment, and then silently turned, and walked up-stairs into the cell, the door of which had been left open. No one of his comrades said a word, but all felt that something dreadful had happened. The officer, who seemed hardly able to control his own emotion, waited for a little time, and then telling the prisoners very gently that it was time to close up the prison, guarded them back to their room.

The explanation Andrews then gave was scarcely needed. He had received his death-sentence! A week from that day had been appointed as the time, and hanging as the mode of his execution. The sorrow of the brave men was indescribable. The many noble qualities of our leader had won not only respect but love. His unselfish regard for every one of his companions in misfortune, his cheerful, kindly manner under the greatest sufferings, had made a deep impression even on his guards,—much more on his comrades.

But there was one gleam of hope. Andrews and his party resolved at once to carry out their projects for breaking out of the jail. These soldiers would have dared anything in the hope of saving their leader; besides, the feeling was general that this execution would be but the beginning. Some of the number had always maintained that no hope existed save the gleam that might come from some desperate attempt for liberty, such as they were now to put forth.

But an additional obstacle was interposed,—Andrews was put down in "the hole" after receiving his sentence. This required the well-worn knife to be again used, sparingly but persistently. Notches were sawed in the planks which held the bolts of the trap-door, and an old blanket or two, with some articles of clothing, were twisted into ropes. When all this was done, although the first flush of dawn began to appear in the east, they dared not risk the chance of their work being discovered the next day, and accordingly resolved to go at once. Andrews had been drawn up out of the hole, and it was agreed to give him the first chance for his life. Andrews and John Wollam were in the loft or attic over the prison room, while all the others, in their assigned order, were ready to mount up through the aperture they had cut in the ceiling. A few bricks in the outside wall had also been removed, and enough of the rude ropes prepared to allow one by one to descend to the ground. The hope was that by taking off their boots and moving very cautiously, each one could go into the loft and out through the hole in the wall, and clamber down the outside blanket-ropes without disturbing the repose of the guard. Those who got down first were to wait beside the jail until all their comrades were on the ground before attempting to dash across the jail-fence and the guard-line outside.

It was an anxious moment. They could see the dim form of the sentry, and hear his measured tread, as he paced back and forth not a dozen yards away. The word was passed from one to another in the prison that all was ready.

Andrews crept out first and swung over the wall, but in doing so loosened a piece of mortar or a brick, which fell to the ground with a loud "thump," and attracted the notice of the sentry outside, who instantly gave the alarm, firing his gun and calling "Halt! halt! Corporal of the guard!" The whole guard was instantly aroused, and the firing became rapid. Andrews, however, dropped to the ground, darted to the fence, and was over before he could be prevented. Wollam heard the noise from the inside, and knowing that caution was now needless, sprang through the wall, and slid with the greatest rapidity to the ground. A number of shots were fired while he was suspended in the air, but the dim light and the hurry and confusion were not favorable to a steady aim, and he, also, got to the ground and over the fence unhurt. Dorsey was third in order, but was too late. Before he could get into the loft the guard were ready to make sure work of any who might follow. He prudently turned to his comrades and said, "It is all up with us!" The whole town was soon aroused. High officers visited the prison to see how many had escaped. They found the remaining eight safely ironed as before, the keys having been brought into use. The natural supposition was that only the two who were missing had succeeded in getting off their irons, and that the others had not escaped because too tightly fettered. They were, however, put down in "the hole" as an additional security, and all damages to the prison carefully repaired, while the guard manifested unusual vigilance. The afternoon airing was forbidden, and all the strictness which had marked the first confinement in Chattanooga returned. The poor captives were made to feel that they had now nothing to expect but the sternest dealings.

One consolation was left them in the hope that their comrades had made good their flight, and that the death-sentence of Andrews could not now be executed. When the firing was first heard the not unnatural inference was that both the fugitives had perished, but they knew that *such* news would soon have been imparted to them; and as days passed by, their hope strengthened that two, at least, of their fated company would get back to the Union lines to tell the story of their adventures and sufferings. How far these hopes were realized will be seen in the sequel.

When Andrews left the prison it was nearly day, so that he knew he could not long continue his flight without detection. He went only a few hundred yards away from the city, and there finding a dense tree, climbed, unobserved, into its branches. It was in plain view of the railroad and the river. All day long he remained in this uncomfortable position, and saw the trains passing almost under his feet, and heard his pursuers speculating as to what could possibly have become of him. The search all over the vicinity was most thorough, but fortunately no one thought of looking into the tree.

At night he came down and swam the river, but becoming entangled in some drift-wood, floated down past Chattanooga, and did not disengage himself until he had lost most of his clothing. His boots had been lost in the first alarm, and he was thus placed in the most unfavorable position for escaping, but he journeyed on as well as he could. Though so much superior, in many particulars, to his followers, yet in trying to escape in the woods he seems to have been as much inferior. As will be seen, Wollam, and, at a later period, many others of the number, were far more skilful or fortunate than he. Early in the morning he crossed an open field on his way to a tree in which he intended to take shelter as on the preceding day, but unfortunately he was observed. Immediate pursuit was made, but he dashed through the woods and regained the river much lower down than the day before. Here he swam a narrow channel and reached a small island, where, for a time, he secreted himself among some drift-wood at the upper end of the island. In all his terrible struggle he seemed to look to the river and to trees for safety. These became fixed ideas, and possibly interfered with his seeking refuge in any other manner. But the loss of clothing at the outset was a fatal misfortune.

A party with blood-hounds now came over from the mainland to search the island for him. The dogs came upon him, but he broke away from them, and ran around the lower end of the island, wading in the shallow water, and in this way throwing the hounds off the track; then he plunged into the dense thicket with which the island was covered, and again ascended a tree. There for a long time he remained securely concealed, while his pursuers searched the whole island. Frequently they were under the very tree, whose high foliage effectually screened him from the gaze of dogs and men. At last they abandoned the search in despair, concluding that he had by some means left the island. Slowly they took their departure to devise new plans of search. Two little boys, who came along merely from curiosity, were all that were left behind.

At length, in their play, one of them looked upward, and said that he saw a great bunch on a tree. The other looked,—shifted his position,—looked again, and exclaimed, " Why, it is *a man !*" They were alarmed and cried aloud, thus announcing their discovery to their friends on shore. The latter instantly returned, and Andrews, seeing himself discovered, dropped from the tree, ran to the lower end of the island, took a small log, with a limb for a paddle, and shoved into the stream, hoping to reach the opposite shore before he could be overtaken. But there was another party lower down the river with a skiff, who saw him and rowed out to meet him. Thus enclosed, he gave over the hopeless struggle, and surrendered to his fate,—inevitable death ! He afterwards said that he felt a sense almost of relief when the end had come and he knew the worst. From the time of losing his clothing in the drift-wood he had but little expectation of ultimate escape. The spectacle of a man condemned to death, starving and naked, hunted through the woods and waters by dogs and men, is one of the most pitiable that can be imagined.

Alfred Wilson, who was one of the eight who failed to escape, speaks in feeling terms of the manner in which their leader was brought back to them on the third day after escaping. He says,—

"At the prison we were startled by a rumor that Andrews had been taken, but we at first gave little credence to it, probably because we did not desire to believe it. But, alas! the rumor was only too true, for soon after, a strong guard of soldiers, having in charge a prisoner, followed by a rabble of citizens, approached the prison. It was Andrews! Oh, how our hearts and hopes sank down within us beyond the power of expression! . . . I could have prayed that death had spared me those painful moments, the most harrowing of my life. He was the most wretched and pitiable human being I ever saw,—a sight which horrified us all, and even drew words of compassion from some of our prison guards. His own brother wou'l scarcely have been able to recognize him. It did not seem possible that the short space of three days could have wrought a change so startling. As he lay there chained to the floor, naked, bloody, bruised, and speechless, he seemed more dead than alive. He had not eaten a morsel since he left us,—during which time he had made the most desperate struggle for liberty and life. He had swam about seven miles in the river in his efforts to keep clear of the dogs. His feet were literally torn to shreds by running over the sharp stones and through the brush. Towards the last he left blood at every step. His back and shoulders were sun-blistered almost to the bone, and so completely exhausted was he that he could hardly move his limbs after he was brought in. His face was pale, haggard, and emaciated. His eyes, which were sunken, gave forth a wild, despairing, unnatural light.

"When we were left to ourselves, we drew around the miserable man, and, after he had somewhat revived, he told us in that low, calm tone of voice in which he always spoke, and which seldom failed to impress the listeners favorably towards the man, the whole story of his unfortunate attempt to escape. He told us he had but little time to live, and that now, after having made every effort to save his life and to rescue us, and failed, he felt reconciled and resigned to his fate. He said he was incapable of doing anything more to help himself, and only regretted that his death could not in some way be instrumental in saving us, his comrades. He counselled us all against the fallacy of hoping for an exchange, or for any mercy from those into whose hands we had fallen. He said his doom foreshadowed our own, and entreated us to prepare for the worst, and, when the time came, to prove to them that we were as brave in confronting an ignominious death for our country's sake as we had been fearless in doing service for her."

A few more words will finish this pitiful story. Andrews, in Wilson's opinion, was somewhat of a fatalist, or at least was haunted with a presentiment of coming doom from the time he had fairly entered upon this expedition. He had not long to wait. He was put back into "the hole," but not before a negro blacksmith had welded a pair of heavy fetters upon his ankles, and connected them with a chain only about eighteen inches in length. A scaffold was prepared for him in Chattanooga, but the indications of an advance by Mitchel, and, possibly, expressions of sympathy on the part of the citizens, induced the authorities at the last moment to transfer the death-scene to Atlanta. His comrades were sent with him to that town. On the way to Atlanta he was taunted with his approaching doom by the crowds, who surrounded every station.

It was the day appointed for the execution. On reaching Atlanta Andrews and his eight companions were conducted to a second-story room, not far from the depot. In a little time a body of soldiers marched up into the building, an officer appeared at the door, and, while all were silent as death, said, in a low, almost faltering tone, "Come on now, Mr. Andrews." He instantly arose, and the low, sad "Farewell, boys," spoken in his calmest, sweetest tones, mingled with the horrible clanking of his chains, as he walked out with the short, halting step his irons compelled. This was the final separation.

The survivors were conducted to the city jail of Atlanta, and there placed in an iron cage. At meal-time the guards told them how bravely Andrews died. His fortitude stilled even the clamorous spectators. The dying agony was protracted by the unskilfulness of the executioner, the rope stretching so that his feet touched the ground. But the earth was shovelled away, and the brave spirit set free. Why should the gallows be accounted infamous when courage and patriotism there meet a hero's death? The cross was once esteemed more shameful than the gallows now, but one death has sanctified that instrument forever!

The grave of Andrews at Atlanta was unmarked, and, in the many changes that have taken place there, it is probably lost forever. The most diligent search on the part of the writer failed to discover it. But the rope adjudged by the court-martial, all of whose members have passed into obscurity with the downfall of the rebellion they served, cannot desecrate his memory. No flowers can be placed on his unknown grave by loyal hands, but loving tears will fall freely for him as long as hearts can feel for the extremity of misfortune that gathered around the last hours of the man who planned and boldly executed the most romantic and perilous enterprise of the Great Civil War.

CHAPTER XIII.

A CONFEDERATE COURT-MARTIAL.

BEFORE describing the adventures of Wollam—Andrews' companion in flight from the Chattanooga prison—we will turn towards the twelve prisoners destined for Knoxville, where a yet more fearful tragedy was in preparation.

On parting from our comrades we were escorted to the cars by Colonel Cleiburne, where we found, much to our gratification, that we were to be guarded by a party of Morgan's guerrillas, whose exploits were then greatly celebrated. Cleiburne recommended us to the humane care of these partisans, saying, "These prisoners are men, like other men, and gentlemen too, and I want them treated as such." This charge from the generous Irishman, for such he was, did much to secure

18

courteous treatment from our guard. Indeed, the position of the irregular soldiers who served under the guerrilla chief was such as to make them admire rather than blame the bold enterprise that led to our capture. They were themselves in citizen's dress, and were not always careful to provide uniforms before penetrating into the Federal lines. A considerable number of their comrades had been captured under such circumstances, and were, by every rule of right, equally liable with ourselves to be treated as criminals. Indeed, the position of some of their captured comrades was still more questionable, for they had assumed the United States uniform whenever they found it to their advantage. The inconsistency of the rebel government in treating our party so harshly is conclusively shown by the fact that they had passed laws for the encouragement of just such irregular warfare.

But we have no complaint to make of these dashing guerrillas. They were very indignant to see us in irons, and offered to be responsible for our safe-keeping if these were removed; but this was not allowed.

As was common in our removals from prison to prison, we had been started without any rations,—not so much, I presume, from wanton cruelty as because it was no one's especial business to furnish provisions. As the journey occupied twenty-four hours (and we were hungry to begin with), our privation would have been considerable but for the generosity of Morgan's men. They bought pies and whatever else they could find at the station eating-houses, and literally feasted us. From the time of our capture we had not experienced such treatment, and only hoped that these generous enemies might have charge of us as long as we remained in Confederate territory,—a hope which was not realized. We never met them again.

We arrived in Knoxville shortly after noon, having spent the night on the cars, and were marched through the hot, dusty streets to the city jail,—an old building of peculiar architecture,—solid, square, and massive, presenting quite an imposing appearance. It was used as a military prison, and was filled from top to bottom with ragged, dirty-looking prisoners. Some Union men, and several rebel soldiers who had been captured while attempting to desert, were with them. These constituted the less-valued class of prisoners, and were permitted to range over most of the building, which, however, was completely encircled outside, and watched in every passage-way, by a strong guard.

The class of prisoners whose offences were considered of a more aggravated character were shut up in cages. There were five of these cages, two of which were at once cleared for our reception. The smaller was seven by nine feet, and four of us were put in it. The larger was perhaps ten by twelve, and held the remaining eight.

We arrived at Knoxville in the latter part of May, and remained until June 10. Outside, the weather was intensely warm, but the enormous mass of iron and stone in the walls of the prison made it comparatively cool within. The days here spent were not altogether unpleasant. Our food was scanty and of indifferent quality, but as long as we were allowed hope I did not feel much disposed to complain of this. Besides, many of the Union men of Knoxville, who visited us, were liberal in the gift of money, and by employing the services of those prisoners who were less strictly guarded, we were able to get many an extra loaf of bread.

We here became acquainted with some Tennesseeans who were long our companions. One of the most remarkable was an old man named Pierce. He presented a most peculiar appearance, having at some period of his history received a terrible blow with a gun-barrel, which left a permanent gash more than an inch deep clear across the forehead from the nose to his hair. From this circumstance he was variously known in the prison as "Forked Head," "Old Gun-

barrel," etc. He presented the singular combination
of great piety and great profanity, singing hymns and
cursing the Confederacy with equal zeal. But his
friendship for Union soldiers knew no bounds, and,
being very bold, he was able to render us many valuable services.

Another East Tennesseean, more widely known, was
Captain Fry, of Greenville, a town near the Virginia
boundary. He was confined in a cage, and considered
by our guards almost equally criminal with ourselves.
Early in the war he had gathered a number of his
neighbors, and, running the gauntlet of guarded roads,
succeeded in reaching our army in Kentucky. Here
he was appointed captain of his recruits, and remained
for some time. When an advance into East Tennessee
through Cumberland Gap was contemplated, the Union
general asked him to return to his home, organize the
loyal citizens of that vicinity, burn the bridges on the
Richmond and Knoxville Railroad, and then to keep
possession of the mountainous region till our forces
could arrive. With the most explicit assurances of
speedy aid, he departed on his perilous mission. Success on his part was rapid and complete. He raised
fifteen hundred men, obstructed all communications,
burned the bridges, and seriously threatened Knoxville itself. A very small Union reinforcement could
then have rendered invaluable services, and all the
men needed for the work were assembled not far from
Cumberland Gap. But the attention of the military
authorities was then turned in another direction, and
the plan of advancing into East Tennessee was accordingly abandoned. No word of the change reached
Fry, who struggled on alone. But the odds were too
great. An overwhelming force of the enemy was
thrown upon him, and after several contests he and his
brave men were forced to disperse. A few succeeded
in reaching the loyal lines, and these mostly enlisted in
our army. Others were captured, and many of them

hanged as rebels! General Leadbetter was very conspicuous in this savage work. Fry himself passed the
whole winter in hiding among the wild mountains of
that section, and in the spring mustered several hundred of those who were fugitives like himself, and tried
to reach the Union lines. Near the border he was
overtaken by a superior rebel force, and after a severe
contest he was defeated, wounded, and taken prisoner.
This was on the 5th of March, 1862, and he was kept
in solitary confinement until placed with us on the 11th
of June following. Captain Fry's subsequent fortunes
were closely united with those of our party—indeed,
with my own—and will be related in due time.

When I bring back in memory the minute impressions of those eventful days, I feel surprise that so
many hours of comparative pleasure were found. We
had here many persons to converse with. We had
light and air, which we had not at Chattanooga. We
procured newspapers with frequency, no attempt being
made to prevent this as in other prisons, and were able
to form some idea of the gigantic contest in which we
were so deeply interested, and which at that time progressed hopefully. We had become most intimate with
each other, and would not allow despondency or brood-
ing over trouble to take hold upon any one of our
number. We also provided employment for each
waking hour, and until those tragic events occurred
which deepened the gloom around us we were comparatively hopeful and happy. I even managed to take
up the thread of my law studies and prosecute them
vigorously. I sent word through a visitor to a law
firm—Baxter & Temple—that I wanted to borrow
"Greenleaf on Evidence," and almost as much to my
surprise as pleasure the volumes were promptly sent.
The prison made quite a good study, and the spectacle
of a man reading law in an iron cage seemed to guards
and visitors alike an excellent jest. But I could afford
to let them laugh, for mine was the gain, not only in

the knowledge acquired, but in causing the prison days to pass less wearily.

Before we had been long at Knoxville we were visited by an officer, whom we had seen frequently in Chattanooga, and who told us that he was judge-advocate of a court-martial about to convene, and notified us to prepare for trial. Neither this intelligence nor his manner in giving it was at all alarming. We knew that we had been ordered to Knoxville for this very purpose, and were only anxious to have the trial soon over, that we might be formally declared prisoners of war, and thus be placed in position to be exchanged, if an opportunity should occur. To this end we asked the judge-advocate if we would all be put on trial at once, and when he answered in the negative, we urged the expediency and justice of that course, assuring him that the cases of all were precisely alike. But he refused with some curtness. We next asked that he would select one of our number to be tried, whose award might determine the position of the whole party, and offering to sign a paper agreeing to this course. This he also refused, with the declaration that the court knew its own business, and that every one of us should be tried on his own merits. The only reason I have ever been able to imagine for this course is that the intentions towards us were much more serious than we had been allowed to conjecture, and that it would have looked too absurd to arraign so large a band of private soldiers from one brigade on the charge of being spies. We asked him for the charge on which the trial was to take place, and with some apparent hesitation he gave it,—the same against all. It was charged, in substance, that we were enemies who were lurking in and around Confederate camps *as spies* for the purpose of obtaining military information. Not one word was said about seizing the cars or anything that we did or tried to do. Wilson spoke out boldly, and said, " But you know we are not spies, and have yourself told us that we cannot be held as such." Then, with what I cannot but consider as deep deception, he replied that their expectation now was to obtain a negative verdict, which would justify them in exchanging us. He further advised us to employ counsel and put our cause in good shape, but not to make ourselves uneasy. The whole conversation left some apprehension upon our minds, but in the case of most of us the inherent hopefulness of youth soon banished it.

Our plan of defence has been partly indicated before. It was to tell just who we were and what we had done, and to claim that we were United States soldiers, detailed on a military expedition without our own consent or knowledge, and simply obeying orders. We were to deny in the strongest terms that we had been lurking about any camps, or that we had sought or obtained any military information. No question was to be answered that would lead to the discovery of the engineer or tend to show that any one had volunteered for this service. As to evidence against us, we knew that our recorded confessions, made when we were first brought to Chattanooga, could be used, and possibly the evidence of those who first captured us. But no one could say anything about our lurking around Confederate camps. We had been within the guard-lines at Big Shanty, but we were no more "lurking" there than a body of cavalry who might charge into a camp. Indeed, we felt sure that the charge, in the form it bore, could not be sustained. To make the greatest impression of candor, our story was sketched in brief, with the approval of the whole number, and, at a subsequent visit of the judge-advocate, handed to him. He took our signatures to it, and it was read on the trials as our confession. It saved our enemies some trouble in the matter of witnesses, and put our case in what we judged the most favorable light.

Baxter & Temple, who had so kindly accommodated me with books, were willing to act as our counsel.

They stipulated that, as fast as tried, we should give them our notes for one hundred and fifty dollars each. They did not care for the money, and, indeed, the prospect of obtaining it was not very favorable. But their own safety required that their help should appear to be purely professional. They assured me privately that they were loyal to our government and would do us any favor they dared. They did promote our comfort by the secret gift of some. money.

The story of the trials may soon be told. The charges and specifications of William Campbell were first handed in. He was a citizen of Kentucky in reality, but claimed to be a member of Company K, Second Ohio, and we were careful to endorse his statement. It was never suspected that he stood in any different relation from his comrades. After the overthrow of the Confederacy the writer obtained copies of these charges and specifications, together with many other papers from the rebel archives. They are still on file at Washington. With the exception of the change of names and position in the army, the charges were precisely alike in all the cases.

"*Charge.*—Violation of Section 2d of the 101st Article of the Rules and Articles of War.

" *Specification 1st.*—In that the said William Campbell, private Company ' K,' Second Ohio Regiment, U.S.A., not owing allegiance to the Confederate States of America, and being in the service and army of the United States, then and now at war with the Confederate States of America, did, on or about the 7th day of April, 1862, leave the army of the United States, then lying near Shelbyville, Tennessee, and with a company of about twenty other soldiers of the United States army, all dressed in citizen's clothes, repair to Chattanooga, Tennessee, entering covertly within the lines of the Confederate forces at that post, and did thus, on or about the 11th day of April, 1862, lurk as a spy in and about the encampment of said forces, representing himself as a citizen of Kentucky going to join the Southern army.

" *Specification 2d.*—And the said William Campbell, private Company ' K,' Second Ohio Regiment, U.S.A., thus dressed in citizen's clothes, and representing himself as a citizen of Kentucky going to join the Southern army, did proceed by railroad to Marietta, Georgia,—thus covertly pass through the lines of

the Confederate forces stationed at Chattanooga, Dalton, **and**
Camp McDonald, and did thus, on or about the 11th day of **April,**
1862, lurk as a spy in and about the said encampments of **the**
Confederate forces at the places stated aforesaid."

All mention of the capture of the train, with the
terrible chase that followed, is entirely omitted from
this paper. Could this be for any other reason than
that this sequel would disprove the fact of " lurking as
a spy," on which the whole charge is made to turn, and
make the whole expedition appear of a distinctive military character? The whole charge of " lurking as a
spy" was constructive—not real. No evidence could
be adduced to show that any one of us had lingered
for a single hour at any one of the three Confederate
encampments mentioned. Neither was there any evidence that our false stories were told inside of any
encampment.

With charges which were simply a recital of a small
part of our own admissions and some inference from
them, the trials were very simple and brief. William
Campbell was taken out first, the above paper read to
him, and he responded, " Not true, so far as lurking in
any camp or being a spy is concerned." The plea of
" not guilty" was then entered for him, our own confession read, one or two minor witnesses called, and he returned to prison. The next day another man was taken
to the court and the same story rehearsed. Thus each
day one trial only took place, and no pleadings were
heard by the prisoner, either for or against himself,
and no sentence was given. The time occupied in each
session of the court was not much more than an hour.
The table around which the court sat was covered with
bottles, newspapers, and novels, and the members occupied themselves during the proceedings in discussing
these. All this was very well if the object was, as they
assured us, merely to put formally on record our true
character as prisoners of war ; but it was most heartless
if the trial was in earnest, and a matter of life or death.

Wilson related to me a ludicrous incident that occurred when he was on trial. No instance of his being anywhere within the guard-lines was proved. A young lieutenant requested to be placed on the witness-stand to testify of one occasion when he knew that the prisoner had passed their picket-lines. His offer was gladly accepted. On being sworn, he stated that he had commanded a picket-post which included the Chattanooga ferry, and this ferry the prisoner admitted passing. Immediately the president of the court arose and said that the young gentleman was mistaken, as he himself commanded the guard that day, and that *no guard was placed at the ferry.* The whole court was thrown into a roar of laughter, and the confusion of our would-be convictor may be imagined.

Our lawyers visited us frequently in the prison for the purpose of consultation, and expressed themselves as delighted with the turn matters were taking. No evidence had been found to discredit or go beyond our own statements. They said that all the plans of the prosecution had been deranged, and that if convicted now, it would be through mere prejudice and perjury on the part of the court.

There was one feature of the trial, however, which I did not like, and against which we protested with all our power. No one who was tried was allowed to be present to hear the pleading of counsel on either side. We could neither hear what the judge-advocate urged against us nor what our lawyers said in our favor. Even at the trial of Andrews, in Chattanooga, he had not been debarred this privilege. But in this, and one other particular to be narrated later, the rebels used our soldiers with less show of justice than had been accorded to Andrews himself.

After three or four of our number had been tried, one of our lawyers read to us the plea, which he said he had read after the trial of each man, and would continue to read. It appeared to me to be a paper of great

ability, and I cannot conceive how it could be successfully answered. Judge-Advocate-General Holt officially speaks of it as "This just and unanswerable
presentation of the case." It was contended that our
being dressed in citizen's clothes instead of Federal
uniforms, which was the only unmilitary incident in
the whole history, ought not to weigh against us, because this was nothing more than the Confederate government had expressly authorized in the case of their
own soldiers, and that making war without uniform
was practised by all the guerrillas in the Confederate
service,—by some from necessity, and by others because
they were thus able better to escape detection, and inflict more damage upon the enemy. A special instance
was cited in which General Morgan had dressed a detachment of his partisans in Federal uniform, and
passed them off as belonging to the Eighth Pennsyl-
vania Cavalry, by which means he had succeeded in
reaching and damaging a railroad within the Federal
lines. Some of these very men were captured by the
Federal government, and were, up to the present, held
as prisoners of war. To decide that we were spies
because we were captured without our uniform would
not only provoke retaliation, but establish a principle
far more dangerous to the Confederate than to the
Federal forces. It was urged that we had stated the
object of our expedition, which was a purely military
one, and as such entirely within the laws of war. No
evidence had been adduced to show that we were other
than what we claimed. The plea closed by asking what
good purpose could be served by sacrificing ignomini-
ously the lives of so many brave men on a charge
which had been conclusively disproved by the evidence,
and which every member of the court knew to be really
untrue. We were not spies in fact, and to call us such
against their own convictions, and on merely technical
and constructive grounds, would be as unwise as it was
cruel. The plea did *not* embrace one argument which

added very much to our hopefulness, and which our
lawyers considered likely to have a great weight with
the court, though they dared not formally state it.
McClellan had not yet been repulsed before Richmond,
and the collapse of the Rebellion seemed imminent.
The same rigid construction which was necessary to
make us spies would assuredly render them all liable to
the punishment of treason, and they were not in a position to make it prudent to invoke the utmost severities
and extreme penalties of the laws of war.   As I glance
back over the lapse of twenty years it still seems to me
strange that the decision of the court-martial in our
favor could have been for a moment doubtful.   But,
alas! reason and sound judgment do not always rule in
human affairs.   Though we knew it not then, the life
of every man in that Knoxville prison was trembling
in the balance.

For one whole week—seven days—the trials went
on, the same forms being used in the case of each man,
who was taken out for an hour and returned, knowing
nothing of his sentence, having heard no pleading
against himself, and being treated in no sense differently
after his trial.   On the seventh day we read that General
Mitchel had advanced to Chattanooga and was shelling
the town across the river, and also, that the Federal General Morgan was advancing from Cumberland Gap, and
threatening Knoxville.   We fervently hoped that the
latter would settle the question of our fate by capturing
the town while we were still in it.   This would have
done away with all further perplexity as to the decision of the court-martial !

This advance did prevent all further trials.   The
officers of the court were hurried off to their regiments
to resist the enemy.   From the newspapers, which some
prisoners managed to obtain every day, and then loaned
or read to all the others, we were kept well informed
as to the progress of events.   Some of the intelligence
they brought thrilled us to our souls.   More than a

week before this we read of the escape of Andrews and
Wollam from the Chattanooga prison. We greatly rejoiced, believing firmly that our leader would be sure
to get to our lines, and then use all his influence to secure some form of help for us. The news of his recapture overthrew all these hopes and filled us with anxious apprehension, although we were ignorant of his
being sentenced to death. Of the fate of Wollam
nothing was stated.

But a more terrible blow was in store. One day a
newspaper was silently passed up to our cage by some
friend outside, and, glancing at it, the first thing that
arrested our attention was an account of *the execution of
Andrews!* With equal silence we sent it into the other
cage. Just before this deadly intelligence came we had
been engaged in story-telling and in various games, for
we were always merry, refusing to indulge in gloomy
forebodings. But this was the sudden opening of an
awful gulf at our feet. All noise and merriment were
suspended, and we passed the whole day in mourning.
We could not talk to our guards as lightly as we had
done before, for there was now blood between us. We
all loved Andrews, and would have undergone any
peril to save him, but there was no possibility now
even of vengeance. And, although his fate was gov-
erned by different principles from ours, we could not
help feeling more distrustful of our own position.

An extra guard, bearing a great number of ropes,
came in the morning after the last trial, and we were
called out of our cages. This was startling, as we had
no hint of their purpose, and the word was even passed
around that we were all to be taken out and hanged
immediately. But one of the outside prisoners found
an opportunity to inform us that he had overheard the
commander saying that he was to remove us to prevent
our capture in case of a sudden Federal dash upon
Knoxville. This convinced us that we were only to
have another of our frequent changes of prisons.

In our cages here we had not been ironed, and, as our fetters had been used on some prisoners sent to Richmond, we were now obliged to content ourselves with a most liberal allowance of cotton rope. It was this provision for tying us which at first excited our apprehensions.

While we were being securely bound I had an amusing passage-at-words with the adjutant, who was superintending that operation. I said to him, as politely as I could,—

"I suppose, sir, our destination is not known?"

"It is not known to you at any rate, sir," was the gruff rejoinder.

This was noticed by the whole party, and I felt rather beaten; but a moment later came my chance for revenge. He turned again to me, and said, in a dictatorial manner,—

"Who was it that run your engine through?"

I bowed, and returned in the blandest tone, "*That is not known to you at any rate, sir.*"

All the prisoners around roared with laughter, and the adjutant, reddening to the eyes, turned away, muttering that he believed I was the engineer myself!

When the process of tying was completed to the adjutant's satisfaction, we took our departure southward, and passed through Chattanooga once more, but, to our satisfaction, did not stop there. We continued southward, in the direction of Atlanta. No rations were taken for us, as usual, and having on this occasion no guerrillas to buy us supplies, we were obliged to fast the whole time. At various stations the populace taunted us with Andrews' death, and charitably hoped we might soon meet the same fate. The remark was often made that we were going to Atlanta to be hanged there, as he had been! Captain Fry, Pierce, and a few other of the East Tennesseans were taken along with us. Before we reached Chattanooga, we had, as I thought, an excellent chance to effect our escape. The journey was so slow that night came on, and our guard, wearied with the frequent delays, had relaxed their vigilance, and most of them slept by our sides. They exceeded us in numbers, and were armed, while we were tied. But our two months' experience had made us adepts in some of the poor, pitiful arts prisoners soon learn. We could communicate without exciting the suspicions of the soldiers, who were sitting in the very seats with us, and scarcely one of our number had failed to so "settle himself" in the cotton ropes that they could have been thrown off at a moment's notice. To be ready at a signal, to dash out the two lights that burned in our car, each of us to seize the musket of the man nearest us while the train was in motion, to secure the doors, and let no one get out, or make any alarm, seemed to me easy enough. Then we could have uncoupled our car, and, *with the arms of our guard*, have started across the country towards the Union lines, which could not have been more than thirty or forty miles west of us. But George D. Wilson opposed the project with all his energy. He thought we might succeed, but some would probably be killed in the scuffle, and all might be captured outside, and then our case be made much worse, while by simply remaining quiet, we were sure of a speedy exchange. He had talked for hours with the captain of our guard, who was certain that our case had been virtually decided in our favor. He encouraged Wilson by saying that he had heard officers high in authority say that it had been necessary to execute Mr. Andrews, as he was a Confederate citizen, and as an example; but that this was enough, and that no other would suffer anything worse than possibly, if no favorable exchange could be arranged, the penalty of being kept to the close of the war. This, in Wilson's opinion, was not far distant. Wilson's opposition made us regretfully yield the attempt. Could the future have been foreseen our decision would undoubtedly have been reversed.

Atlanta, we found, was our destination. **Here,** almost in the centre of the rebel States, the Confederates were as yet free from interruption by Union armies. Andrews had already perished in this city, and here our own fate was to be determined. As we marched, with ropes bound tightly round our hands and pinioning our arms, from the depot to the Atlanta city jail, a crowd gathered around us, as usual, and a man, calling himself the mayor of the city, addressed himself first to Captain Fry, telling him that he knew his history and would soon have the pleasure of hanging him. Then turning to us, he boasted that he had put the rope around Andrews' neck and was waiting and anxious to do the same for us!

The city prison was much smaller than that at Knoxvile, but was quite a large edifice. The lower story was occupied by the jailer and family. The upper story contained four rooms, two on each side of an entry, into which the staircase from below led. We, in company with Captain Fry, were given one of these rooms. The other Tennesseeans brought from Knoxville with us were put into another, just across the entry from us. Our comrades, who had been left behind at Chattanooga, had been in this building ever since the death of Andrews, and in the third room. The fourth room was on the same side as our own, and had a succession of occupants,—frequently negroes who had been in search of the North Star. This jail was to be our home for many eventful months.

For some days our food was comparatively good and abundant. Turner, the jailer, was a kind man, and, in a mild way, of Union sentiments. He showed us all the favor in his power, and, indeed, became so much suspected that an odious old man named Thoer was sent to watch him. The change in our condition was at once manifest. Our fare became worse and more scanty than in any former prison. The constant vigilance of this spy kept the jailer from doing anything

to mitigate our sufferings. But in this prison we had
one great relief. Our ropes were removed and no
chains or handcuffs put upon us. Within our prison-
cell we were free. Here we remained in quiet for a
week, thinking the worst of our trials now over. Little
did we imagine how fearful a storm was about to
burst over us.

CHAPTER XIV.

THE CROWNING HORROR.

THE event described in this chapter will never be
effaced from the memory of any witness. Nothing
more terrible or more gratuitously barbarous is recorded
in the annals of civilized war. The seven men of
whose death I am now to write were all young,—from
eighteen to twenty-five. With good prospects, and
well connected, they had entered the army at the bidding of patriotism, ready to endure every peril to in-
sure the triumph of the old flag. Their only offence,
when stripped of all technicality, was that of accepting
a dangerous service proposed by their own officers.
They had entered on this service in the same spirit that
they would have obeyed an order to head a desperate
charge on the enemy's fortifications. Had they perished
in the enterprise itself, their fate would have been but
the common fortune of war. But more than two
months had passed since they had been in the power
of their enemies, who had repeatedly testified admiration for their heroism, as well as for their gallant bearing in captivity. Prominent officers had held friendly
conversations with them and assured them of ultimate
safety. Now, without a moment's warning—— But
I must not anticipate the narration.

One day—the 18th of June. 1862—while amusing

ourselves with games and stories in our prison-cell, we saw through the barred window a squadron of cavalry approaching. This only excited a languid curiosity at first, for it was a common thing to see bodies of horsemen in the streets; but soon we saw them halt before the gate of the high prison-wall and throw a line of soldiers completely round the building. This was no ordinary occurrence. What could it portend?

A moment after we heard the clink of the officers' swords as they ascended the prison stairway in unusual numbers, while we waited the event with deep solicitude. They paused at our door, which was unlocked by the jailer, and the names of the seven who had been tried at Knoxville were called over, one by one, and each man as he was called led out of the room. Samuel Robinson was very sick with fever, and was not able to rise without assistance, but two guards helped him to his feet, and he was taken out with the others. Then the door opposite to ours, on the other side of the hall, was opened, and the Tennesseeans in that room put with us, while our comrades, with the whole number of officers, went into the vacated room, and the door was closed.

With throbbing veins we asked one another the meaning of these strange proceedings. A confused sound was heard through the closed door opposite, as of some one reading, but we could distinguish no words. Some of us supposed they were taken in there to receive their acquittal; others, still more sanguine, maintained that they were now being paroled, prepara tory to an exchange.

I was also suffering with malarial fever at that time, but rose to my feet oppressed with a nameless fear. A half-idiotic man who was among the Tennessee prisoners came to me and wanted to play a game of cards. I struck the greasy pack out of his hands, and bade him leave me.

Our terrible suspense was not of long duration. The

door opened and George D. Wilson entered first, his hands and arms firmly bound, and his face pale as death, but with form erect and firm step. Some one asked in a whisper a solution of the dreadful mystery, for his countenance had appalled every one.

"*We are to be executed immediately!*" was the awful reply, whispered with thrilling distinctness.

Behind him came the others, all tied, ready for the scaffold! They were to be hanged at once. Not a day nor an hour was given for preparation. From their hopefulness and fancied security they were snatched in a moment to die as felons! Surely no rule of war, no military necessity, no consideration of policy, required such frightful and murderous haste. I have never heard a word in defence of this military massacre. Even Andrews, our leader, was given a week for preparation before the execution of his sentence. The most atrocious criminals are always allowed a short respite. For a long time I cherished the belief that some misunderstanding of orders, some terrible error, and not deliberate cruelty, led to this frightful haste. But the following death-sentence seems to leave no room for doubt. In the very centre of the Confederacy, with hundreds of troops at their disposal for guards, there could have been no military necessity for hurling these poor men into eternity without one hour's warning!

The following is a literal copy of the death-sentence read to the doomed men during the few minutes they were separated from us:

"HEADQUARTERS DEPARTMENT EAST TENNESSEE,
"KNOXVILLE, June 14, 1862.

"*General Orders,* No. 54.   *VII.*

"At a general court-martial held at Knoxville by virtue of General Orders Nos. 21 and 34 (Department Headquarters, April 15 and May 10, 1862), whereof Lieutenant-Colonel J. B. Bibb, of the Twenty-third Regiment Alabama Volunteers, was president, was tried George D. Wilson, private Company ' B,' Second

Ohio Regiment, on the following charge and specifications, to wit:

"*Charge.*—Violation of Section 2d of the 101st Article of the Rules and Articles of War.

"*Specification 1st.*—In this, that the said George D. Wilson, private Company 'B,' Second Ohio Regiment, not owing allegiance to the Confederate States of America, and being in the service and army of the United States, then and now at war with the Confederate States of America, did, on or about the 7th day of April, 1862, leave the army of the United States, then lying near Shelbyville, Tennessee, and with a company of about twenty other soldiers of the United States army, all dressed in citizen's clothes, repair to Chattanooga, Tennessee, entering covertly within the lines of the Confederate forces at that post, and did thus, on or about the 11th day of April, 1862, lurk as a spy in and about the encampment of said forces, representing himself as a citizen of Kentucky going to join the Southern army.

"*Specification 2d.*—And the said George D. Wilson, private Company 'B,' Second Ohio Regiment, U.S.A., thus dressed in citizen's clothes, and representing himself as a citizen of Kentucky going to join the Southern army, and did proceed by railroad to Marietta, Georgia,—thus covertly pass through the lines of the Confederate forces stationed at Chattanooga, Dalton, and Camp McDonald, and did thus, on or about the 11th day of April, 1862, lurk as a spy in and about the said encampments of the Confederate forces at the places stated aforesaid.

"To which charge and specifications the prisoner plead 'Not Guilty.'

"The court, after mature deliberation, find the accused as follows: Of the 1st specification of the charge, 'Guilty.' Of the 2d specification of the charge, 'Guilty,' and 'Guilty of the Charge.' And the court do therefore sentence the accused, the said George D. Wilson, private Company 'B,' Second Ohio Regiment (two-thirds of the members concurring therein), as soon as this order shall be made public, 'to be hung by the neck until he is dead.'

"The proceedings in the foregoing case of George D. Wilson, private Company 'B,' Second Ohio Regiment, are approved.

"The sentence of the court will be carried into effect between the 15th and 22d days of June, inst., at such time and place as may be designated by the commanding officer at Atlanta, Georgia, who is charged with the arrangements for the proper execution thereof

"By command of
          "Major-General E. KIRBY SMITH.
                    "J. F. BRETON, A.A.A.G.
"To Commanding Officer of post at Atlanta, Ga."

It will be noticed that the sentence was to be exe-

cuted as soon as made public. The time fixed was between the 15th and 22d days of June. This was the
18th. The sentence had been received the preceding
day, and the time employed in clearing a spot of wooded
ground then lying east of the city cemetery, but since
included in its bounds, and in erecting a scaffold there.
But no word of the awful preparations had been allowed
to reach us. According to the orders of General E.
Kirby Smith, several days' respite might have been allowed ; but in a communication to the Confederate Secretary of War, Colonel G. I. Foreacre, post-commander
at Atlanta, says, " General Smith only sent from Knoxville instructions and orders to have seven of them
hung, which was promptly attended to by myself."

After the sentences had been read came the farewells,
—which, in their full meaning, we could scarcely realize,—farewells with no hope of meeting again in this
world ! Our comrades were dear as brothers to us, and
to stand helpless while they were dragged away to the
scaffold froze our blood and crushed our hearts.

These doomed men were brave. On the battle-field
they had never faltered in the presence of danger.
They were ready to die, if need were, for their country ;
but to die on the scaffold,—to die as murderers die,—
this was almost too much for human nature to endure.

Then, too, they were destitute of the best support a
man can have in the presence of death. Although
most of them had been of excellent moral character,
yet they had no firmly-grounded religious hope. The
near prospect of eternity, into which they were thus to
be hurled without a moment's preparation, was black
and appalling. Wilson had been a professed disbe-
liever in revelation, and many a time had argued with
me for hours at a time. But in this awful moment he
said to me, " Pittenger, I believe you are right now !
Oh, try to be better prepared, when your turn comes to
die, than I am !" Then laying his hand on my head,
with a muttered " God bless you !" we parted. I saw

no more the one I had loved and trusted as few others in the world.

Shadrack was profane in speech and reckless in action, but withal exceeding kind-hearted, lovable, and always merry. Now turning to us with a voice the forced calmness of which was more affecting than a wail of agony, he said, "Boys, I am not prepared to meet my Jesus." When asked by some of us, in tears, to trust in His mercy, and to think of heaven, he answered, still in tones of thrilling calmness, "I'll try! I'll try! But I know I am not prepared."

Samuel Slavens, who was a man of immense strength and iron resolution, turned to his friend Buffum, and could only articulate, "Wife—children—tell—" when utterance failed.

John Scott had been married only three days before he came to the army, and the thought of his young and sorrowing wife nearly drove him to despair. He could only clasp his hands in silent agony.

William Campbell smiled grimly as we pressed his bound hands, and said in response to our declarations, "Yes, boys, this *is* hard."

Marion Ross bore himself most firmly of all. He had been more gloomy and depressed than any other member of the party previously, and did not seem to share fully in our hopes. Now his eyes beamed with unnatural light, and there was not a tremor in his voice as he said, in full, clear tones, "Tell them at home, if any of you should escape, that I died for my country, and did not regret it."

These parting words occupied but a moment, and even then the officers standing in the door seemed impatient to finish their horrible work!

In this manner the poor men were hurried to their doom. Several of them, in passing, had the privilege of shaking hands with our comrades in the other room. Robinson, though too sick to walk, was dragged away with them.

Thus we parted. The rough wagon, with a wood-rack for a bed, drove off with our comrades, surrounded by cavalry. In about an hour it came back, *empty.* The deed of shame was done.

Later in the evening the provost-marshal came to our door, and, in response to eager questions, informed us that our friends "had met their fate as brave men should die everywhere."

The next day we obtained from the guards, who, in the absence of their officers, were always willing to talk with us, full particulars of the sevenfold murder.

When all had been mounted on the scaffold Wilson asked permission to say a few words, which was granted, —probably in the hope of hearing some kind of a con-fession. If such was the expectation, they were much disappointed. It was a strange scene,—a dying speech to a desperate audience, and under the most terrible circumstances conceivable.

But Wilson was equal to the occasion, and when he had once begun to speak, the force of his words was such that the mob remained silent, making no attempt to interrupt him. Unterrified by the near approach of death, he spoke his mind freely. He told the rebels that they were all in the wrong, that he had no hard feelings towards the Southern people for what they were about to do, because they had been duped by their leaders, and induced by them to engage in the work of rebellion. He also said that though he had been condemned as a spy, yet he was none, and they well knew it. He was only a soldier in the performance of the work he had been detailed to do; that he did not regret to die for his country, but only regretted the manner of his death. He concluded by assuring them in prophetic words that they would yet live to regret the part they had taken in this rebellion, and would see the flag of our country wave in triumph over the very ground occupied by his scaffold.

This address made a deep impression on the minds

of all who listened, and I often afterwards heard it
spoken of in terms of deepest admiration. When he
ceased the signal was given, and the traps fell!

Then followed one of the disgusting exhibitions
which so often disgrace all kinds of public executions.
Five only remained dangling in the air. Campbell
and Slavens, being very heavy, broke their ropes, and
fell to the ground insensible. When they revived,
they asked and received a drink of water. Then they
requested an hour to pray before entering the future
world. This most reasonable petition, which would
not have been denied to the most hardened murderer
under civilized rule, was sternly denied, as if they
wished to do their utmost to murder both soul and
body. As soon as the ropes could be readjusted they
were compelled to mount the scaffold once more, and
were again turned off.

CHAPTER XV.

PRISON RELIGION.

THE afternoon following the execution of our brave
comrades was one of indescribable sorrow, gloom, and
fear. We knew not how soon we might be compelled
to follow in the same path and drink the same bitter
cup. As has been before narrated, we had offered at
Knoxville to accept the award of the court in one of
the cases as the sentence of all, since there was not the
slightest difference among us. At that time, however,
we were confident of acquittal. Now that confidence
had utterly vanished, and no one of our number anticipated anything but speedy death on the scaffold.

But even without the addition of apprehension for
ourselves, the parting from our loved friends, whose
voices were still ringing in our ears, while they them-

selves had passed beyond the gates of death into the unknown land of shadows, was enough to rend the stoutest heart. Few words were spoken, but tears and sobs were frequent.

I could not shed a tear. A fierce fever burned in my veins, and my head seemed as if on fire. For hours I scarcely knew where I was, or the loss I had sustained. Every glance around the room, which revealed the vacant place of our friends, would bring our sorrow in a new wave upon us again. Slowly the afternoon wore on in grief too deep for words, and despair too black for hope.

At last some voice suggested prayer. We had no chaplain, and few of us were professedly religious, but the very thought of prayer seemed to bring relief, and was eagerly accepted. We knelt around the bare prison-walls, as so many prisoners have done before, and tried to draw near to God. We felt as if already cut off from the world. Captain Fry first prayed aloud. His voice was broken by sobs, but he did not now pray for the first time, and we felt our faith leaning on his as he poured out strong supplications for that Almighty help we so sorely needed. He prayed that God's love might be revealed to us, and that we might be able to trust the Saviour even on the gallows When he ceased another took up the thread of petition After him, another and another followed, until all but two had prayed aloud, and even these were kneeling and sobbing with the rest. As the twilight deepened our devotional exercises grew more solemn. In the lonely shadow of coming night, with eternity thus tangibly open before us, and standing on its very brink, we prayed with inconceivable fervor. These exercises continued far into the night, and wrought their effect deeply in our hearts. From that night I recognized God's right to my allegiance. I did accept Christ as my Saviour, and determined to confess His name before men, whether I lived or died. This resolution in my own case—and I doubt not the same result was produced in other hearts—restored the fortitude that had been so rudely shaken, and I felt nerved for any fate.   Strangely enough, with this resignation to the worst came the glimmer of a hope, unfelt before, that possibly life might yet be spared.

This hour wrought a complete and permanent change in the routine of our prison-life.   Games, sports, and stories were no longer our leading pursuits.   The cards we had been accustomed to play for pastime only—an old greasy pack obtained from the compassion of some soldier on guard—were thrown out of the window, and that game given up forever.   Each morning and each evening we had a prayer-meeting,—not simply a single prayer, but all praying in turn.   We asked for and obtained a Bible from the jailer, and read a chapter or more as part of our exercises, and sang hymns, so that our meetings became as much like those we had witnessed in the distant but never forgotten days of freedom as we could make them.   There was wonderful pathos in the very rudeness of the singing, for our sweetest voices were silent in death.   The remark was often made, "If Ross was only here to lead the singing!"   The one who read the Bible lesson was considered the leader of the meeting, and, for a time, we took this position by turns.   In place of "Do they miss me at Home?" we sang the more inspiring and helpful "Jesus, Lover of my Soul," and "Rock of Ages."   The jailer, the guards, and all who came near the prison noticed the great change.

I had one peculiar difficulty which, to many readers, will appear almost whimsical, but to me was most real.   Our hope of ever regaining liberty, or even preserving our lives much longer, was but slight; yet my greatest difficulty in finding satisfactory religious consolation had reference to a possible release.   I had been a diligent law student, and had managed to continue the study even in the army and in prison.   But now it

was impressed upon my mind, with daily increasing
force, that I must submit the decision of my future
career to God. If I took this matter into my own
hands, I could not feel that I was completely true to
Him. Underlying this feeling was the further conviction that if I made such a submission of my future
profession to God I would be led into the ministry, and
the thought of this was very repulsive. Yet the longer
the struggle continued the plainer duty became. If I
gave myself to Christ, it seemed a necessary consequence
that I should accept any work He gave me to do. If
I feared that He would guide me in a certain direction,
this was sure proof that I was not resigned to His will,
and, according to my views, not a true Christian. At
last the choice was made,—I resolved to follow my
sense of duty, no matter where that should lead,—to
the ministry or anywhere else. When this conflict was
over there was no great emotional excitement,—only a
sense of peace and rest. I could wait calmly in the
prison until led forth to die, if such should be my
doom, and then go forth out of life feeling that I was
loyal to God, and that I should remain His, into whatever worlds the gate of death should open. If, contrary to all probability, the prison-gate should open for
my passage back into the free world, from which I
seemed almost as effectually separated as if death had
already intervened, I promised still to be loyal to Him.
This was the essence of the inward change I date from
that time. My standard of action before had been
pleasure, inclination, the world's notion of honor and
morality. Even this had not been held too strictly, as
the reader of these pages has discovered. But afterwards, however imperfectly maintained, my standard
became the will of God, as revealed in the Bible, and
my own sense of duty as enlightened by His Spirit.
No great joy, such as is often expressed in conversion,
came at first. But it was even better than any joy to
feel that I now had a strong arm upon which I could

lean,—that there was one person to whom I could go at any time, and who was not indifferent to my fate.

I now read the Bible with a clear purpose, and with a light on its pages that never before beamed there. Its very history was full of new meaning. Its grand beginning, the growth of wandering tribes into great empires, the pathos of the Psalms, the sublimity and eternal hope of the prophecies, and, above all, the life and death of that loving and lowly man who was greater than Psalmist or Prophet,—all these passed before me in the old Atlanta jail, until the place seemed like a new isle of Patmos. I had a strong bent towards scepticism, though I had not yielded to it, and found it hard to exercise simple faith in all the Word of God. But, little by little, my doubts became weaker and my conviction of truth clearer.

For a considerable time the whole of our party took turns in the leadership of our devotions, but finally this work devolved on the writer, and, after some months, the guards and other prisoners began to call me the "preacher," though, as yet, I was a member of no church, unless our prison band can be dignified by that title.

Two Southern ministers visited us at this period. The first requested permission of the guard, and was allowed to enter with the express provision that his conversation should be confined to religious topics. His name was Scott, but I am not sure what denomination he belonged to, and his conversation gave no clue. His first question did not contribute to a good understanding. He asked how we could be so wicked as to enter the Federal army, to fight against the Southern people and free their negroes? We were sorry enough about many things, but had not yet repented of those particular sins, and therefore answered a little tartly, by asking how he and his friends could be so wicked as to rebel against a good government? A heated dispute followed. Our visitor talked so loudly and vehemently that the officer of the guard entered and told him that he "had given those men religious counsel enough for one time and had better leave." He never came again, and we were not sorry.

Our jailer, Mr. Turner, had a very kindly feeling towards us, and hearing us so often singing and praying, asked if we would not like to talk with a minister. Knowing that ministers were not all alike, we assented. Rev. George G. N. MacDonell, of the M. E. Church South, then visited us. We were glad to see him, and a very profitable conversation took place. A little offence was occasioned by his first prayer, in which he petitioned that our lives might be spared, if consistent with *the interests of the Confederacy.* But we made no comment, and were richly rewarded for our complacency. He not only gave us Christian sympathy and counsel above all value, but on leaving sent us some excellent books. When the first lot of books was finished—of which we took the best of care, reading most of them aloud—we returned them, and received others,—continuing the process of borrowing until we had perused nearly the whole of the good man's library. Only those who know what a terrible trial it is to pass day after day with no definite employment, no company, and no means of diverting thought from one never-ending round, can form any idea of the great boon thus bestowed upon us. The Christian kindness and disinterested benevolence of this minister will never be forgotten. But even these books were not sufficient. I sold my vest—not expecting to live until cold weather—and my pocket-book,—which my captors had left when they took all its contents,—and with the proceeds the jailer bought me three little books—all gems,—"Paradise Lost," "Pilgrim's Progress," and Pollok's "Course of Time." These I deliberately set to work to memorize. It was a pleasant and profitable employment, helping very much to shorten those interminable days.

Our room was of greater size than that in Chattanooga; the windows larger, and our number reduced; yet the heat was fearfully oppressive.   One of the party, Mark Wood, was very sick. He had been prostrated with fever for nearly a month, and at this time his life was despaired of.   This was not thought by the others to be any great misfortune to him, and they accordingly administered consolation in a style worthy the best of Job's friends. They would say, " Now, Wood, I wouldn't try to get well, if I were in your place. They will only hang you if you do. Better try to die and save them the trouble." Wood, however, did not relish this counsel, and, becoming contrary, he recovered, "just for spite," as he often declared.

The black waiters of the prison were very friendly. They assisted us by every means in their power, and seemed willing to take any personal risk on our behalf. It was not long before they found that we desired few things so much as to read the news, and they tasked their ingenuity to gratify us.   Newspapers were prohibited, as they had not been at Knoxville. But the waiters would watch until the jailer or some of the guard had finished reading a paper and laid it down, when they would slyly purloin it, put it into the bottom of the pan in which our food was brought, and thus hand it to us unsuspected. It had to be returned in the same way to avoid suspicion. Our ministerial friend also, as he acquired confidence in us, gave us reason to think that he was not so much devoted to the Confederacy as his first prayer (made in hearing of the guard) indicated.   He asked permission of the jailer to give us some old files of religious papers, and sent in a bundle weekly, or oftener. They were acceptable, but their value greatly increased when we found that an old religious paper might have a new daily folded carefully inside! These acts of friendship were deeply grateful to us, and lightened many a weary hour.

One morning our jailer came to our door and asked if we knew John Wollam. We were startled, and hesitated to answer. For three weeks we had heard nothing of Wollam, and hoped that one member of our devoted band had escaped. Now we knew that the jailer was in possession of some news, and while we burned to hear it, we feared the possibility of doing Wollam an injury by acknowledging the acquaintance. But while we deliberated John himself came up, and put an end to our doubts by greeting us heartily. The door was unlocked, and he entered. All the survivors of our party were now together, as those who had been separated from us at Chattanooga were put into our room immediately after the execution of our comrades. Our number, including Captain Fry, who remained in our room, was fifteen.

The first thing in order, when left alone, was for John to tell us all his adventures from the time he and Andrews had broken out of the Chattanooga dungeon. He was fired upon while still suspended in the air by the blankets upon which he was descending, but fortunately the hands of the guards were too unsteady to inflict any injury. He succeeded in getting safely to the ground, and then out of the prison-yard and through the guard-line.

In his efforts to escape Wollam displayed qualities which would have done credit to an Indian. A few moments' running brought him down to the river-side in advance of all pursuers. Finding no means of crossing, the brilliant thought struck him of making his enemies believe he had crossed. This idea was instantly acted on. He threw off his coat and vest, dropping them on the bank of the river, and then walked a few rods in the water to throw any hounds that might be following off his track. He next slipped quietly back and hid in a dense thicket of canes and rushes. He heard his pursuers on the bank above him, and all around, talking of their various plans. At last they found the clothes, and at once concluded that he had taken to the river. Accordingly they ferried the blood-hounds to the other side, and searched for the place of his exit from the water. As might be expected, the dogs were unable to find that, and after a due time spent in consultation, the Confederates concluded that he had been drowned and gave over the search.

Wollam spent the day in great anxiety, but night gave him the opportunity of leaving his hiding-place. He made his way cautiously down the river on the Chattanooga side for some miles. At length he found a canoe, in which he drifted down the stream by night, while hiding it and himself in the bushes by day. On two occasions he would have been saved if he had only known it. General Mitchel had captured a steamboat and fitted it up as a cruiser, with which he patrolled the river as far as his lines extended. In his night-voyaging Wollam passed this extemporized gunboat twice, but fearing that it was some rebel craft, he crept quietly by in the shadow of the shore without discovery.

At length he felt sure that he was inside the Union lines, and beyond the probable danger of capture, and therefore ventured boldly forward in the daytime. This was a fatal mistake. The danger of capture is never so great as in the debatable ground between two armies, where both exercise their utmost vigilance. This boundary in most cases is also a shifting one. It was so in this instance. A band of rebel cavalry on the shore saw the lonely voyager, and, riding on ahead, procured a boat and came out to meet him. He was unable to escape, and thus the poor fellow was captured on the very brink of safety. As usual, he tried to persuade them that he was a Confederate, but unfortunately a certain Lieutenant Edwards, who had assisted in his previous capture, happened to be present, and at once recognized him by his bold and reckless bearing. He was then taken to join us at Atlanta.

Our provisions here became worse and less, until the starvation point was very nearly reached. Constant hunger was one of the torments of our life. We only received a very small fragment of half-baked corn-bread, without salt, and a morsel of pork,—the latter always spoiled, and frequently covered with maggots. But none of it was wasted ! Several had very little appetite, because of malarial or intermittent fever. The allowance of *such* food was abundant for these, but the others ate all that the sick spared. Many a Barmecide feast was spread by the description of rich dainties that would be enjoyed if " at home" once more ; and what was even worse, the same banquets would be spread in dreams, from which the tantalized sleepers awoke more hungry and miserable than ever. I am not sure that the aching head and burning fever were more painful than the constant pangs of unsatisfied hunger. However, I need not linger over these details. In the mere matter of starving I presume we suffered no more than thousands of our fellow-soldiers in Andersonville and other prisons. Alfred Wilson, whose iron constitution bore up well under all hardships, and whose appetite was always good enough for all the rations of every kind he could get, felt these privations most keenly. He says of the food that it was " almost enough to convulse the stomach of a hungry dog. I have found by experience, and I think I will be corroborated by all the men who have been in rebel prisons and have suffered the protracted pangs of hunger and starvation, that man, when forced to it, is as ravenous, reckless, unreasonable, and brutish in his appetite as the lowest order of animal creation." In other prisons, it was not uncommon for the inmates to fight over their miserable allowance ; but our common sympathy and discipline were so strong that few disputes arose, and these were quickly settled by the general voice. The religious influence that had grown up in our midst also tended powerfully to prevent any interference of the stronger with the rights of the weaker.

Indeed, the completeness of our voluntary discipline and the systematic manner in which we employed our time was little less than marvellous. To sleep was always in order, when possible, but the disposal of waking hours was not left to the will of each person. The only game permitted was that of checkers or drafts, and over the rude board carved on the floor eager players bent during all the hours allotted to amusement. Then we had a couple of hours daily for debating, and discussed questions of every kind. No little ingenuity and skill were thus exercised. Often great political questions occupied our attention, and evoked real and strong differences of opinion. Strange as it may seem, there were but two of us—Buffum and myself—who avowed ourselves out and out abolitionists. The name had not yet lost all its reproach, but we held our own in argument, especially when we pointed out the natural result of slavery in making men barbarous and inhuman even to whites, as illustrated in our condition. *That* argument never failed to give us the advantage!

We also set aside two hours in the forenoon and two in the afternoon for reading. During this time not so much as a whisper was permitted, and few schools have kept better discipline. Any one not wishing to read was permitted to sleep or occupy himself in any quiet manner. Frequently some one was selected to read aloud for a time, but this only took place by general consent, that those who wished to read silently might be undisturbed. The extraordinary character of these exercises will be better appreciated when it is remembered that we had no "light reading," but mainly theological works, with a few volumes of travels, biography, and poetry,—just what the good minister's library could furnish, for we read everything we could get. The Bible was not forgotten. When the supply of books ran short, we resorted to our memories. All the

prominent incidents of our lives had been told in our
terribly close association, and we next began to repeat
for the common benefit the books we had read so far as
we could remember them. One night about dark I
began to tell something about a weird book I had read
a few months previously. A few questions elicited
fuller detail, and it was after midnight before the story
was finished. Buffum, especially, was so deeply impressed that when released he took the earliest opportunity of getting and reading the volume, but he gave
me a great compliment by saying that the original was
not half so good as the copy. The changed circumstances, perhaps, made a more natural, if less flattering,
explanation of his diminished interest. We also had
our regular hours for gymnastic exercise,—wrestling,
boxing, acrobatic feats, etc. One of our party, Hawkins, having once been connected with a circus, now
trained us in all the exercises that our enfeebled condition and close quarters permitted. Much of the
health and vigor that we retained during so long an
imprisonment was due to our systematic and diversified
employments.

This careful division of time, and endeavor after
constant employment, was, doubtless, of great advantage, but it could not change the fact that we were close
prisoners in a stifling room, and far from our home.
Those summer days, as month after month glided away,
were terribly long and oppressive. The tediousness and
vain longing for action pressed upon us more and more
closely. We fought the dreadful weight with all the
strength of our wills, but even will-power grew feebler.
The engineer Brown, who was one of the most restless
of mortals, all nerve and fire in action, capable of enduring tremendous hardship if it were only of an active
character, would pace the floor back and forth like a
caged tiger ; when this, too, grew unendurable, he
would stop at the door, shake its woven iron bars till
they rang again, and say in the most piteous tones (of

course, meant only for *us* to hear), " Oh, kind sir, please
let me out! I want to go home!" The feeling he
expressed was shared by all. Never before could I
realize the full value of liberty and the horror of confinement. In previous prisons the novelty of our situation, the frequent removals, the painful excitement
of trials, prevented the blank monotony of imprisonment from settling down upon us as it did here, after
the first few weeks of our stay in Atlanta rolled by,
and no whisper regarding our probable fate reached us.
It was like the stillness and death that brood over the
Dead Sea!

We would sit at the windows in the sultry noon and
look out through the bars at the free birds as they flew
past, seemingly so full of joyous life, and foolishly wish
that we were birds, that we, too, might fly far away and
be free.

At long intervals, two of us at a time would be permitted to go down into the jail-yard to do some wash-
ing for ourselves and the party. This great privilege
came round to me at last. It was then three months
since I had stepped out of that prison room, and the
unobscured vision of open air and sky made it seem
like another world. I remember looking up at the
snowy clouds, my eyes dazzled by the unusual light,
and wondering, as I gazed in admiration upon their
beautiful and changing forms, whether beyond them
lay a world of rest in which there were neither wars
nor prisons. Oh, how I longed for freedom! to be
where I could look up at the sky every day and go
where I wished! Yet with the thought came a great
fear. If I was ever removed from the pressure of immediate danger, and allowed to mingle in the interests
and cares of the thronging world, might I not forget
my prison-made vows and lose my claim to the world
beyond the clouds and stars? Such a sense of weakness and helplessness came over me that I felt greatly
relieved when, my task being done, I was conducted

back to the dark and narrow prison room, where the contrast between freedom and bondage was less palpable !

All this time we hardly permitted ourselves to indulge a hope of getting home again. The friends we had known in happier days were separated from us by an impassable gulf; and when fancy called round us the loved scenes and friends at home, it was like treading upon forbidden ground. But when the long day had dragged its hours away, when we were weary with fighting against weariness, the night removed every restraint, and for a few golden hours love and freedom were ours again.

Often in dreams have I seen the streets and buildings of my own town rise before me, and have felt a thrilling pleasure in contemplating each feature of the landscape around as I wended my way in fancy towards the old log cabin forever consecrated by affection. But the waking from such dreams of earthly paradise was sad beyond measure. The evening hour, when the burning heat had abated, and when we were settling to rest,—though it was on the bare floor, and without even a stone like that upon which Jacob pillowed his head, —was our happiest time. Then prayer and song and more cheerful conversation prepared us for rest and often for happy dreams. But the morning hours, when we wakened, hungry, sore, unrefreshed, with no food but our miserable bit of vile bread and spoiled meat, and a long day to look forward to,—these were always dreary. After prayers, and our apology for a breakfast, we grew more cheerful, and again took up the task of living.

An anecdote here will fitly illustrate the affection and exaggerated reverence felt for what we, to the great annoyance of the guards and citizens, persisted in calling "God's country." I had been reading aloud a sermon of Bishop Bascom's, from a book loaned us by our friend, the minister. The topic was "The Joys of

Heaven." All listened with delight to his magnificent descriptions, but when the reading closed, engineer Brown, who was of a matter-of-fact disposition, asked, " Now, candidly, boys, would you rather be in heaven, safe from all harm, if it is as good as the preacher says, or be in Cincinnati?" This roused a very animated discussion, but at its conclusion, when we took a vote on the subject, the majority decided, honestly, no doubt, that they would rather be in Cincinnati,—for a while, at least !

The expedients to which the tobacco-chewers of our party were driven to obtain a supply of " the weed" were at once amusing and pathetic. They were even more eager for it than for their food. They begged from the negroes, jailer, guards, visitors,—anybody who could supply the valued article. The little they got was husbanded with the utmost care. One chewing was not sufficient. No " quids" were thrown away, but carefully laid up, dried, and again used. When no more narcotic could be so extracted, they were once more dried and smoked in cob pipes !

When Andrews broke out of the Chattanooga jail, he gave Hawkins a large, fine coat, which was too heavy to be carried. This was now sold to the jailer, and the proceeds furnished quite a treat of provisions.

We found some diversion in opening secret communication with every room in the prison. Those on the opposite side of the entry were reached by means of a small stick, which was shot from the crack under one door to the corresponding crack under the other. Each door was double,—one thickness of heavy wood, which was shut only at night, and precluded all communication ; the other of light iron bars. A string tied to the stick pulled over any message we might desire to send. Between our room and the other on the same side of the hall there was an unused chimney, into which stove-pipes led on each side. By removing the elbows we could talk through, but there was the danger of being overheard. To remedy that, a long lath **was** forced off the side of our room in such a way that it could be put back again when desired, and this **was** used in passing notes back and forth through this concealed passage. This "telegraph" was very useful when we afterwards undertook an escape.

I can preserve no order of time in relating the events of these tedious months, which slowly rolled away their ponderous length. It was an almost perfect isolation from the world, with little hope of ever again mingling in its busy currents. As each month closed, we were startled by the thought that we were still alive,—that the thunder-bolt had not yet descended,— and we surmised and wondered how much longer it could be delayed. At last a small ray of hope began to rise, very feeble at first, and based only upon the incomprehensible reprieve we were enjoying. As week after week glided away eventless—marked only by the monotony that is more wearying to heart and brain than the most severe anguish—this hope grew stronger; though it was so little assured that the most trifling circumstance—such as the strengthening of the guard, or the visit of an army official—was sufficient for the time to overturn it. It was the 12th of June when we entered that room. It was the 18th of October before we left it amid events of the most startling character, which will form a fit topic for a new chapter.

CHAPTER XVI.

LIBERTY OR DEATH?

ONE morning the guard brought up four Federal soldiers, who were shut up in the front room. As soon as we were alone we resorted to our usual method of telegraphing to learn who they were. To our great surprise and pleasure we found that two of them—Coleman and Helbling—were of the Tenth Wisconsin, a regiment of our own brigade. They gave us many most interesting items of news,—among others, that our comrades had long since given us up for dead, and were vowing vengeance on our behalf. They were greatly surprised to find so many of us still alive. The other two were of the regular army, who had been captured on the coast of Florida. They remained with us until we were taken to Richmond long after. From them we gained a complete detail of the movements of our army since our departure. We were greatly grieved to find the military situation far less favorable than it had been four months before. The transfer of General Mitchel from Tennessee to the Atlantic coast we also regarded as unfavorable to our interests. These soldiers were the means shortly of leading us to a desperate resolution.

We frequently talked and plotted about escape. This is the one topic that prisoners never weary of. We long before resolved that if any movement was made towards a court-martial, we would make one desperate effort for life; for the result of the trials in the case of Andrews and our poor comrades assured us that this formality would not be undertaken for any other purpose than that of putting us to death, under a show of law. After the lapse of a considerable time we had hopes

that they would not dispense with this ceremony, and
that we would thus have warning which might be useful. But many of our number—those especially who
were vigorous in health, and, therefore, were more
ready for action—wished to make the attempt at any
rate. But time rolled on, and the dreaded preparations for a trial were not made. Why we were left in
this uncertain condition for four months we could not
tell. It might be that, in the rush of military events,
we were forgotten, or it might be that the rebel authorities considered the hanging of eight men as sufficient
to show their estimate of the enormity of our crime.
This latter view grew upon the minds of some to such
a degree that we boldly resolved to test it, even if it
did bring our fate more swiftly upon us,—resolving
that if our action should result in calling a court-
martial we would then break from our prison or die
in the attempt. Indeed, the scanty fare, the uncertainty, and the longing for liberty had become so completely unendurable, that the prospects of perishing on
the bayonets of the guard had little terror. But our
resolution was to write a letter directly to Jefferson
Davis, the President of the Confederacy, reciting our
case, and asking to be put on the footing of prisoners of
war. I acted as scribe, and used language as strong
and yet respectful as possible. While writing, the whole
party gathered around, and volunteered suggestions.
Said Brown, " Be very humble to him, Pittenger. We
can take all back, if we get out." Buffum raised quite
a laugh by saying, " Tell him, Pittenger, that ' all we
ask is to be let alone.' " This was an extract from one
of Jefferson Davis' own addresses. But it did not go
in the letter. The following is a copy of the document,
obtained from the Confederate archives:

"ATLANTA JAIL, August 17, 1862.
"To HIS EXCELLENCY JEFFERSON DAVIS,
"President Confederate States of America.
"RESPECTED SIR,—We are United States soldiers regularly
detailed from our command to obey the orders of Andrews. He
21*

was a stranger to us, and we ignorant of his design, but, of course, we obeyed our officers. You are no doubt familiar with all we did, or can find it recorded in the trial of our comrades. Since then, Andrews himself and seven of us have been executed, and fourteen survive. Is this not enough for vengeance and for a warning to others? Would mercy in our case be misplaced? We have already been closely confined for more than four months. Will you not, sir, display a noble generosity by putting us on the same footing as prisoners of war, and permitting us to be exchanged, and thus show that in this terrible war the South still feels the claim of mercy and humanity?

"If you will be so good as to grant this request we will ever be grateful to you.

"Please inform us of your decision as soon as convenient."

Signed by all the survivors,—eight of the Twenty-first Ohio, one of the Second, and five of the Thirty-third, all of Sill's brigade, Mitchel's division.

This paper was forwarded from one officer to another in an ascending grade, and the indorsements on it, and the correspondence which followed, shed much light upon the position and fortunes of our party. But this light did not come to us until long after.

The letter was marked (erroneously as to its address), as follows:

"Petition from the survivors of Andrews' party, who took the engine on the Georgia State Railroad in April last, to Major-General Bragg, commanding Department No. 2."

The first indorsement is that of Colonel Lee, provost-marshal at Atlanta:

"Respectfully forwarded to General Staughton.
                    "G. W. LEE,
                            'Commanding Post."

                    'HEADQUARTERS DEPARTMENT No. 2,
                        "CHATTANOOGA, August 21, 1862
"ADJUTANT-GENERAL C. S. ARMY, Richmond, Va.

"SIR,—I have the honor to inclose herewith the petition of W. W. Brown and others, soldiers of the Twenty-first and Second Ohio Regiments, U.S.A., and to request information in the matter.   I am, sir, very respectfully,
                    "Your obedient servant,
                        "BRAXTON BRAGG,
                            "General Commanding."

The next indorsement shows a favorable disposition —at least in part:

[Indorsement.]

" Respectfully submitted to the President.
" I recommend that they be respited until further orders, and detained as hostages for our own people in the hands of the enemy.

" G. W. RANDOLPH,
" Secretary of War."

The Secretary of War seems to have had the impression that we had been also tried, and that sentence of death was pending over us. Under such circumstances a respite would have been a valuable boon.

But President Davis is inflexible:

[Indorsement.]

"Secretary of War, inquire whether there is anything to justify a discrimination between them and others who were executed for the same offence. J. D."

The inquiry thus ordered was at once begun:

[Indorsement.]

" Write to Major G. W. Lee, provost-marshal at Atlanta, and inquire why fourteen of the engine thieves were respited while the others were executed, and whether there is anything distinguishing their case.

" G. W. RANDOLPH,
" Secretary of War."

Only the responses to these inquiries were preserved on file at Richmond, and are now in Washington. They show the degree of confusion and misunderstanding which prevailed at the rebel capital:

" HEADQUARTERS, ATLANTA, GA., Sept. 16, 1862.
" HON. G. W. RANDOLPH, Secretary of War, Richmond, Va.
" SIR,—Your communication of the 11th inst. is duly to hand In reply, I have respectfully to say that the arrest, incarceration, trial, and execution of the prisoners you refer to occurred before I took charge of this post by your order. I found a number of prisoners on my arrival, and among them the men named in the petition transmitted.

"Inclosed I transmit the papers handed over to me by my predecesssor. Since the reception of your letter I have endeavored to find Captain Foreacre, and ascertain something more, explaining what I was not conversant with in the transaction, but as his business takes him away from the city, I have not as yet had an interview with him. I will still seek occasion to find him, and give you all the information learned from him. You will please find inclosed the names of the engine-stealers and bridge-burners who are confined in the jail of this city. It is entirely out of my power to answer you as to 'why fourteen of the engine thieves were respited while the others were executed, and whether or not there is anything to justify a discrimination in their favor?' as I am not informed in relation to the proceedings of the court-martial that tried the men.

"I am, sir,
"Respectfully your obt. servt.,
"G. W. LEE,
"Commanding Post, and Provost-Marshal."

The inclosures consist of the seven death-sentences, one of which has already been given, and the following lists, which show a number of glaring errors. According to the first we had all been court-martialled, but only the seven sentenced. The second is wrong in the placing of several names. The manner in which the word "spies" is interlined in the "charges" of the first list is also suggestive.

"*List of Prisoners sent to Atlanta, Ga., June 13, 1862, from Knoxville, Tenn., by command of Major-General E. Kirby Smith:*

Names.	Residence.	Charges.
		Spies.
1. Wilson Brown	Ohio.	Court-martialled and sentenced....Engine stealing.
2. Marion Ross	"	"　"　"　"　"
3. W. H. Campbell	"	"　"　"　"　"
4. John Scott	"	"　"　"　"　"
5. Perry G. Shadrach	"	"　"　"　"　"
6. G. D. Wilson	'	"　"　"　"　"
7. Samuel Slavens	"	"　"　"　"　"
8. S. Robinson	"	"　"　"　"　"
9. E. H. Mason	"	"　"　"　"
10. Wm. Knight	"	"　"　"　"
11. Robt. Buffins	"	"　"　"　"
12. Wm. Pettinger	"	"　"　"　"
13. Captain David Fry	Green Co., Tenn	Bridge-burning and recruiting for Federal army.
14. G. W. Barlow	Washington Co., Tenn	Obstructing railroad track.
15. Thos. McCoy	Morgan Co., "	⎫
Peter Pierce	Campbell Co., "	Prisoners of war.—Federal soldiers.
John Barker	Estill Co., "	
Bennut Powers	Lincoln Co., "	⎭

Names.	Residence.	Charges. Political Prisoners.
Ransom White........Morgan Co.,	Tenn.	Citizen aiding the enemy.
John Walls.............Blount Co.,	"	Trying to go to Kentucky.
John Green ....Union Co.,	"	Rebellion.
John Thompkins.....Washington Co.,	"	"
Henry Miller...........Sullivan Co.,	"	....Suspected as a spy.
William Thompson.Arrested at Bristol..........	" "	"

" Respectfully submitted by order.
     " WM. M. CHURCHWELL,
       " Colonel, and Provost-Marshal."

"List of Prisoners in Atlanta City Jail, September 16, 1862.

ENGINE-STEALERS.

M. J. Hawkins,	W. Reddick,
J. Parrott,	D. A. Dorsey,
W. Bensinger,	J. K. Porter,
A. Wilson,	M. Wood,
E. H. Mason,	W. W. Brown,
W. Knight,	R. Bufman,
W. Pettinger,	David Fry,
	J. J. Barker.

BRIDGE-BURNERS.

T. McCoy,	P. Pierce,
B. Powers,	Jno. Walls,
Jno. Green,	R. White,
H. Mills,	J. Tompkins,
G. D. Barlow,	Jno. Wollam."

The next day Provost-Marshal Lee wrote again as follows:

       " HEADQUARTERS, ATLANTA, GA.,
         " September 17, 1862.

" HON. G. W. RANDOLPH, Secretary of War, Richmond, Va.

" SIR,—I respectfully forward to you hereby all that I have been enabled to obtain from my predecessor, Captain Foreacre.

" The documents relating to the cases, so far as I know anything about them, were forwarded to you on yesterday.

       " I am, sir, very respectfully,
         " Your obedient servant,
           " G. W. LEE,
     " Commanding Post, and Provost-Marshal. '

The following letter, inclosed from Captain Foreacre, is wrong in saying that some of the party had been tried but not sentenced. Yet this was the obvious belief of the Confederate authorities :

"ATLANTA, GA., September 16, 1862.
"HON. G. W. RANDOLPH, Secretary of War, Richmond, Va.

"DEAR SIR,—Your letter of September 11, 1862, to Major
Lee, provost-marshal, has been shown me by him, and, as far as
I am acquainted with the matter, General Smith only sent from
Knoxville instructions and orders to have seven of them hung,
which was promptly attended to by myself.

"The remaining fourteen were reported to this office only for
safe-keeping,—some having been tried, but not sentenced, and
others not tried. The only office which can properly answer your
inquiry is that of Major-General E. K. Smith.

"I have the honor to remain,
"Your obedient servant,
"G. I. FOREACRE."

No record of any further inquiry remains. Whether
the matter was there dropped, or orders issued for opening the whole question by a court-martial, remains uncertain. But these documents make it almost certain
that all the party, or at least the twelve who were sent
to Knoxville, were destined to be tried and condemned;
that at the abrupt breaking up of the court, no record
was put on file of the cause of the interruption; and
that the authorities at Atlanta and Richmond expected
the court at Knoxville, which they assumed to have
finished its work, to give orders for our disposal. That
court never reconvened. Its members were dispersed
all over the South. The commanding general, E.
Kirby Smith, was transferred to a distant department.
We were forgotten, and thus the strange respite we
enjoyed is explained. But would it continue?

Some of the Confederate officers had formed a theory
of their own to account for the death of seven of our
number and the sparing of the remainder. They assumed that those put to death were volunteers, while
the others were detailed by their officers. But there
were no grounds for such a supposition.

While this correspondence was in progress, Colonel
Lee came to our door one day, and had a long talk
with us about our expedition and prison experiences.
He finally told us of receiving a letter from the Secre-

tary of War at Richmond asking why we had not all
been executed! He asked us the reason, and one of
the party, who had not totally forgotten his experience
of duplicity in the early part of our enterprise, said
that it had been thought that there were some miti-
gating circumstances in our case. The marshal said
that he could give no reason, but had referred the
Secretary to the court-martial at Knoxville, and that
he was now awaiting orders concerning us. On our
request he promised to visit us again when he should
receive an answer from Richmond. We told him of
the manner in which our comrades had been put to
death without warning. He admitted the wrong, but
disclaimed responsibility for it, as it occurred before he
came into command.

We waited anxiously for his return for several days,
but waited in vain. It was urged that we had heard
enough already, and that now, if ever, we ought to
strike for life. But I was of another opinion. The
enterprise of escaping was of enormous difficulty, and
success, at the best, doubtful. I did not think that, in
our enfeebled condition, after six months of terrible
hardship and partial starvation, we were the men we
had been. It was my judgment that nothing but the
certainty of death on the one hand could give the necessary vigor, spring, and desperation to command success
on the other. Despair might nerve us to throw ourselves with resistless fury on the bayonets of the guards,
but this fury would come only when the last hope was
dead. My reasoning prevailed, and we waited a little
longer.

But evidence came soon that ended hesitation. More
of the guard was kept on duty at once, and greater
vigilance was everywhere apparent. We fancied that
the old jailer regarded us with unusual compassion.
But through the stove-pipe, from our friends in the
other room, came the decisive information. The prisoners there saw the provost-marshal ride up to the

gate, have the jailer called out, and heard him give orders to watch those engine-thieves closely, as he had been notified that a court was ordered for their trial. The same evening the jailer said to them that he was very sorry for the poor Yankees in the other room, for every man of them would be hung! This word was conveyed to us, and longer doubt would have been folly.

We were now ready for the emergency, and had fully discussed and settled our plans. We were in the upper story of the jail. Our room was entered by a double door,—one of heavy plank, and one of iron slats. If this was opened, we would only be in the entry, and would have still to go down-stairs into a hall and pass another door before we could gain the jail-yard. This, in turn, was surrounded by a board fence eight or ten feet high, and having but a single gate, which was usually closed. Seven fully-armed soldiers were constantly on guard, with an unknown reserve close at hand. We could depend on help from no one of the prisoners except Captain Fry, so that we were but fifteen, and even two or three of these were too sick to be of great value in a fight. Then we were in the skirts of the town, fully a mile from the nearest woods. One advantage, and the only one on which I relied, was that of surprise. We knew what we were to do, and the strong motive that impelled it.

All plans looking to sawing out and swinging to the ground at night, as in Chattanooga, had been canvassed and rejected. What we meant to do was to break out in open daylight and overpower the guards. The most favorable time was when the doors were opened for bringing in our supper, which was a little before sundown, as by starting then we would soon have the cover of darkness. It was arranged to seize the jailer when he came to remove the pans in which our supper was brought, and to keep him perfectly quiet while all the doors were being unlocked, for we wished to release all the other prisoners. At the same moment the other members of the party, divided into two squads, were to cautiously descend the stairway, pounce upon the guards, and take their guns from them. If this was done in *perfect quiet*, the guards were to be locked up, and we, taking their arms, would march out on our homeward journey. As soon as discovered we were to break into parties of two and strike out for Union territory by widely-diverging lines.

All our plans were completed. We had patched our clothes as well as possible, and made cloth moccasins to protect our feet, many of our shoes being worn out. We only waited the coming of the appointed hour.

Slowly the sun sunk down the west; slowly the shadows lengthened in the east, till the gloomy shade of the jail had nearly reached the crest of the hill that usually marked our supper-time. We bade each other a solemn farewell, for we knew not if we should ever meet again on earth, or how many of us might be cold and lifeless before the stars shone out. We prayed fervently, though we dared not kneel or speak aloud. Captain Fry, who was tender-hearted as a child, wept at the parting. He had two large coats, and as he could not take both with him in the expected rush, he generously gave one to me. I needed it extremely, for I was very nearly destitute of clothing. He and I were to be companions, according to a previous arrangement.

Everything was put in readiness. I had carefully piled in a corner such of the books belonging to the minister as we still retained, and had written him a note of thanks for them. Anything that could be used as a weapon was now put within reach.

At last the supper-hour came. We could not afford to lose a morsel of the scanty food, and ate it in silence. The jailer was not accustomed to come into the room, but merely opened the door and admitted the negroes who bore the pans filled with corn-bread. Old Thoer,

22

the watchman whom everybody hated, was fortunately away. It was well, or he might have suffered. Turner we respected, and were determined not to injure if we could help it. After the jailer had given their food to the inmates of the other rooms he came back to ours and swung open the creaking door to remove the food-pans. This was the signal.

It was a thrilling moment! On the action of the next few seconds hung the issues of life or death. I confess that for one instant the blood flowed to my heart with a sharp, piercing throb, and there came a sudden and terrible fear lest the fever-weakened body would not in this crisis obey the dictates of will. But this ceased before the door had swung wide enough open to admit the passage of a man. The others were pale but determined, and a single glance told me that there would be no faltering. As for Captain Fry, who was to initiate the movement,—supported by myself,—and whom I had seen weeping a few minutes before, he was perfectly calm, and his face wore a pleasant smile! As soon as the door had swung far enough he stepped adroitly through it as if this were the most natural thing in the world, and said, very quietly,—

" A pleasant evening, Mr. Turner."

" Yes, — rather — pleasant," responded the jailer, looking bewildered by this movement, as he no doubt was.

" We feel like taking a little walk this evening," continued the captain, while the door was forced clear back, and three of us stood abreast in it ready to spring.

The astonishment of the jailer now knew no bounds. " What ?—how ?—where ?" he gasped, in broken ejaculations.

Fry's countenance grew darker as he clasped the old man in his arms, and said,—

" We have stayed as long as we can stand it, and are now going to leave and let the other prisoners out ; so

LIBERTY OR DEATH.

Page 255.

give up the keys, and make no noise about it, or it will
be the worse for you!"

Turner tightened his grasp on the keys, whispered,
hoarsely, " You can't do that," then threw himself back
and began in a loud tone, "Guar—" when my hand
closed across his mouth and stifled the incipient call for
help.   He bit my finger, but did no great damage.

Then came the rush of the prisoners,—quick, stealthy,
cat-like. Not a sound was audible a dozen yards away.
The negroes huddled in a corner of the room in stupid
fright, but had sense enough to be quiet.   Turner
struggled violently, for he was a man of great strength,
but Fry and I kept him mute ; the keys were twisted
from him, and Buffum was soon at work on the locks
of the other doors.   Quietly the assaulting column descended the stairway and burst out upon the guards
outside. If they committed a fault, it was in being
too quick. In one minute Buffum would have had the
other doors unlocked, and then, throwing aside the dis-
armed jailer, Fry, Buffum, and myself, reinforced by
all the prisoners who chose to go with us, would have
stood by their side in the second charge. This trifling
circumstance did make a considerable difference in the
result,—at least, to some of us.

Seven sentinels were on duty,—three in the back
yard, four in the front yard. The charge upon the former was completely successful, their guns being wrested
from them before they knew their danger, and they
were kept perfectly quiet under the threat—which
would have been executed—of instant death.

The attack in the front yard was made with equal
gallantry and skill, but not with equal success. Two
rebels stood near the front door of the prison, and these
were secured in the same manner as their comrades at
the rear, and held in silence. Had the remaining two
been close at hand, I have no doubt they would have
fared as their comrades, and thus the unparalleled feat
of twelve unarmed prisoners taking the loaded muskets

from seven guards on their post would have been accomplished. But, unfortunately, the last two stood at the open gate. Their conduct was not brave but it was wise, for, without firing a shot, they ran out through the gate, screaming the alarm in tones that roused the whole neighborhood. The reserve guard was close at hand, and at once rushed to the rescue.

The whole action, from the time Fry stepped out of the door until the wild cry was raised at the gate, was probably less than sixty seconds. Fry and myself were preparing to secure the jailer, for we knew not yet that the attack was made. Buffum had opened two doors, and was working at the third when the wild, thrilling cry of alarm arose from below. Those within adjured him to open, and the brave man, though his own chances of life were lessening each second, worked till the door opened, and then violently flung it wide, with an impatient "*there!*" while he bounded down the stairway like a hunted deer.

All secrecy was at an end, and the only remaining hope was in headlong flight. Our comrades in the yard saw their peril, and were in a little better position than those of us who were still inside the jail. They let go their terrified enemies, flung away the guns, which now could only impede their flight, and, scaling the board fence, made for the woods nearly a mile away. Even for the foremost of them it was a fearful race. Rebel bullets whistled around their ears, but none of them was hit. Indeed, I am inclined to think that it was a fortunate thing for our comrades that the rebels had guns to carry, and stopped to fire whenever they came near a fugitive. Otherwise hundreds of fresh, vigorous soldiers—for there were soon hundreds on the scene—could have run down a dozen half-starved prisoners.

Fry and myself started down-stairs together as soon as Buffum had opened the last door,—only a moment after the alarm had been given, but moments were

more precious then than common months. The captain was a little in advance. His eagle eye took in
the situation, as in two leaps he cleared the stairway.
He saw there was no chance in the front yard, now
filled with armed rebels, and darted to the back door,
found a passage to the yard fence, scaled it just before
a complete guard was stretched around the prison, was
fired at on the fence, but descended in safety, and ran
in a different direction from the other fugitives. Finally, a soldier levelled his musket at him, and he fell.
One of our own men who saw this, and no more, reported that he was killed, and we long mourned the
brave man as dead. But this was only a stratagem to
gain his breath for a moment. His pursuers turned
towards other game, and he rose, and, after a second
hard chase, gained the cover of the woods. Thirty
days after he had reached Nashville in safety.

I was to have been his companion, according to the
allotment we made before leaving the prison, and our
boys almost envied me the advantage of being with
so experienced a mountain traveller. But a moment's
misfortune made this advantage unavailing, and doomed
me to further sufferings. My eyes have always been
defective, and especially sensitive to sudden variations
of light. When I came from the dark prison room
(the hall was equally dark) into full light, for a moment
I could see nothing distinctly. I lost sight of Fry. It
would not do to stand still, and I rushed for the prison-
gate. Many a time defective vision has been a source
of annoyance and vexation, but never so much as then.
Before getting to the gate I could see better, and was
confronted by two soldiers, who were tossing their guns
about in a distracted manner, and crying, "What shall
we do? Oh, what shall we do?" They did not look
dangerous, and I ran by; but just in the gate I met a
stream of fresh guards coming on the run. Of course
they halted me, and equally, of course, I did not halt,
but turned back towards the jail. There were other

guards around, one of whom snapped his gun at me when not two yards away. I eluded them, got into the jail again, and out at the back door. This time I reached the top of the yard fence, but a dozen muskets were lifted from the outside to fire. To jump down on that side was inevitable death. One chance only remained. Possibly the gate now was not watched! I sprang back into the yard, and other guards were after me. The prison-door was open, and I entered, seeking to pass through it as before, and get outside the gate for a clear race. But the front door was now guarded also, and, as I turned, I found my pursuers in the back door. I was fairly trapped,—back in the prison again! It was a terrible situation. If I could crush between the two men who stood with loaded muskets in the door, their comrades were outside, and it was simply death to attack them. In sheer desperation, I turned my back upon them, not caring whether they fired or not, and walked up-stairs to a window, from which I could see something of the fearful race still going on, and note the streams of troops pouring towards the prison. My guards pointed their guns at me, but did not offer to come near, and when I walked from the hall window into a room,—not our own, but another which commanded a better view,—I found in it the four Federal soldiers, its former occupants, who had made no attempt to get away, the alarm and the rapid firing which followed convincing them that it was safer to remain where they were.

Parrott and Reddick were recaptured inside the wall, like myself. Buffum got over the wall about the same time as Captain Fry, but was less fortunate. A soldier singled him out, and squarely ran him down. When hardly able to drag another step, and with the inexorable armed runner within a rod of him, Buffum tried a "Yankee trick." (He was a native of Massachusetts.) Sinking down exhausted, he said, "I surrender. You can go on and get that other fellow," pointing to one a

few rods away. " No," answered the man, with a great
oath, " I've got *you*, and I mean to *keep* you." So he stood
with his gun aimed until some of his comrades arrived,
and poor Buffum was marched back to jail. Had the
man taken his advice, and looked for a bird in the
bush, the one in hand would doubtless have flown.
Mason and Bensinger were also captured outside of the
wall, making a recapture of six and an escape of nine,
—a better result than I had supposed probable when
we planned the attempt.

From the window of the front room where I then
was I had a good view of the proceedings below. In
a short time a large body of troops, including a regiment of cavalry, were drawn up in front of the jail.
I heard Colonel Lee give his orders. He said, " Don't
take one of the villains alive. Shoot them down
wherever you find them," with many similar expressions, which were possibly meant for the benefit of
those inside the prison as well as for the troops. He
also ordered pickets to be placed at the ferries of the
Chattahoochee, along the railroad, and also at all cross-
roads,—an arrangement that pleased me, for we had
agreed to avoid those very places. Our intention had
been to travel in the night-time through the woods, and
to cross the rivers on logs as far from ferries as possible.

Hearing some confused sounds of distress from the
room of the Tennesseeans, I inquired the cause, and
learned that a young man, named Barlow, who alone
of their number had attempted to escape, had broken
his ankle. This injury was received in jumping from
the outside fence. He was driven back to the prison
room, where surgical aid was refused, and he finally
died after great suffering.

Of all who were up-stairs at the time the alarm was
given, only Fry and one other man succeeded in escaping. The latter was a deserter from the rebel army,
and being very active and fleet, reached the shelter of
the woods in advance of all the fugitives.

From the window I could hear the guards, all night long, talking over their adventures. Generally they praised their own bravery liberally, but occasionally some one who had arrived later would suggest that it was not much to their credit to let unarmed men snatch their guns from them; but such suggestions were not kindly received, and the work of self-glorification went on. One of them expressed astonishment at the speed of the Yankees, who had been so long kept in jail; another accounted for it by the abundant practice in running Yankee soldiers had received in battle!

All night long I lay in a hammock which one of the regular soldiers had swung by the window, but now kindly resigned to me, and listened to the boastful conversation below.

"Sadly I thought of the morrow."

There was little reason to doubt that full vengeance would be dealt to each man who remained in the enemy's power. The news we had received, and which we had agreed in crediting, was the end of all hope. Death, which had stared us in the face so often, could not be far distant now. Another escape would scarcely be left by the aroused vigilance of the enemy within the realms of possibility. And such a death! No vision of glory to dazzle the sight, and hide the grim monster from view, or wreathe him in flowers. No eye of friends to behold the last struggle. No sympathy,—nothing but ignominy and an impenetrable darkness, beyond which no loving eye might ever pierce! But even as the cold horror of the scaffold, and the vision of the heartless, jeering crowd rose freshly before me, I looked out in the clear night, and up to the shining stars, and remembered that I had one Friend, —a Friend who would not fear to stand with me on the scaffold, and who had Himself tasted the bitterness of a public execution. Was it for me he had died,—to

show me that no outward shame is too great to be borne
by the true heart? With the thought came a still and
heavenly peace, while my hope, finding no place on
this side, overleaped the darkness of death and dwelt
upon the scenes of promised happiness beyond. It is
in such hours that the value and supporting power of
religion is fully realized.

The next morning the jailer put me back into the
room formerly occupied. When all had gathered, we
were only six in number,—Mason, Buffum, Bensinger,
Reddick, Parrott, and myself. We had enough to talk
over for many hours. The jailer, too, had his story to
tell. He said that some man put his hand over his
mouth and nearly smothered him, but added, with
great satisfaction, "I bit his finger terribly, and gave
the rascal a mark he will carry to the grave with him."
However, though he did bite hard, his teeth were not
so sharp as he thought, and he had only managed to
inflict a slight bruise. I kept my hand out of sight in
his presence for a day or two, and he had no idea that
I was the person of whom he complained, as his fright
prevented his clearly distinguishing anything. He was
rather cross for a while, and always brought up the
guards when he came to feed us.

About the middle of the day some officers came to
see us, and talked very roughly. With many threats,
they demanded to know what direction our comrades
had intended to travel. I was glad of this, as it assured me that some were still at large. They professed
to have killed several, and declared that they meant to
kill the others as fast as they were taken. In answer
to their demand I told them the truth, as I thought
that would do them as little good as anything else. I
said,—

"They intend to try to get to the Union lines; and
they said that it made little difference which way they
went, for our forces have you so completely surrounded,
that travelling in *any* course will do equally well."

Being unable to get anything more definite, they retired.

Not until our own release did we learn with certainty the fate of our eight comrades. Nothing in this whole story seems more wonderful than their adventures and ultimate success. Two went South, two West, and four others, in two groups, went Northward. To recite the adventures of all would detain us too long, but the reader will expect some account. We will give two of the four narratives in some detail, and the others more briefly.

CHAPTER XVII.

ROMANTIC ESCAPES.

J. R. PORTER and John Wollam kept in company when they ran for the woods. The latter will be remembered as having previously escaped from Chattanooga in company with Andrews, and eluded his pursuers for a long time.

It was October 16 when they started, and they reached the Federal lines at Corinth, Mississippi, November 18, being thus two days over a month on the way. They endured the greatest hardships. When in wooded country they travelled both night and day, subsisting on wild grapes, chestnuts, hickory-nuts, walnuts, and some few sweet potatoes. In a few instances they got a little morsel of corn-bread from some negroes. This was not always a gift. Several times they slipped into the fields where the negroes were at work and stole their scanty dinners. Necessity knew no law. For one whole week they had no bread, nor any other food, except the nuts gathered in the woods.

Their sufferings with cold were also very great, as their clothes were light and almost worn out, and the nights very chill. Twice only they slept in houses. One night they travelled till they were chilled and weary, and almost perishing with cold, when they fortunately discovered a nest of hogs. It was no time to be choice; so routing out the inmates, they took posses sion of the warm bed, and slept soundly till morning!

They found many streams on the way, which they were obliged to wade, or float across on logs. Porter was a man of clear religious faith and great constancy, while Wollam was full of resources, though somewhat reckless. He longed for the Tennessee River, down which he had floated alone once before, and somewhere on which he knew Federal troops were to be found. It was twenty-two days, however, before this stream was reached, at a point forty miles west of Chattanooga. The worst of their trials were now over. They pressed a canoe into the service, and used it as Wollam had done before, paddling and floating down stream at night, and hiding it and themselves, in the most secret place they could find, during the day. Two persons under such circumstances have great advantages over a solitary traveller. Not only does companionship assist in keeping hope alive in each breast, but one can watch while the other rests, and thus their resources are husbanded. The voyagers met with no remarkable adventures until they reached the head of Muscle Shoals, which they could not pass on account of low water. Abandoning their canoe here, they made a circuit of forty miles by land, and came back to the river below the Shoals. Here they "borrowed" a skiff, and continued their journey until within twelve miles of Pittsburg Landing, where they finally left the river. Twelve miles of travel brought them to Corinth,—a post occupied by Union troops,—where they were received with all the welcome that could be given to comrades long considered dead. They had passed over three hundred miles in a straight line,—probably double that distance by reason of the circuits they made, and this without assistance, and while shunning all about them as foes.

Engineer Brown, W. J. Knight, and E. H. Mason were thrown together in the hurry of escape, although only the former two had intended to travel in company. Mason's intended comrade was recaptured. Dorsey and Hawkins were also, at first, in the same squad. The first night, while hiding in the woods, Mason became very sick, and for two days remained within a short distance of Atlanta. This was very dangerous, and he finally told Brown and Knight to leave him and make good their own escape. This the heroic boys refused to do, but, on the contrary, took him to a house, as he was growing rapidly worse. They were well received, and given some food in the kitchen. Just as they had finished it, three men, who had probably seen their arrival, came in at the front door to arrest them. This was an almost unique incident in the history of our expedition,—the attempt to arrest any members of the party without having an overwhelming superiority in numbers,—and, as might have been expected, it miscarried. Our comrades did not deny being escaped prisoners, but when told that they must surrender and go back to Atlanta, Brown, who hardly knew the meaning of fear, gave in his soft, silvery voice the very decided reply, "No, we won't; now see if we do," and with Knight sprang through the back door. There was no alternative but to abandon Mason; but the other two were the strongest and most agile of our number,—had always been our leaders in all athletic sports, and were able to give a good account of themselves either in a race or fight. They ran round the end of the house and then struck towards a piece of woods half a mile away, keeping under the shelter of a fence which extended towards the woods. The Confederates ran out at the front door with their shot-guns just as the fugitives were flying along the fence. Not wishing to try a foot-race, the former mounted their horses and galloped

LIEUTENANT WILSON W. BROWN.

(Union Engineer.)   Page 264.

out from the house down a lane that led to the main
road, attempting thus to head them off, while the owner
of the house where they had stayed unloosed his pack
of hounds, which were soon on the trail in full cry. The
fugitives changed their course to avoid the chance of a
shot from the road, and to keep at right angles with it.
Before the woodland could be reached, the dogs closed
in upon them, and the struggle which followed was
short and decisive. Brown and Knight, seeing the
dogs gaining upon them, selected a place where loose
stones were abundant, and gave their barking foes a
reception which must have astonished them. Stones
weighing a pound or more, hurled at close quarters by
the strong arms of desperate men, are not to be despised
by the most savage of blood-hounds. The whole pack
were soon crippled or driven into hasty flight.

But by this time the horsemen were near, and our
hunted comrades were obliged to run again at full speed,
changing their course, with the purpose of eluding their
armed pursuers. They got into some brushwood, and
by " seesawing and tacking" hoped to get out of sight
of the horsemen. But the dogs still followed the trail,
though they dared not come near, and the brave pair
would no doubt have been run down in time, by the
aid of dogs and horses, had they not found a little creek,
in which they waded long enough to throw the dogs off
the scent; then the expanse of timber about the creek
soon hid them from their human foes.

That day they reached Stone Mountain, about eighteen miles east of Atlanta, and afterwards travelled only
at n ght, due north, with the North Star for their guide.
From their daytime hiding-places they frequently saw
parties of patrollers, but were never discovered.

Mason was taken without resistance and sent back to
Atlanta, where he joined us, being the sixth and last
man recaptured.

Brown and Knight did not venture again to a house,
and suffered greatly for want of food. From the house

they had left so precipitately they travelled six days with
nothing to eat save what the woods furnished. They
even chewed brush to appease the gnawings of hunger.
On the seventh day they obtained a great feast by
catching a goose, which they ate raw, and also procured
a little of the corn left in a field by the huskers. Two
days after, they found a tree of apples, very poor, but
precious to them, and, after having devoured as many
as they could, carried a supply with them. Before
night, however, they had still better fortune. They
discovered a drove of half-grown pigs. To get one
was not easy, but these men were not readily baffled.
Their plan was soon laid: Knight hid behind a tree
with a club, while Brown tolled a confiding member of
the drove by biting off bits of apple and throwing
towards him. He backed past the tree where Knight
was concealed, and when the pig in following came near
enough, the latter felled it with one powerful blow, and
they bore it away in triumph. That night they found
a burnt brush-heap, and, as some of the coals were not
extinct, they made a fire and feasted on roast pig. They
carried off what they could not eat, and it took the
edge from famine for a long while.

When ten days out they crossed the Chattahoochee
on a raft made of rails tied together with bark. At
length they came into the mountains, where travel at
night for famishing men was intolerably difficult. But,
though they knew it not, they were near friends. The
border country between Tennessee and North Carolina was always predominantly loyal. Accident led to
the discovery of those who were glad to give them
help. In crossing an old clearing, which seemed deserted, they came out unexpectedly in front of a lonely
looking log house, where two men stood on the porch.
Brown and Knight were so hungry that they resolved
to take the risk of asking for dinner. As there were
only two men, they thought they could not be arrested,
especially if they first got something to eat. They pre-

tended to be rebel soldiers, who had been sick and were now trying to get back to their regiments. The mistress of the house gave them food, but eyed them closely, and soon accused them of being "Yankees." Denial was useless, and they "soon found each other out." These Union people put them on the Southern branch of the Underground Railroad, and they arrived at Somerset, Kentucky, on the 25th of November,—a month and nine days after leaving Atlanta.

The course of the next pair, Dorsey and Hawkins, was also northward, and in nearly the same track. In the early part it presents marked peculiarities, especially in the fact that much help was obtained from the negroes. These sympathized with all fugitives on general principles, and still more when the fugitives were Union soldiers. The latter part of this narrative passes over the same ground as the former. It is a trifling but noticeable coincidence that four of the eight who escaped came to the town of Somerset, Kentucky, and two others to the ship "Somerset."

Dorsey shall tell his own story, with a few abridgments. He hurt his ankle in the first terrible run, and this caused him great suffering. He also met a countryman just before reaching the woods, but having armed himself with a large stone in each hand, and looking dangerous, he was not stopped. The rapid firing of the enemy led him to believe that many of our number were killed. We take up his story at the entrance of the forest. The first touch is very graphic.

"Passing a little way into the woods, I found Brown and Knight leaning against a tree, gasping for breath. I leaned against the same tree. None of us could speak. I thought for a moment or two that each breath would be my last. As we recovered a little, one gasped, 'Guess we'd better go, boys.' On we went, but not so fast as before, for none of our pursuers were now in sight. We were soon joined by Hawkins, Mason, and the escaped deserter, so that we were six in all. We lay in an open field that night, judging it to be safer than the woods, and huddled together as a partial protection from the cold. All night long we heard the baying of the hounds and the frequent discharge of firearms. The distance from which these sounds came indicated that the pursuers were beyond us, and that our best chance was in hiding and allowing them to pass still farther ahead. The next day we were fortunate enough to discover some luscious wild grapes, which we devoured with the greatest relish. Our mouths afterwards were very sore, and the grapes may possibly have been the cause of the injury. The same day we were surprised by some citizens with shot-guns, but outran them and escaped.

"Brown, Mason, and Knight left us, the latter being sick. The deserter continued with us a day longer. He then wished to visit a house for food, but we, though very hungry, did not think it advisable, and parted with all good wishes. I have heard that he got safely to Washington, D. C., but, returning to his home in Northern Georgia, was arrested and executed as a deserter from the Confederate army, into which he had been conscripted at first.

"On the fourth day out we met two of our pursuers, who were apparently coming back discouraged, but easily eluded them by hiding under some bushes. We now began to travel more rapidly, hiding by day and continuing on our way by night, directed by the stars, which Hawkins understood very well.

"On the eighth day out we came to the ferry of the Chattahoochee River, far to the northeast of Atlanta. We took rails from a neighboring fence, and began to build a raft, when we observed a lighted torch approaching the opposite side of the river. When it came nearer we saw that the party accompanying it were negroes, two in number, with four dogs. Hawkins, who had spent some years in the South, and understood the disposition of the negroes, felt disposed to trust them. Accordingly, we asked them to ferry us over, which they readily did, we giving them a little tobacco we had, and which we could not use because of our sore mouths. They professed themselves Unionists, and we told them that we were Union soldiers. The fact of belonging to the railroad party we did not disclose until we were within the Union lines. One went for provisions, while the other remained with us, as if to allay any suspicions we might entertain. They told us that we were forty-eight miles northeast of Atlanta, in the region of deserted gold-mines, and proposed to hide us in one of those mines, supply us with quilts and provisions until we were well rested, and then direct us on our northward way. It would probably have been better to have accepted their kind offer, which I think Hawkins wished to do, but I had some fear; so we declined.

"The one who had gone for provisions returned with a goodly supply of boiled pork and beans, mashed Irish potatoes, sweet potatoes, and corn-bread. What a feast! It was the first food worthy the name we had eaten for six long months! We did it ample justice, and what was left carried away with us. Our African friends also gave us a piece of a broken butcher-knife.

that was of great service. They also gave us invaluable directions, telling us where the rebel troops lay, and where we could
find a colored slave, who would ferry us over the Hiawassee
(which runs down from North Carolina into the Tennessee), as
they had done over the Chattahoochee. We assured them that
they would soon be free, and parted with a mutual ' God bless
you !'

"With thankful hearts we pressed on, made a good night's
journey, and then laid by until evening of the next day. Seeing a house on the edge of the woods, we watched it until assured
that only an old man and woman were there, when we went boldly
up to it and asked for supper, which was given with some reluctance.

"Early in the evening journey we came to a small stream, and
attempting to cross on a fallen tree, I fell into the water, and was
thoroughly soaked. From this cause I suffered greatly with cold.
Some hours after we came to a barn, the mows of which were
filled with corn-blades. We were glad to bury ourselves out of
sight in the fodder, where we grew warm, and slept all day. It
was comfortable, but we paid for it by a terrible fright. Some
cavalrymen came into the stable under the mows and took out
their horses. We could hear their conversation and the jingle
of their spurs, and scarcely dared to breathe. But they left us
in safety. We stayed a day longer, as the bed was the best we
had found since our first capture. But a negro boy came up to
hunt eggs, and found us. He was so frightened that we could not
pacify him, and, fearing an alarm, we hastened to the woods once
more. Some negroes were again met, starting on their favorite
amusement,—an opossum-hunt. On application they gave us a
magnificent treat,—a hatful of apples, a half 'pone,' and two
or three pounds of boiled beef on a bone. This supply lasted for
several days.

"On the night journey we were much annoyed by the barking
of dogs at the houses we passed. Once we were seen, but, pretending to be rebels on the way to our regiments, we succeeded
so well in lulling suspicion that an old man sent a message to his
son, who was in the rebel army, by us, and added some corn-
bread for the messengers.

"I here became more lame than ever, by reason of an unfortunate misstep, and had to walk by leaning part of my weight
upon my faithful comrade. We came to a wide river we could
not cross, and, going back into the fields, lay on the damp ground
till morning. If I ever *tasted* cold, it was then. Hawkins became reckless from suffering, and was disposed to go to a house,
even at the risk of capture. But I demurred, and we waited for
an opportunity to communicate with the ever-faithful negroes.
We found a hut, and, watching it some time, saw none but a
black woman there. She readily responded to our appeal for
help, gave us a hot breakfast, a fire to warm by, and some
parched corn to carry on our journey. She also directed us to a
23*

ford. Thanking her from our hearts, we returned to the river, got over, and concealed ourselves in the woods on the other side.

" With the coming of night we once more took up our weary way. Towards morning we saw a large encampment of whites and colored people. All were asleep except one of the latter. We approached, and, in a whisper, asked him who they were. He told us of the retreat of Bragg's army from Kentucky, and that these were a band of fugitives coming South with their slaves to avoid the Union army. To us this was a serious matter. A large army, with all its baggage, and the country full of pickets, directly in our front, was a great addition to our danger. The colored man gave us all the scanty information he possessed about the position of the army. Hawkins, spying a covered skillet near the fire, winked at our friend, got an assenting nod, and reached for it. It had two baked sweet potatoes, which we appropriated, and departed as noiselessly as we had advanced. Twenty-four hours after, we had reached the Hiawassee River. We called lustily for the ferryman, and, to our exceeding delight, were answered by the very slave our colored friends on the Chattahoochee had said would be willing to ferry us over.

" With his counsel, for we trusted him with the secret of our being escaped prisoners, we resolved to go down the Hiawassee to its junction with the Tennessee. To do this, however, it would be necessary to pass round the rebel camp at Charleston, a few miles farther down the river. This was Friday, and, by waiting until Saturday, the young man could get a pass good until Monday, and could pilot us around Charleston. We resolved to wait. He treated us royally,—shared his scanty allowance of food with us, for he had only a slave's rations, doctored my ankle, kept us in his best bed—*a feather one*—overnight, though, for prudential reasons, we hid in the woods during the day, and, on starting, gave us a bottle of molasses and a piece of pork. We floated down near camp in a ' dug-out' canoe, then left the river and *surrounded* the enemy. Our pilot was obliged to leave us before we got back to the river below the town, but he put us on the banks of a small stream, which we had only to follow down to its mouth. This we reached by two P.M., and amused ourselves by cracking walnuts and hickory-nuts in a solitary place until dark, when we hunted up an old dilapidated canoe. It was a miserable boat, and gave us enough to do in bailing as well as paddling it. We soon saw a better craft, with good paddles, tied up, and, as the owner was not there, we 'traded' without difficulty.

" The stars were shining brightly when we again pushed off, and the water was as clear as crystal, though not deep. We dried our wet clothes, and felt very much more comfortable. Save an occasional whisper between us and the soft ripple of the oars, silence was unbroken. This was the most peaceful and satisfactory night's travel we had yet made.

" At daybreak we hid the boat and nestled away in some dry leaves, and after the sun got high enough to warm us, slept by

turns till afternoon. Then we noticed an island half a mile farther down the river, and, as we had seen nobody the whole day,
and the place appeared perfectly solitary, we resolved to explore
it. Nothing was found, but we saw a house on the east bank,
which we watched until sundown, and seeing only women about
it, resolved to try for supper. We got a good square meal, but
judge our dismay at finding a good number of ladies, and, soon
after, a few men, also, at the place. It was a 'quilting,' and
they were to dance that evening. But we told a new story. We
had been working at a saw-mill in the mountains, were now out
of employment, and were going to Chattanooga to look for a job.
They warned us that we would be arrested at Chattanooga, and
would have to go to jail or join the army. They seemed to care
nothing for the war, and to have no disposition to molest us.
We assured them that we would be all right in Chattanooga, as
we were *personally acquainted with General Leadbetter.* They
looked doubtful, and in parting they said, in a rather insinuat
ing manner, that they wished us a safe journey *to Chattanooga.*
Probably they were Unionists, but we dared not risk a discovery.
I tried, unsuccessfully, to steal a quilt, which we greatly needed.
The night was overcast, the water was very shallow in places,
and some tree-tops were in the way. We had to get out, pull
our boat out of these obstructions and into deeper water, and
then, wet to the skin, to re-embark and paddle on.

"About midnight we came to what seemed to be a ferry, where
the river was deeper and wider than it had been before. Suddenly two shots were fired at us. We lay down in the bottom
of the boat, and, taking in our paddles, let her float down stream,
while we did not move a muscle. I suppose it was a picket of
the enemy, who, after firing once, concluded that our boat was
only a floating log, and took no further trouble. After getting,
as we supposed, out of danger, we again seized the paddles, and
an hour of vigorous work brought us to the river's mouth, and
out on the broader Tennessee.

"We were very reluctant to abandon the river navigation, but
it was manifestly dangerous to continue it further, and useless as
well, unless we were prepared to take the risk of running by
Chattanooga. So we rowed to the north side of the Tennessee,
and turned our trusty craft adrift, while we started across the
mountains. The first road we crossed gave evidence of the passage of a large body of troops, and thus warned us that we were
probably in danger of becoming entangled in the scouts and de-
tachments of Bragg's army, now on its retreat from Kentucky.
Two boys we found by a fire in a school-house—they had been
out 'coon'-hunting—confirmed this report. Soon we saw their
camp-fires, and ascending a mountain, where we supposed we
would be safer than in the valleys, waited for morning. When
it came, an appalling sight met our view,—a large division of
Bragg's army, with its seemingly endless baggage-trains, well
guarded by cavalry, was spread out beneath us. All day long

we watched their movements from our eyrie with breathless
anxiety. We resolved at night to turn to the northeast instead
of keeping due north, as we had intended. Before we had gone
far, Hawkins whispered in my ear, 'Dorsey, we mustn't crack
any corn to-night.' Rebel pickets and scouts were no doubt on
every side of us. The mountain-side was steep and covered with
loose stones, where travelling, even by day, would have been difficult; at night, in the presence of the enemy, it was terrible!
We came to a picket, and were only saved from running right
into it by the snuffling of a horse. We slipped away a short distance from the road, and lay down. Soon a squad of cavalry
passed up the road, and we crossed it right behind them, anxious
to get out of that dangerous neighborhood while the sound of
their hoofs drowned any noise we might make. We moved very
cautiously, again ascended the mountain-side, and near daybreak
came to a halt and went into camp,—that is, hid in the brush.

"When the light came we could see the enemy no more, but
heard his wagons rumbling off in the distance. The immediate
danger from that source was over. Our stock of provision.
which was only a little parched corn, was almost exhausted; and
as the mountain seemed to be uninhabited, we resolved to move
forward in the afternoon. We found a negro, who, for a wonder,
could not or would not give any provisions or information. Late
in the night we rested, tying some bushes together to make a
rude shelter, and both sleeping, for nature was almost overcome.
Food and water were also very low, but in the morning we pressed
on, halting when our waning strength failed, and going on when
strength allowed.

"Very impressive were some of the hours spent in watching
on the Cumberland Mountains. One of us would sleep in perfect trust, while the other watched and thought. The lofty peaks,
the wide landscape, and the rising and setting sun were doubly
solemn in the profound silence, and amid the mighty forests of
that region. I can never forget the beauty of nature associated
with so much of peril.

"But there were other hours of very prosaic toil. Once we
had to force our way on hands and knees through a mass of briers
a quarter of a mile wide. Several times we hunted persimmons
by moonlight,—Hawkins shaking them off, while I crawled on
hands and knees *feeling* for them. Many adventures similar to
those already narrated were encountered. Near a ford of the
Sequatchie River we found a quilted skirt hanging out, which we
appropriated, tore in two, and, making a hole in the middle of
each piece for our heads, found ourselves possessed of passable
undershirts, which we needed sorely, as it was now colder than
ever. The ford was waded with our clothes taken off and tied
on our heads.

"For two days more we travelled and rested alternately in the
mountains, hungry, wet with the rain that now began to fall,
and as solitary as if we were the only inhabitants of the globe.

DORSEY AND HAWKINS IN THE CUMBERLAND MOUNTAINS.

Page 272.

Near sundown of the second day we heard some wood-choppers far below us. We were so weak that we repeatedly fell as we descended the mountain-side. Hunger was so extreme that we resolved to try for food from them, using the best story we could frame. We told them we were Confederate soldiers, who had been left in a hospital, from which we had run away, and were now trying to get to our regiments; also that we were without money, and wanted food. They refused to do anything for us; said that soldiers had already eaten them nearly out. This reception encouraged us. To test them further we talked of *our cause*, its justice, certainty of success, etc. They did not pretend to agree with us, and, finally, told us that we were in what had been called 'Lincoln District,' because only two votes were cast there for secession. The conversation led them to a flat avowal that they were Union men. We then cautiously revealed the fact that we were soldiers on the same side, and the hospitality which had been denied before was now readily extended."

This proved to be a station on the "Underground Railroad," which had been organized since the opening of the war for the escape of Union men and prisoners to the Union lines in Kentucky. After the fugitives had completely proved their character, they were put under the conduct of a local celebrity, known as "Red Fox," from his skill in eluding the enemy. He conducted them for some distance, and gave them directions to the next point, and from this they were directed to another. Thus they were forwarded swiftly and in comparative safety. Dorsey dwells with great gusto upon the good food and generous treatment received from these loyal mountaineers, who had no hope of a reward, but were glad to do anything for their loved and imperilled country. His expressions of gratitude are also frequent and hearty. One man gave them the only dollar he had, and would not hear of a refusal. Some very narrow escapes were run even after they were thus among friends, but they finally reached Somerset, Kentucky. At first they were received with some suspicion by the Union officials, but, as soon as their true character was established, they enjoyed the enthusiastic welcome accorded to each one of the railroad party who returned from "the valley of the shadow of death."

CHAPTER XVIII.

FROM ATLANTA TO THE GULF.

No fugitives passed through more romantic adventures than Wood and Wilson. The southward course they took saved them from an energetic pursuit, but their unwillingness to trust the negroes exposed them to imminent peril of starvation. The idea that any of our party would seek for the Gulf blockading squadron probably never entered the head of any pursuer. It was well that this route was chosen by Wilson, for. in no other way could he possibly have succeeded in carrying his sick comrade with him. The manner in which poor Wood, who had been for months suffering from fever, and was scarcely able to walk about the jail, was taken from "Atlanta to the sea" by a starving comrade, would seem a most improbable invention if met in a work of fiction. I extract the complete account of the escape, with a few unimportant omissions, from "The Adventures of Alf. Wilson," written by himself, and first published in book form in Toledo, 1880. The account begins in the Atlanta jail-yard. The necessity for immediate flight was first seen by Wood, who exclaimed,—

"'Alf, come on, quick! the boys are getting over the fence at the back of the jail; hurry up, for there's a company of guards coming double-quick.'

"This was my old comrade, Mark Wood, and his voice was the first warning I had of the danger that threatened me, or of the necessary change in our programme.

"'Then bounce that fence!' I yelled. We both reached the top of the high fence at the same instant, and not a second too soon, for, as I glanced over my shoulder from the fence-top, I saw the guards with gleaming muskets pouring in at the gate, and before I could throw my leg over and spring off a volley was fired, the balls rattling and whizzing all about us. One bullet struck the picket under my thigh, and so close that the splinters lacerated my flesh, and as my feet struck the ground on the outside, I said to Mark, ' I am hit.'

" ' Get up and run like —— !' exclaimed Mark.

" I was on my feet in an instant, not knowing whether my thigh was shattered or not. As I ran I clapped my hand there to see if it bled freely. I pulled away a lot of splinters, and had the satisfaction of finding that I had received only a slight flesh wound made by the picket splinters. Never did I make better use of my legs; there was need of it, too, for the balls were spatting about us in the dirt uncomfortably near. They came so thick and closely at one time that I was almost certain that one or both of us would be hit; but we answered their cries of ' Halt ! halt !' by springing forward with all the speed we could command.

" It was about a mile before we struck the cover of woods, and then the trees were so scattering that they afforded only a doubtful place for concealment. It was now every man for himself, and, like the Duke of Wellington at Waterloo, we longed for darkness or some other friendly interposition in our behalf. Wood had come up with me, and we dodged stealthily from one thicket to another until it began to grow quite dark, when we breathed easier and acted more deliberately, although we well knew we were not out of danger yet.

" About this time, we became aware that we were approaching a public road. We soon had warning that it was much better to halt, and not attempt to cross the road. The sound of galloping horsemen in great numbers and the clanking of sabres could be heard near by. We were so nearly out of breath that we could run no farther for the present, and, on looking hastily about, discovered a low, scrubby pine-bush surrounded with shrubbery. We both darted under its protecting shelter, and lay flat on the ground on our faces, neither having spoken a word to the other for some minutes, on account of our great exhaustion. We were so near the road that we could plainly see all the movements of the rebel cavalry, who were deploying their line something in the manner of skirmishers.

" This presented an unexpected difficulty in our way. If we had reached the road two minutes sooner we might have crossed without being seen, but we could not have been there an instant sooner than we were, unless we had had wings, for we had both run until we were ready to fall in our tracks. We had become separated from the rest of the party, but could still hear the reports of muskets, and knew that the pursuit was still going on, but how many of the escaping party had been killed was beyond our knowledge, though I had seen Captain Fry reeling and stumbling in a manner that led me to fear he was shot. We were thus compelled to lie quietly for some time. While we were waiting here the cavalry was relieved by infantry, and formed into squads to scour the woods.

"The place where we lay was not over fifteen steps from where the infantry sentinel was stationed. We could hear every word he spoke to the man on the next post. Their comments on the affair at the jail would have been amusing to us under less serious circumstances, and I wish I could give their words exactly now, for they were ludicrous enough.

"Some time late in the evening, while we were still lying under the bush, we became aware that some one was approaching us very quietly. In the dark we could recognize the dim outlines of two men, and we felt certain, as they came so near us that we could have almost touched them, that it was two of our comrades; but we dare not even whisper to them, lest we should cause them to betray themselves, and, perhaps, us too. They were, evidently, from the cautious manner in which they moved, aware that they were very close to the rebel guards. These men, I afterwards learned, were Porter and Wollam.

"After waiting a short time to see if they were discovered, and hearing nothing of them, we began to crawl out, concluding that there was no probability of the guards leaving that night. I should judge the sentries were stationed about thirty paces apart, and to get out there was no alternative but to pass between them. I selected a place and crawled to the other side of the road safely, and then lay perfectly still, while Mark did the same. My hair fairly stood on end as he wriggled along, for it seemed to me once or twice as if one of the sentries would certainly discover him before he would reach me. This was one of our most narrow escapes.

"We were no more than safely across the road when a new and unseen obstacle, in the shape of a high fence, presented itself, over which we must climb before we could breathe free. We crawled carefully to the fence, and by great patience and much care, one at a time, managed to get over without attracting the attention of the guards. We felt as if we had accomplished quite an achievement when at last we had escaped beyond the fence a few steps and found ourselves in an open field, where we could push ahead noiselessly, and when, at last, we got away entirely out of hearing, we struck out on a full run. At the far side of the field we came to a small stream, in which we travelled some distance in the water, to take precaution against pursuit by dogs. Soon after, we struck a thick piece of 'woods on the slope of a hill-side, which we continued to ascend under the thick foliage for some time. But, at last, exhausted Nature asserted her full sway, and we were compelled to lie down and rest out of sheer inability to go farther.

"Up to this time, I think, neither of us had spoken any more than if we had been dumb. As we threw ourselves on the ground, without breath or strength to go farther, we began to realize the weak, helpless condition we were in. It did not appear as if our limbs were strong enough to carry us five miles a day. When we looked forward to the long journey ahead of us, the hunger and fatigue, it looked a little discouraging. I think, however, a portion of this sense of physical prostration was caused by the sudden relaxation from the great mental strain and excitement which had been upon us from the time of the jail-break and immediately preceding it. This, with the intense exertion in running, in our enfeebled condition, had wellnigh unnerved us. We were wild, too, almost, with joy at our escape.

"But we had but little time to rest, rejoice, or feel thankful in. Many contingencies yet stood between us and the goal of our hopes. Many armed enemies; many long, weary miles of travel; many rivers lay across our path, and many days of hunger and many sleepless nights, if we would succeed.

"Before we escaped from the prison I studied over the subject of routes very carefully. I had seen enough of night travel in the mountains about Chattanooga and along the Tennessee River, and well knew that the probabilities of our being picked up, should we go in that direction, would be very much greater. I therefore decided in my own mind that I would strike out for the Gulf, and try to reach some of the vessels of the Federal blockading squadron. While this would be much the longest route,—the distance, as near as I could calculate, being over three hundred miles,—I thought there would be less vigilance and liability of pursuit in that direction. In this conjecture it turned out that I was correct. The country was entirely unknown to me, except a slight general idea I had of it from the school geographies. I only knew that the waters of the Chattahoochee River, which flowed west of Atlanta, entered the Gulf.

"While we rested on the hill-side I communicated, in a whisper, to Mark my views, and he readily agreed that he would go in any direction I thought best. Accordingly, we rose up and walked to an open place where we could see the stars, and soon determined our course, which was to be slightly south of west, and at once we set out as fast as we could travel. We spoke no words as we walked on, and went as noiselessly as possible, for we were on the look-out for scouting parties of cavalrymen that might be prowling about.

"We soon came to the railroad track leading from Atlanta to Columbus, and knew from this that our course was about right. Our march led us through some rough country, and we were compelled to rest quite frequently, so that when it began to grow light in the east we estimated that we were about eight miles from the prison. We sought out a secluded retreat for the day, and after getting each of us a stout stick, which would answer either as a weapon or a walking-stick, we lay down and slept until late in the afternoon. We woke up much rested, but were so lame and our feet were so sore that we could hardly take a step without excruciating pain. We were hungry, and the scanty morsel of corn-bread we had brought from the prison the

24

previous evening did not go far towards satisfying our sharp appetites. But it was all we had, and we ate it and were thankful, although we did not know where or when we would get our next rations.

"I now saw a difficulty in this attempt to get away that we did not encounter in our first attempt to reach the Federal lines. Our clothes had become dirty and ragged, and we had a sort of jail-bird look, that it seemed to me would betray us if we were seen. I was brought to a realization of this fact as I looked at Wood, when we sat together in silence beneath the great tree where we had taken shelter, waiting for the friendly mantle of darkness to shield our movements. And I suppose my own appearance was no more prepossessing than his. The miserable garments he wore did not cover his nakedness. His face was begrimed with dirt almost set in the skin. He had become thin and emaciated with fever, and had a ravenous appetite; his eyes were sunken in his head and seemed to have the wild, unnatural glare of a madman, which at times almost made me shudder. The poor fellow's pitiable appearance, as he sat there despondently and longingly gazing down on the beautiful valley below, was such as to appeal to a heart of stone. Yet I knew that it was unsafe for us to go to a house, and we agreed not to be seen by a human being if we could avoid it. I felt certain that if we should meet any one, our appearance would at once betray us. We were in a country where we could not expect to find a friend, unless, possibly, it might be the negroes, of whom, as a class, we knew but very little. We were so weak, and the mental strain and long-continued anxiety, in which we had lived from day to day, had had the effect of making us, I may say, foolishly suspicious and timid of everything. We were startled at every sudden noise, and crouched like sneaking wolves from the sight of man.

"While in the midst of unpleasant thoughts, Mark broke the long silence by raising his head and saying, ' Alf, it is time for us to go.'

"Our journey that night took us through a corn-field, where we pulled a few ears of corn and chewed it as we went along. I remember it was hard and made my jaws very tired, but it helped to quiet my gnawing hunger. It was much better than nothing. After a toilsome night's journey, guided by the stars, and over a very rough country, in which we entirely avoided roads, we again secreted ourselves as the streaks of gray began to appear in the east, and, after scraping up a pile of leaves, lay down for the day. When we awoke, late in the afternoon, we found that our feet were so bruised and sore, and that we were otherwise so lame, and withal so weak from hunger, that it taxed our endurance to the utmost to take a single step. We each took from our pockets an ear of corn, and after crunching and swallowing what we could, we put the rest in our clothes and hobbled off, making but very slow time for the first mile or so. It was in the month of October, and the nights were pretty cool, which, in our poorly-clad condition, compelled us to keep moving all the time to keep comfortably warm.

"The next morning came and still we had not reached the river. Again we hid ourselves and slept through the day. When night came and we tried to walk, we found our feet in such a deplorable condition that it did not seem possible for us to go farther. Mark crawled some distance on his hands and knees, and, looking back at me, said in an appealing tone, ' Alf, what's a fellow's life but a curse to him when he has to drag it out in this way? I would rather be dead and done with it.'

" I encouraged him, telling him the worst was over and we would soon reach the river. I suppose we had shaped our course a little too far south, and thus made the distance longer than it would otherwise have been. We struggled on for some time, crawling where the ground was stony, and stopping very often to temporarily quell the pain in our feet. I was a little ahead, and, as the breeze fanned my aching temples, I thought I heard to our right the lull of running water. I told Mark and cheered him up. We forgot our tortures for the time being and scrambled on quite lively, and soon after had the satisfaction of standing on the banks of the Chattahoochee.

" De Soto did not feel more joy when he first discovered the Mississippi, the great Father of Waters, nor was the ecstasy of Balboa greater, when, from the cloud-capped summits of Darien, his eyes first beheld the vast expanse of water which he named the Pacific Ocean. Like that great discoverer, we waded out into the water, carrying neither naked sword nor the banner of our country like he, to take possession of our discovery in the name of our rulers, but to bathe our painful feet and cool our parched throats.

" We made certain of the direction the river current ran, and started southward in high hopes, although the temptation to go northward to our friends was very strong. We now wanted a boat, and, not long after we started, fortune had another pleasant surprise in store for us, for we came upon a skiff safely moored, with lock and chain, to a tree. After carefully inspecting the surroundings to see that no prying eyes were peering on us, we ' loosened' the lock with a stone, and in a few minutes after were smoothly gliding down the current of the great river, and I doubt if two more joyful mortals ever navigated a canoe than we two, with that stolen little craft.

" What a happy change! Our weary limbs and painful feet now had a rest, and yet we were gliding noiselessly on our journey. What wonderful teachers hardship and stern necessity are! Discontented mortals do not half appreciate the blessings they have until they have been pupils in the school of adversity. I felt as if this chilly night's ride, in a little stolen boat, on a strange river, whose shores were hidden by Plutonian shadows, was the best and most grateful that I ever had, or ever expected to enjoy.

" We pulled off our old boots and bathed our lacerated feet in

the water, and quenched the tormenting thirst caused by the in-
digestible hard corn, which was now our only nourishment. We
kept our paddles pretty busy, as we wished to get as far away as
possible from where we took the boat before the dawn of day.
When daylight began to appear, we paddled our craft into a
bayou, safe from view, and secreted ourselves in a thicket for the
day.

"Four days and nights had now passed since we had eaten
food, except the morsel of corn-bread we brought out of the
prison. We lay down to sleep the day away, but between our
great hunger and the swarms of mosquitoes we could get but
little rest. I could, while sleeping, see in my dreams tables
spread and groaning with loads of good things to eat; bread,
meat, cheese, coffee, biscuit, and butter were all within my reach,
and were vanishing before my ravenous appetite, when, in the
midst of the great pleasures of this feast, I would suddenly
waken to a sense of the reality of the case, and what a madden-
ing disappointment I would feel. With this disturbed sort of
rest we worried through the day, the demands of hunger and our
stomachs getting the better of nature's demand for rest, until at
last we grew desperate, and at early twilight, in the evening,
pulled out of the little bayou, determined on a raid of some sort
on a house for food.

"We spied a house some distance from the river-bank, which
we thought from appearances we could capture with a plausible
story or by force.

"On approaching, we saw in its immediate vicinity quite a
number of negro cabins, and in the yard surrounding the house
about twenty blood-hounds chained to the fence, indicating that
these were the premises of an extensive planter. The only occupants of the house were an old man and woman. We apologized
for disturbing them, and told them we were soldiers who had been
on furlough returning to our regiments at Atlanta, and wished
directions to the ferry (we had discovered a ferry as we came
down); also, that we were hungry and wanted to get something
to eat, provided they felt like feeding hungry soldiers without
money, as we had had no pay for some time, and were both money-
less and in bad health, Mark's appearance proving this latter
assertion. It was quite dark, however, and they could not see
us very distinctly, but they evidently credited our story, for they
told us to be seated and we would soon be made welcome to such
food as they had.

"They were a couple of quite intelligent but unsophisticated
old people, in comfortable circumstances, living, as most South-
erners did, away from any highway, and we gained their confidence so far as to feel ourselves assured from suspicion. I had
been in Dixie so long that I had acquired, from the guards and
citizens, their vernacular of speech quite perfectly; besides this,
we had learned the names of officers and the number of different
regiments, such as the Eighth Georgia Cavalry, Fifth Tennessee

Infantry, etc., until we were able to tell quite a plausible story, if not too closely questioned.

"We asked the old man if there was any late news. He said, 'Nothing, except that the Yankee raiders had seized the Atlanta jailer, overpowered the guards, and a number of them escaped and had not yet been caught.' We expressed great surprise that such a piece of audacity could be made successful in Atlanta. The old man said, 'They were a desperate, dangerous lot of scoundrels, who ought to have been hung long ago.' He said many of them stood up and fought the soldiers with clubs and bricks, even after the guards had shot them through, and finally they jumped the high fence and ran like deer.

"In the mean time we had devoured everything the good woman had set before us on the table. We were ashamed, but our hunger was so much stronger than our sense of shame that we could not leave off, and, if we had not been in a hurry, we would have waited for her to have prepared another meal for us. She said she regretted that she had not more cooked to set before us, but we told her she had been very kind, and thanked them, at the same time bidding them good-night, when we started off, as they supposed, for the ferry. A short time afterwards we were in our boat pulling down-stream with more vigorous energy than we had before. We kept up a steady stroke of the paddles for some hours, feeling that each stroke placed so much more distance between us and the prison.

"While we were thus moving along with steady, cautious stroke, high in the hopes of the future, I suddenly, quicker than a flash, found myself lying flat on my back in the river. What on earth had happened I did not know, the accident had been so sudden. I thought of earthquakes, whales, sharks, torpedoes, and many other things. Luckily, one of my feet caught on the side of the boat, and I drifted with it until Mark came to my assistance and pulled me out. The cause of my mishap had been a ferry-boat wire, which was stretched across the river, and hung just low enough to catch me fairly as I sat in the stern of the boat. It struck Mark, but he sat in the middle, and fell into the bottom of the boat. We were going at a good speed, and the collision came so suddenly that it is a wonder we did not fare worse. Fortunately, there were no guards at the ferry, so we had no cause to apprehend discovery or molestation. My greatest mishap was a thorough wetting, for the night was frosty and cold, and caused me to chill.

"This was followed in the after part of the night by a stupor that I could not shake off, and my continued efforts at the paddle had wellnigh exhausted me. Mark could not manage the boat very well, as he had tried it a number of times. But I felt that I must have rest and sleep, and so gave the boat over into his hands, enjoining him to keep it in the current. I lay down in the bottom of the boat, and soon sank into a state of forgetfulness and sleep. I do not know how long I had slept, but some

24*

time in the night Mark aroused me, and told me we could go no
farther, as we had come 'to the end of the river.' It was some
time before he could awaken me fully to consciousness, so that I
could comprehend our situation.

"At last I began to look around, to determine what Mark's
'end of the river' meant. I soon discovered that he had run the
boat away under a ledge of the mountain, and a dim light could
only be seen in one direction. All else around us was impenetrable darkness. I took the paddle, and worked the boat in the
direction of the light, and in a little while we emerged from beneath this overhanging mountain ledge, and again reached the current of the river, down which the boat was soon rapidly gliding.
Mark now discovered that the 'end of the river' had not yet been
reached, but he did not care to take charge of the boat again

"Shortly after this adventure we perceived that we were not
to have smooth sailing all the way. The river began to grow
rough, and the water ran over benches and ledges of rocks, and,
in places, with great velocity, so much so that we narrowly escaped being 'broken up' on several occasions during this night's
journey. We passed over a number of places that we would not
have dared to risk in daylight, when we could have seen the danger. It seemed to grow worse and worse as we went on, when
daylight warned us that it was time to tie up and hide, which we
did, and, the day being warm and pleasant, we had a comfortable
rest,—the best since our escape.

"On the following night we came to a mill-dam, where the
water, judging from the noise, poured over in great volume and
force. We manœuvred around for some time above it, not
knowing what to do, but finally discovered what appeared to be
an apron near the centre of the dam, and decided to risk running it. Accordingly, we rowed up-stream some distance to get
under good headway, then turning the head of the boat down-
stream, we bent to our paddles with all our might. We came
down with the velocity of an express-train. What we supposed
might have been an apron, was nothing but a break in the dam,
and over it we shot like an arrow, shutting our eyes and holding
our breath. In an instant after, we landed (luckily right side
up) away below in the midst of the angry, foaming torrent, and
plying our paddles right vigorously, and keeping the bow of our
boat down-stream, we rode out safely, but then and there 'swore
off' on running mill-dams in the night.

"We continued our journey, though the river was still rough
and growing worse. We were constantly among rocks and
foaming, headlong torrents of water, while steep rocky walls
confined the stream to very narrow limits, and dark, shadowy
mountain peaks loomed up in the background, reminding us of
the Tennessee about Chattanooga. We went on from bad to
worse, until at last, during the latter part of the night, we were
incautiously drawn into a gorge, where it seemed that the destruction of our boat was inevitable. Such was the force and

velocity of the water, that we lost all control of the boat, and in one instant would be spinning around in a furious eddy until our heads were fairly dizzy, and in the next we would be dashed against the rocks until it seemed as if our boat would be splintered to pieces. We regarded our escape here as the narrowest we had made, and as quick as we could do so with safety we landed on the rocks and, with many regrets, abandoned our little craft to begin a tedious, toilsome land journey of three days and nights over rocky hills, bluffs, and mountains along the river.

"Just as we landed from the boat Mark started to walk out, and, losing his balance, fell headlong into the river. With considerable difficulty I fished him out, and, the early morning being quite cool, the poor fellow was chilled through and through, and it was with the greatest difficulty that I finally succeeded in getting him up into the mountains, and continued to exercise him by walking, so as to get up a good circulation of his blood. But he became so benumbed that I finally let him lie down, and gathered a lot of cedar boughs and piled them thickly over him, and then crawled in with him myself, and kept him as warm as possible. Here we slept and rested until late in the afternoon of that day, which became very warm under the bright rays of the sun.

"Our progress was very slow, and towards the last extremely painful. The old bruises and blisters on our feet, which were not entirely healed, came back worse than ever, and much of the time we crept along on the rocks on our hands and knees, believing that if once we could get below this range of mountains, we would find navigable waters. We came in sight of several isolated cabins in these wild, rocky hills, where we managed to beg a little food on two different occasions, which helped us very much. The suffering we endured on our last night's travel I cannot describe. It seemed as if we must give up and die where we were. But at last, when daylight came, to our great delight we saw the spires and smoke-stacks of a town in the distance. We knew this to be Columbus, Georgia, and that when we got below it the river was navigable clear to the Gulf.

"We now deemed it prudent to hide ourselves for the day, which we had not done in the mountains, and wait for the friendly cloak of darkness. When night came we made a long, careful detour away out around the suburbs of the town, and at last had the satisfaction of again reaching the river-bank, below the town, where we found good shelter among the dense grape-vines and drift-wood. By this time it was nearly morning again, and, like beasts of prey, we betook ourselves to a safe hiding-place.

"During all the time we had been in the vicinity of the town we had heard a constant clattering sound, as of a hundred workmen with hammers. This noise came from near the river, where there appeared also to be a great light. When daylight came the noise still continued, and we were near enough so that we could see that it was caused by a large number of workmen engaged on a vessel, which they were covering with iron. The boat appeared to be very large and of great strength, and evidently was intended for a warlike purpose. On closer inspection the following night I found that she was a powerfully-built gunboat, which they were evidently in great haste to complete, as the hammers of the workmen never ceased on her, night or day, nor for a single moment.

" This gunboat was none other than the rebel ram ' Chattahoochee,' a formidable iron monster, built as an engine of destruction for the blockading fleet in Appalachicola Bay. The first knowledge the Navy Department had of her was through Wood and myself. The ram, on her first downward trip, blew up near the mouth of Flint River, and never reached the Gulf.

" Our great anxiety now was to secure a boat. Wood was so lame he could not walk, and I was not much better. This delayed us here two days and nights. During the nights I was prowling about, up and down, trying to discover some sort of a craft that would float. In my reconnoitring about the gunboat I had discovered an old skiff chained to a stump quite near and in plain sight of the workmen, to some of whom, no doubt, it belonged. I secured a stout stick for a lever, and crept to the stump to which the boat was chained, when, watching my opportunity, I got a pry in such a manner as to break the lock on the chain. The lights shone so brightly that I could plainly see the men's eyes, and I very much feared they would notice me. However, I worked off with the boat carefully, and half an hour after I had Mark aboard, and we were pulling rapidly downstream. We found our prize to be a leaky old concern, and one of us was constantly busy keeping her bailed out.

" After we had drifted down some miles, we spied three boats tied to the shore on the Alabama side of the river, and as we had been giving our attention entirely to the Georgians all along, we concluded to trade boats on that side of the river, provided we could secure a better boat. Just as we had loosened the one we selected, three men with a pack of dogs came down the hill towards us, and the head man, evidently the owner, began hallooing to us and calling us slanderous names, such as thieves and the like. We did not stop to bandy words with the fellows, but speedily shoved all the boats into the river, and took a course up the river, as though we were going towards Columbus. They rent the air with curses upon our heads. In the course of fifteen or twenty minutes they had secured the boats we shoved into the stream, and with the lights they carried we could distinctly see that they were bent on pursuing us. We took a wide circuit, and then headed downward under cover of the willows, behind several small islands near the Georgia shore, and came out in the main stream far below the islands, while we had the satisfaction of seeing the lights of our pursuers disappearing up the river and prowling about the upper end of the islands, which we were now leaving far behind. We soon lost sight of them, and the strong presumption is that they never succeeded in finding their boat.

" We increased our speed, and kept under the shadows of the wooded shores as much as possible, congratulating each other on our lucky boat trade. With a good boat and an open river we felt now that our chances of escape were exceedingly good, and our spirits were buoyant and hopes high, although our stomachs were craving food. But on we swept, hour after hour, down the broad river, happy in the thought that we were fast placing scores of miles between us and the hated prison. The rest given our feet had much allayed the pain we suffered, and when morning came and we had secreted ourselves for the day, we slept well, but awoke in the afternoon ravenously desperate for want of something to eat.

" We went out, and, reconnoitring a little, discovered a cornfield. Making sure that there was no one about, we stole into the field and found plenty of corn and pumpkins. The hard corn and river water did not go well together, and proved to be an unpleasant diet to us, so we broke up the pumpkins, ate freely of the seed, and filled our pockets with more for lunch, each of us taking also a few ears of corn. By the time we got back it was nearly dark, and we pulled out. The pumpkin-seed diet, poor as it was, helped us wonderfully, and we made a big night's journey, passing a steamboat upward bound, which we dodged by pulling under the shadows of the timber and low-hanging bushes.

" Thus we progressed, travelling by boat at night and laying by in the daytime. If any reader of this story has ever made a trip on the lower end of the Chattahoochee River, I think he or she will agree with me when I say that the river scenery is peculiarly monotonous and causes a sense of loneliness. It is a vast water-path through dense forests of cypress and other swamp-growing timber. On either side, to the right and left, were endless swamps covered with water, and the river-channel was only observable by its being free from logs and gigantic trees. Great festoons of gray and sombre moss hung suspended from even the topmost limbs of these trees, reaching clear down to the water, and floated and swung to the music of the sighing winds. Perhaps it was the circumstances in our case that made us feel so, but I remember it as a dismal, lonesome journey. Sometimes we would not see a sign of civilization for forty-eight hours at a stretch.

" Besides the torments of hunger, our nights were made almost unendurable by the swarms of blood-thirsty mosquitoes, which came upon us in clouds. I did think that I had learned considerable about mosquitoes in my boyhood days in the Black Swamp of Northwestern Ohio, but for numbers, vocal powers, and ferocity I will ' trot' the Chattahoochee swamp fellows out against any others I have ever ' met up with.' The ragged clothing, which yet clung to our backs, did not much more than half cover us; especially was this the case with Wood, who was, I may truthfully say, half naked, and was thus doubly annoyed by the omnipresent 'skeeters.' And my own condition was but little better. To protect ourselves from the pests, we thatched our bodies all over with great skeins of moss, and two more comical-looking beings than we were, thus rigged out, it would be hard to find, but it baffled the bills of our tormentors.

"We had two other annoyances,—moccasin-snakes and alligators. The latter, with which the water swarmed as we went farther towards the Gulf, were a terror to me. They were a ferocious, hungry, dangerous-looking beast at best. We knew but little of their habits. The largest water inhabitant I had ever seen was a Maumee River cat-fish, and the most dangerous, a Black Swamp massasauger. Night or day these 'gators," as the Southern negroes call them, like the mosquitoes, were always within sight and hearing. Sometimes during the day, in order to keep out of the water, we would take shelter in a pile of driftwood. When we would wake up, after a short nap, every old log and hommock about us would be covered with 'gators.' They would lie listlessly and lazily, with eyes almost shut, looking hungrily and quizzically out of one corner of their wicked peepers, as if waiting for us to leave, or for a chance to nab one of us by the leg or arm and run. Mark grew superstitious of these creatures. He said he had read of wolves following a famished buffalo in the same manner, and that sharks would hover around a ship from which a corpse was to be cast overboard, and that, too, even days before death had occurred or was even suspected by the sailors. But the 'gators' were cowardly fellows, and, on the least demonstration on our part, would scramble into the water. Still we feared that they might steal upon and lay hold of us with their powerful jaws while we were asleep. We had learned that they were not apt to attack, except when the object of their voracious appetites lay quiet; but, when once they did lay hold, that they were hard to beat off. They will drag their victim, be it man or beast, instantly under the water, where the struggle soon ends.

"After enduring hunger as long as we possibly could, we were finally forced a second time since leaving Columbus to go in search of something to eat. This, I think, was about five or ten miles above Chattahoochee landing. It is not necessary to relate the particulars of our search for a human habitation, and the story of deception we told. It was a little before dark when we struck out on foot so weak, hungry, and faint that we could not walk many steps without resting, in search of something or anything we could devour. We were successful, or partially so, at least, and came back safely, much strengthened, as well as elated over our good luck, when, to our great dismay and chagrin, we found that our boat had been stolen during our absence.

"It was evident some one had seen us land and watched until

we left, and then taken the boat. I cannot describe our feelings. We scarcely knew what to do. The night was very dark, and it rained incessantly. We waded about in the water, tall grass and cane, and after a while found a little mound or hommock, which projected above the water, and on which we perched ourselves for the night. Such a dismal, long, rainy night as it was, too! It did seem as if the mosquitoes would carry us away piecemeal towards morning, when the rain had ceased. Had it not been for the food we had eaten, I believe we would have given up in despair. When morning came, we waded up and down in the cane and grass all forenoon, and about the only discovery we made was that another river came in just below us, and we could not go farther without a boat.

" During the afternoon I descried something on the far side of the river that looked like a boat partly sunk in the water, one end only of which was out. The next trouble was to get to it, as the river was about three-quarters of a mile wide, as near as we could judge. We found an old piece of plank, which we lashed on three flat rails with a grape-vine, and with a piece of narrow stave for a paddle and to fight off 'gators,' I twined my legs firmly around the centre of the frail craft, while Mark pushed it off into the stream and stood at the edge of the grass watching me. The raft sunk down until the water came about my waist, but I stuck to it, and after about an hour's hard work I effected a landing on the far side, and not long after found myself rewarded in the possession of a much better boat than the one we had lost the night before. I was not long in bailing out the water and rowing her back to where Mark was, whose gratitude found expression in tears and hearty hand-shaking, as he crept into the boat with me.

" We now plied our paddles energetically for a while, until we felt sure we had passed out of reach of the owners of the boat, when we put into the cane and secreted ourselves until night. After this mishap in losing our boat, we resolved that we would not both leave again while our journey lasted, starve or no starve. During the following day, while we were laid up waiting for night and fighting mosquitoes, I went out, skulking about to see what I could see, and in passing through an old field found some fish-hooks and lines in an old vacant cabin. I appropriated them, and we found them a godsend to us, for they proved the means of keeping us from actual starvation.

" We must have had a touch of scurvy, for our mouths and gums had become feverish, and our teeth were loose, and would bleed constantly when we attempted to chew the corn. This was the condition we were in when, providentially, we became possessed of the fish-hooks and lines.

"And now for a feast on raw cat-fish, of which we caught a plentiful supply as we journeyed on in the night. I have previously neglected to mention that I had with me an old one-bladed knife without any back, which was our only weapon, defensive or offensive. This old knife I had secreted when we were in the Atlanta prison, and had kept it with me as a precious treasure during all our wanderings. With this knife and our fingers we managed to skin and dress the fish, which we ate raw with our soaked corn. Matches we had none, nor had we been able to get any, and so we had no fire. I could eat only a mouthful or two of the raw fish at a time. My stomach was weak and feverish, and rebelled against the flesh. Still it tasted palatable.

" Mark, poor, hungry fellow, tore it from the bones in great mouthfuls, like a ravenous wolf, until I would beg of him to desist, fearing the results. He would sit and crunch the bloody flesh, and look at me with a wild, strange stare, and never speak a word. His eyes were sunken away in his head, almost out of sight, and as he would seize a fresh piece the pupils of his eyes would dilate with the gloating, ferocious expression of a panther or other carnivorous wild beast. I had frequently heard of men losing their reason and going mad from the effects of protracted hunger, and I sometimes shuddered as I looked at its telling effects on poor Mark's wasted frame, and the unnatural glare of his eyes. He would mutter and groan in his sleep, and sometimes scream out as if pierced by a knife, when he would suddenly start up and call my name. Towards the last of our journey his condition was much of the time a cause of great anxiety to me. Still, after we began to eat the fish he seemed much better, and I only feared the unnatural quantities of the raw flesh would kill him.

" We were now nearing the bay, as was plain to be seen, for on each succeeding morning the river had grown wider. Finally we became well satisfied that we were nearing a large town, which afterwards proved to be Appalachicola, and this made us anxious to learn something of the state of affairs below,—whether there were rebel picket-boats, or obstructions, such as torpedo-boats and the like.

" About this time we discovered a cabin some distance from the shore, and, to have a plausible excuse, I took an old pipe Mark had, and filled it with a few crumbs of tobacco which I fished from my old coat-linings, and then taking a piece of rotten wood which would retain fire, I left Mark with the boat and walked over to the house to get a light for my pipe. The occupants of the cabin proved to be an old Scotchman and his wife. He was very inquisitive, and asked more questions than I cared to answer. But I managed to evade suspicion, and at the same time gained considerable information. I learned that we were about five miles above Appalachicola, and that the Federal blockading squadron was stationed at the mouth of the bay, eighteen miles below the city. I hurried back to the boat, and found Mark rejoicing over a little armful of sweet potatoes he had stolen from a negro's canoe, which he had discovered in my absence.

" We got into the boat and at once paddled to the other side of the bay or river, where we entered into an inlet or creek, up which we ran for some distance, when we came to a dense cane-brake. Here we secreted ourselves and built a little fire, roasted fish and potatoes, parched corn, and dined in right royal style, although we felt the need of a little salt. Two hungry wolves never ate more ravenously than we did, although we were obliged to restrain ourselves, and leave off while yet hungry. It was with the utmost difficulty that I absolutely forced Mark to quit. After eating enough for four men, as I thought, he still begged for more. I finally induced him to go to sleep, and stored away some of the cooked fish and sweet potatoes for the next day.

"The information we had gained was invaluable to us, al-though I felt I had obtained it at some risk. When night came on we pulled out and passed down on the opposite side of the bay from the city, slowly and cautiously. We had moss in the bottom, on the sides, and in the seats of our boat for our comfort. As soon as we had gone well past the city, whose bright lights we could plainly see, we crossed the bay to the city side below the city, in the hope of finding a more sea-worthy boat. We were unable to find any other boat, however, and pulled on down the bay as fast as we could. While going down the bay that evening, we ran along in the midst of a large school of huge fish of some description, from which we apprehended danger every instant. These monsters would swim along on all sides of us, with great fins sticking more than a foot out of the water, and extended like a great fan. One of these fish could easily have wrecked our boat with its huge body. We hoped to reach the blockading fleet before daylight, but the night grew cloudy and we were unable to tell what course we were running, as the bay grew wider and wider as we went out. We decided the best thing we could do was to pull for land, which we reached after midnight, pretty well exhausted with our hard work at the paddles. We tied up our boat and went to a thicket near by and slept soundly.

"When we awoke in the morning, we were cheered by the beautiful surroundings,—all just as nature had fashioned them, for the habitation or handiwork of man was nowhere to be seen. Our couch had been a bed of prickly grass, that caused a sting-ing, itching sensation all over our bodies. We had slept in a wild orange grove.

"We made a hasty breakfast on our fish and potatoes left from the night previous, and started for our boat; but imagine our surprise when we found it distant at least two hundred yards from the water. Mark, who had lived in the old country, ex-plained to me that this was the effect of the ocean tide, which had gone out since we landed, and would not come in again until that night. There was no safe course left us but to drag our boat to the water, which we did, after tugging at it for about an hour.

"When we were again on the water we could see the spires and high buildings of the city we had passed, but no sight of ships could we see. We took our course as well as we could, and pulled for the open sea. A little boat, which seemed to be a fishing-smack under full sail, passed away to the leeward of us, coming out from the city, and caused us no little concern, but she passed off, and either did not notice us or care to inquire who we were. We plied our paddles industriously until about the middle of the afternoon, when we spied an island away in the distance. We had been out of sight of land for some time and the view of the island cheered us up a little, for we knew if a rough sea came on that our little boat was liable to get swamped. This island was much farther away than we had supposed. As we neared it we were in some doubt as to whether we should pass to the right or left of it, when our decision was made by the discovery to the left and away in the distance of something that had the appearance of dead trees.

" In the same direction, and right in our course, was something that appeared like a bar or gravel-bank. We supposed the old trees stood on another low island or bar beyond. But as we neared this bar, that which at first seemed to be dead trees began to take the shape of ship-masts, and we imagined that we could see something that looked like the dark outlines of black smoke-stacks in the blue, hazy distance This made us quite nervous, and we pulled away at the paddles with renewed vigor and strength. Before we were scarcely conscious of it we were close upon the bar, and began to be puzzled how we should get by or around it, for it was longer than it appeared to be when first seen. Presently we discovered a narrow, shallow channel through it, and we were not long in getting our boat through. As we were going through, Mark gathered in a lot of rough, muddy-looking lumps, which I supposed were boulders, and soon called for my old broken-backed knife, after which I saw him open one of the muddy chunks and eat something from it. Says I, ' Mark ! you starving Yank ! what in thunder are you at now ?' ' Taste this,' says he, as he opened another muddy chunk, and I lapped up from the dirty shell the sweetest oyster I had ever tasted.

" We were in the midst of a great oyster-bed, the like of which I had never before seen. I had never, in fact, seen an oyster in the shell before. Mark gathered up as many as he could as the boat passed along, and when we reached the still water we made quite a little feast on them as we paddled on. I think I never tasted anything so delicious. We were still very hungry, and the moist, rich, salty flavor of the oysters seemed to suit our weak, famished stomachs to a nicety.

" But our little feast was soon cut short by the certain discovery that the dead trees were nothing less than the masts of vessels. We could now plainly see the yards, cross-trees, and great smoke-stacks. We dropped the oysters in the bottom of the boat, and, though quite exhausted, the sight of the vessels so renewed our strength that we made the little boat scud over the still water at a lively rate. Soon we could see the long, gracefu'

SAVED AT SEA.

streamers waving from the peaks of the masts, and the outlines of the dark, sombre-looking hulls of the ships.

"We were now nearing the ships very fast, and were a little anxious to see their colors, as we had become so suspicious of everybody and everything that we half feared running into the clutches of our enemies. But we were not long in suspense, for suddenly a little breeze sprang up, and I shall never forget my joy on seeing the old flag, the glorious old stars and stripes, as they unfolded to the ocean breeze, and seemed to extend their beneficent protection over us, after nearly eight months of terrible bondage. We could see the field of blue, studded with its golden stars, and the stripes of white and red! Yes, it was our flag, old *E Pluribus Unum!* We threw down our paddles in the boat, and stood up and yelled and screamed and cried like a couple of foolish boys lost in the woods. We could not restrain ourselves. Mark wanted to jump overboard and swim to the ships, although we were yet, perhaps, nearly a mile away,—at least too far to swim in his condition. After we recovered our senses a little, we picked up the paddles and began rowing again, directing our course towards the largest vessel.

"It seems now like a dream to me,—that joyful day,—the most joyful, I was about to say, of my life. I believe there were three vessels in sight. In steering for the largest one, although it was the most distant, we had to pass some distance in front of the bow of a smaller ship or boat. We were now getting so close that we could plainly see the officers and men on the decks in their neat, blue uniforms. We could see the port-holes in the sides of the ships, and the black muzzles of the cannon projecting out. This gave us much assurance, and we said to ourselves, 'Good-by, rebs! We are out of your clutches at last!'

"We were rowing our insignificant-looking little boat right along, just as though we intended to capture the biggest vessel in the fleet, when a gruff voice from the ship, whose bow we were passing, commanded us to 'Come to, there!' At the same time we saw a grim-looking old sea-dog, in nice uniform, leaning over the rail, motioning us in with his hand. We turned the bow of our little boat towards him, and, when we came within better speaking distance, he interrogated us, in stentorian voice, about as follows:

"'Who in —— are you, and what are you paddling under my guns in this manner for?'

"We were half-terrified by the old fellow's angry, stern manner, and did not know but we had at last fallen into the hands of a rebel cruiser under false colors. We did not know what to say to this unexpected, angry interrogation. We paddled on very slowly, while the sailors and officers began to gather in little squads, and look at us with mingled curiosity and merriment.

"Presently, the officer hailed us again, with about the same questions. I now stood up in our boat, and answered that we were two men trying to get back to God's country, among friends. I was now quite uneasy, and suspicious of the situation, and kept my eyes on the officer, for I perceived he was the commander. I shall never forget his stern but puzzled look as we came up under the bow of his vessel. We had been so over-joyed and excited that we had forgotten to pull the old moss, which covered our nakedness and protected us from the sun, from our backs, and we must have looked like scare-crows or swamp-dragons. I cannot speak so well of my own appearance then, but can see Mark Wood, just as he was on that joyful day, and a more comical, forlorn, starved-looking being cannot well be imagined.

"In our boat were a few cat-fish partly skinned, some oysters in the shell, some ears of scorched corn, a lot of moss, and our old boots, for our feet were yet sore, and we went bare-footed when in the boat.

"After scrutinizing us in silence for some little time, as we drifted up closer and closer, he again demanded of us some account of our strange conduct and appearance. I told him we were enlisted Federal soldiers, and belonged to the command of General O. M. Mitchel, in Tennessee, to which he growled something about our being 'a —— long ways from camp.' I then explained to him briefly that we were fugitives, and the causes that led to it; that we were nearly famished with hunger, and that, after skulking through mountains and river by night, we had at last sought protection under the old flag and the guns of his ship.

"I could see that his manner towards us had changed. He plainly saw the indications of our distress. He said he had heard of the raiding expedition we spoke of, and commanded us to row up to the ladder and come up the ship's side. We did so, and Wood went up the steps first. The poor fellow's agitation and joy were so great, and he was so weak, that he could scarcely raise his feet from step to step on the ladder or stairs. The commander, seeing his weak, faltering condition, leaned over the rail, as Wood came up, and, reaching out, took hold to assist him, and, as he did so, the rotten bit of old moss, which covered Mark's shoulder and back, all pulled off, and exposed his emaciated, bony skeleton, which, in truth, was nothing but skin and bones. The well-fed, sleek-looking sailors seemed to look on in horror, but not more so than the generous-hearted commander, who was moved almost to tears as he was reaching over to help me as I came to the top of the step-ladder. They stared at us in silent wonderment, while the sailors looked down into our little boat with comical curiosity."

We need not linger over the royal reception the poor fugitives met, or their joy as they partook of the hospitality of the commander, or even their still greater

joy when they returned to friends and comrades, who
had long mourned them as dead. From the bright termination of their sufferings we must turn, with deep
reluctance, to the story of the unfortunate six, still in
the power of the enemy.

CHAPTER XIX.

FROM ATLANTA TO RICHMOND.

WHEN we resolved to break jail it was our firm belief that failure or recapture meant death. Yet no
sooner was the excitement over, and we quietly back
in prison, than hope began to whisper once more. Possibly there was some mistake in the report which led
to our desperate effort, or, if it was indeed true, the escape of the larger part of the band might derange the
plan, or change the purpose of holding another court-
martial. It is sure that our anticipations of worse treatment were not realized. I cannot account for the agreeable surprise we experienced in this particular. Those
who are convinced that the mitigations of our lot were
caused by any representations made by the Union authorities at Washington after our comrades had escaped
must be mistaken, because the change took place *before
one of the fugitives had reached the Union lines.* Wilson
and Wood at Washington, as well as the others of our
number who escaped, did make prompt representations
to our government, which may afterwards have been
of service to us. But these could scarcely have affected
us during our stay in Atlanta, as the time was not sufficient. Possibly, it was thought by the Confederates
that the little remnant of the band, which had already
suffered so much, was not worth persecuting further.
25*

However it is explained, the succeeding two months we remained in Atlanta, after the attempted escape, was the least rigorous imprisonment endured by us in the South.

Colonel Lee thought the jail no longer safe, and ordered us to be taken to the city barracks. These were in the centre of Atlanta, looking out on one of its busiest public squares. Our room was also far better than had been given to us before. It was large, well lighted, and provided with a great open fireplace, in which a fire was kept continually burning. Our door was never closed, but a sentinel stood in it, watching us, and the gas was burned all the night. The Confederate soldiers roomed all around us, and the whole large house—a former hotel, I think—was surrounded by a line of sentinels. We were in the second story, and our windows were not barred. We could stand by them, and watch the busy throng outside for hours at a time. All our surroundings were now of a soldierly and civilized character. Our treatment was also more courteous and considerate than formerly.

Probably much, if not all, of this change for the better may be attributed to the character of the man in whose charge we were now placed. Jack Wells, as he was familiarly called, had been a lieutenant in the regular army of the United States before the war, and had not forgotten the traditions of the service. He had no feeling of resentment against us; on the contrary, would come around to our room and talk by the hour, telling us some great stories of his adventures and receiving as great in return. His worst fault was intemperance, being frequently half drunk and not seldom going beyond that point. In these cases, and when in a communicative mood, he would tell us that he did not care a cent which side whipped in the war,—that he only held his present position to avoid being conscripted, and because he preferred having a commission as a volunteer to being compelled to fight as a private conscript. But he was an excellent disciplinarian, and we nowhere had less chance of escape than from under his watchful eye and among his well-drilled soldiers. He would allow no trifling with his authority, and was ready to punish with fearful severity, as some of our Tennessee comrades—who were citizens, not soldiers—found. In fact, he seemed to care very little for those who were not soldiers.

One of these men—Mr. Pierce, who had accompanied us from Knoxville—one day threw his allowance of provisions back again into the tray in which it was being passed around, with a gesture of contempt, but without a word being spoken. The supply was very scanty and bad; but, as we could get no better, we only thought that the old man was very foolish thus to give up the little that he was offered. But this was not the end. In a few minutes a file of guards entered, took Pierce out, and tied his hands before his knees, with a stick inserted across under the knees and over the arms, in that most uncomfortable position known to soldiers as "bucking." They left him in the cold hall all night. He was able to eat his morning allowance without difficulty!

The next Tennessee sufferer was a Mr. Barker. One of the guards often used to tease the prisoners by asking them how they liked being shut up in a prison, "playing checkers with their noses on the windows," etc. A complaint to the commander would probably have caused a cessation of such taunts, which it was foolish to notice in any way. But Barker answered, that *he* need not feel so proud, for he would certainly be driven before long to work like a slave in the cotton-fields, to help pay the expenses of the war. The guard reported the insult, and Barker was taken to the punishment-room and there suspended, head downwards, till he fainted. This was repeated two or three times, and he was then put into a dark cell, only four feet square, without food, for twenty-four hours.

I was personally very fortunate here in receiving the favor of the commander, which I used to the advantage of my comrades as well as I was able. Having nothing to read, for the kind minister had not visited us since the attempted escape, and being determined not to be idle, I began to practise short-hand regularly each day. I had learned it before, and now wrote with a pencil on any scraps of paper I could find. Wells watched me while thus engaged, made a good deal of sport of the "spider tracks," but came in the next day and asked if I would not do a little writing for him. I was perfectly willing, provided it was not contrary to my allegiance to the United States. He laughed at the qualification, and showed me that it was the daily prison reports that he wanted made out. I did not see that this kind of work would do any harm, and undertook it. His office adjoined the prison room, and he gave orders that I was to be allowed to go from one room to the other at pleasure, but no farther. In fact, when in the office, there was always a special guard standing at the door. A hundred schemes of escape flashed through my brain, founded upon the additional privileges I now had; but I soon found that the guards were instructed to watch me all the more closely on account of my license. Wells himself laughed, and said that he would ask no pledges of me, for it was his business to keep us, and ours to get away—if we could! The qualification was well put. The only time the eye of a guard was off me day or night was while in the office, and that had only one door, by which the guard who brought me to the office always stood till ready to take me back to the common prison room. Yet I hoped something might occur by which I could help my comrades and myself.

One day I had the heartfelt pleasure of saving a man's life. While I was in Wells' office writing a requisition for provisions a person dressed in the uniform of a rebel officer was brought in under arrest.

He appeared to be very drunk, but remonstrated so very hard against being put into the rooms which had common prisoners that Wells consented to let him stay in his office, to get sober enough to give an account of himself. He had five hundred dollars in gold, which had been taken from him,—a marvellous possession, which Wells asked me to feel the weight of,—but as the officer furiously demanded his money, it was given back to him. As the charge against him had not yet been made known, Wells believed that it was only that of drunkenness,—an offence with which he had great sympathy. When the man got his money he sank down on a lounge in a drunken stupor. Wells had some business to transact, and soon went out. Sergeant White, the second in command, was with us, but he, too, soon took his departure. I was busy writing, but, hearing a step, I looked up and saw the stranger approaching me. A startling change had taken place. No trace of drunkenness was visible, but in place of it a terrible expression of anxiety and determination. I glanced about the desk to see that the heavy inkstand was in easy reach, for I had never seen a more desperate face. He leaned over my chair, and whispered, " You are a prisoner ?"

" Yes, sir."

" One they call engine thieves ?"

I nodded assent.

" I know you," said he; " I know all about you. I was here when your comrades were hung. Brave men they were, and the cruel deed will yet be avenged. I am not afraid to trust you. The commander here don't know who I am yet, but he will soon learn, and then I will have to *die*, for I am a spy from the Federal army." Then he added, with a most appealing look, " Can't you help me to escape, before it is too late ?"

I was amazed, and for a moment doubtful; but a few hasty questions, put to test his knowledge of the

Federal army and his present character, set my doubts at rest. Then I asked, " What can I do for you?"

He answered, " Can't you write me a pass and sign the commander's name to it?"

I shook my head.. If a pass written in such circumstances had been worth anything, I would probably have written one for myself and comrades before that time. Wells, who did not trust me at all, had guarded that very point in his orders.

Then my new friend proposed that we together break past the guard and run for it. I had no wish for such a trial with only one to help. There was my guard at the office-door; two more guards in the hall; a barrack-room, with always a dozen or more soldiers in it, at the head of the stairway; two guards at the front door; and a line of sentinels around the whole building.

But as I glanced around the room my eye rested on a fine overcoat of Wells' lying on the foot of the office bed, and an idea struck me. The prisoner was a short, thick man, about the same size and build of Wells. Said I, "Take that overcoat," pointing to it, "and throw it around you, and just walk out as independently as though you owned the entire establishment. It is now nearly dark, and the chances are that you will not be halted at all."

His countenance lighted at once. "I'll do it!" he exclaimed, with suppressed eagerness. To fold himself in the cloak, nearly crush my hand as he said "Thank you! Thank you!" and to open the door and walk out, was the work of but a moment. I listened as his firm step died away along the hall, but there was no challenge, no sound that betokened any discovery. The soldiers, seeing the familiar coat, must have supposed its rightful owner in it, and allowed it to pass unhindered. A moment after Sergeant White came in. I feared he would notice the prisoner's absence, but he did not. I got him engaged in story-telling as soon as possible, to postpone any inquiries.

For some five minutes I succeeded very well, when Wells entered, cast an uneasy glance about the room, and at once exclaimed, "Sergeant, where is that officer? Did you put him in another room?"

The sergeant answered that he had been out, and that when he returned he saw nothing of the man.

It was Wells' turn to be startled now. He sprang over to me and demanded sternly, "Pittenger, where's that officer?"

I was not in the least terrified. In fact, I was greatly amused, and for the moment forgetting the purpose formed two months before, of always avoiding untruth as well as all other evil things, I answered, "What officer?"

"That officer I put in here."

"Oh! that drunken fellow?"

"Yes; where is he?"

"The last I saw of him, he picked up his coat and said he was going to supper."

"Going to supper, was he? Ho! I see! Sergeant, run to the guards and tell them if they let him out I'll have every one of them hung up by the heels."

Wells was in a towering passion at once. The alarm was sounded, and for a few minutes a terrible commotion prevailed, but nothing was seen of the drunken fugitive, whose importance began to be known. Soon Wells returned, and demanded in a peremptory tone, "Pittenger, why did not you give the alarm when he started?"

I answered carelessly, "Oh! I did not know that my business in the South was to guard prisoners."

"Of course not," he returned; "but I wish you had called me this time."

Then after a moment's silence, he continued, "You said he took his coat. Had he a coat?"

"I suppose so, sir," I returned, "or he would not have taken it."

"He brought none in. Where did he get it?"

"Off the foot of that bed."

Wells sprang to his feet as quickly as if he had been galvanized, kicked the chair on which he had been sitting clear across the room, and exclaimed, "*My over-coat!* sure as ——! Worth eighty dollars! The villain!"

No intelligence of this spy reached Atlanta while we remained there. Wells told me that there was no doubt he had gotten entirely away.

While in this place, I had the opportunity of learn-ing that there were many lovers of the old Union in Atlanta. These visited us, and, although always in the presence of the guards, managed to express their kind-ness in very tangible ways. They told us much of their hopes, and of the strength they numbered. A certain Dr. Scott was very liberal in his contributions to our wants. I had afterwards the pleasure of repay-ing his kindness, when he had been forced to flee for his life, and arrived destitute in the North. The money we thus obtained, together with some small presents Captain Wells bestowed, when pleased with the writing I did for him, gave us the means of living almost luxuriously. One dainty I remember with es-pecial delight. Sweet potatoes were very abundant and cheap, and we were allowed to buy as many as our means permitted, and roast them in the ashes of the wood fire which always glowed on our hearth. The great mealy potatoes, raked out and dusted off and eaten hot, constituted a feast good enough for a king! I have never since found any sweet potatoes equal to those we devoured by the bushel in the old Atlanta barracks. This abundant living made some amends for the six months of famine that preceded it, and gave strength, which was still to be sorely tested before the day of deliverance. The memory of those beautiful autumnal days, when we could look from our unbarred windows upon the sky and the street, when we could gather around the fire and under the gas-jet in the evening, when hunger no longer pinched, and when health, which I had long missed, came back, when some consideration was shown for us even by our guards, and when visitors often whispered words or gave signs of sympathy for our cause as well as for ourselves, is not altogether unpleasant. True, we were still prisoners, and our fate as uncertain as ever; but it was easy to persuade ourselves that these more pleasant surroundings were the promise of still greater good.

Our religious exercises were here continued as persistently and publicly as in the jail. There were serious difficulties to overcome. Some of our own party seemed to consider that our release from the dark cells of a criminal prison removed the necessity of morning and evening prayer. We were not alone, and the soldiers who were "off duty" came to our door when it was first reported that "the Yankees were having prayer-meeting," and greatly annoyed us by interruptions and by a continual series of comments upon the exercises. We endured this for a time, but at last I appealed to Wells. He gave us protection from the guard, saying that he could not stand praying himself, but if we could get any good out of it we were welcome, and should not be disturbed. The opposition of the prisoners soon gave way also, and our morning and evening devotions were seasons of great interest. Even prisoners from other rooms came to their open doors that they might hear the reading and prayers, and join with us in song. Faith, hope, and courage were sustained by this recognition of God more than by all other agencies combined.

An effort was here made to get recruits out of the prison for the Confederate army. Especially were the regular soldiers who were in our company importuned. But our band were not asked. I presume they thought we could not be trusted. Had the offer now been made I would not have accepted, though I would have done so without hesitation at any time preceding the death

26

of our friends. Now my religious principles would
have prevented me from taking the oath of allegiance
to the Confederacy for the mere purpose of breaking it
by desertion. But I was glad the temptation was not
offered to any of our band.

At length there came to us most startling news,—a
court-martial was again convened! This was the first
since the ever-memorable one at Knoxville, and we
awaited its action with breathless interest. A week of
sickening suspense passed and no summons came for
us. Had we been ordered out for trial we had resolved
to try again to escape, even if the effort only resulted
in throwing us on the bayonets of the surrounding
guards. But when news came that the court had ad-
journed, we were as much rejoiced as we had been
fearful before. It did look as if they intended to per-
secute the feeble remnant of our party no further; and
passing from the extreme of despondency to that of
hope, we began once more to indulge the blissful expec-
tations of exchange. But our time had not yet come.

The weeks rolled on. Few things worthy of note
occurred. The same monotony which makes prison-
life so dreary robs it of interest when recorded. We
would rise in the morning from our hard bed—the
floor—and wash ourselves by pouring water on each
other's hands; then eat our scanty rations when brought.
Then the effort was to kill time until dinner came, which
was about four o'clock. It was not abundant, but if
we had a bundle of roasted sweet potatoes to add from
our own stores, as often happened, it was not so bad.
Then we did anything to keep busy until the gas was
lit. This was kept burning all night, not from any
favor to us, but only that the guards might see that we
were not arranging any plan for escaping.

This was the most cheerful hour of the day, for
under the soft inspiration of the gaslight conversation
flowed freely, and all the incidents of our past lives
were rehearsed. Wells or some other rebel officer

would often enter and talk with us. Arguments and discussion on all manner of subjects were introduced, and often continued until the midnight bells were striking in the town. Then would come our evening prayers as we lay down to dream often of home and friends and freedom. In the morning the same round recommenced. Thus days glided into weeks, and weeks passed into months. The golden hues of autumn deepened into the sombre colors of early winter, and still we were in Atlanta. It almost seemed as if we would never be anywhere else.

At length there came a day of wonderful joy. A number of officers, including the provost-marshal, came to the barracks, and, inquiring out our room, had us all drawn up in line. One of them stepped forth and addressed us, saying that he had good news to communicate, which they had been hoping to receive for some time past. He continued, " You have all been exchanged, and all that now remains is to send you out of our territory by way of Richmond and City Point."

Each of them then came along our line and shook hands with us,—the Tennesseeans and regular soldiers included, twenty in all,—offering congratulations on the happy terminations of our trials, and wishing us much joy on our arrival at home.

Our feelings were indescribable, but strangely mingled. There was an overwhelming rush of emotions which forbade utterance,—rapture exceedingly great, and yet mingled with a deep touch of sorrow that our seven dead—murdered—comrades were not with us to share the joy of this hour. And the eight also who had managed to get out of the clutches of the rebels by their own daring,—we were uneasy about them. Only a day or two before we had seen in an Atlanta paper, obtained, as usual, through the negroes, who were waiters here as well as at the jail, an article clipped from the *Cincinnati Commercial*, telling of the arrival of Porter and Wollam at Corinth, as narrated above. Of the others we had received no reliable information, but supposed that some of them at least had perished. The provost-marshal told us that three had been shot and left in the woods, but we did not fully credit him.

Notwithstanding all this, the prospect of liberty was enough to make our hearts overflow with gratitude to God. I was so agitated that when Wells asked me to write a requisition for provisions for the trip to Richmond I could not do it, and had to transfer the work to more steady hands. It was nine o'clock in the morning when we received the glad news, and we were to start for home—*via* Richmond—at seven in the evening. As the time for departure drew near, we again lit the gas, and made up a fire, the ruddy blaze of which was an emblem of cheerfulness, to take a farewell view of the room in which we had spent so many not altogether unhappy hours. Often afterwards did we remember that bright hour of expectation.

We were forbidden to take any blankets with us, being told that we would soon be where blankets were plenty. The pieces of carpet we had managed to secure as blankets were therefore left behind, with the exception of two small strips, which were afterwards very serviceable. A great surprise met us when we were ordered to start. We were not tied! This was the first journey on which we had been sent so carelessly, and it afforded the strongest presumption that the exchange was a reality.

All was now in readiness for our departure, and we took a last look at rebel Atlanta. The guards fell in on each side of us, and we wended our way along the dark streets. Wells, even drunker than usual, accompanied us to the cars, where he hiccoughed an affectionate farewell. I carried away one good article of dress, —a nice felt hat. The day before Wells clapped it on my head, telling me that I looked better in it than in my own shabby cap. I supposed that it was only a freak, and that he would reclaim it again, but he did not. It was much out of suit with my other garments, but I wore it until I had a chance to sell it for a great price —in Confederate money !

Sergeant White commanded our escort. He had always been kind to us, and, like his superior, did not care which side came out best in the war, so long as he was not hurt. The guard was only ten in number, while we were twenty and unbound,—a ridiculous falling off from former precautions.

We were crowded into box-cars, and soon began to suffer severely with cold, for the night air was most piercing. It was the 3d of December, and we had only summer clothing, which was, in addition, very ragged. About three o'clock in the morning we left the train at Dalton to wait for another train to Cleveland, as we were not to go through Chattanooga. This was our last passage over the railroad we had so much wished to destroy nine months before.

The stars were sparkling in light and frosty brilliancy when we stopped, and the keen and icy wind cut almost through us. We nearly perished before the train arrived, and enabled us to continue our journey.

In the morning we found that our three days' rations, which were to last to Richmond, were barely sufficient for breakfast. We ate everything, and trusted to buying something with the remaining money our Atlanta Union friends had given us. When that failed we had our old resource,—the endurance of hunger.

During this day's ride on the cars we discussed the question as to whether it would not be best to capture the guard and escape. The task did not seem hard. The guards were very careless, and we could at any time have had as many guns as they had. They sat on the same seats with us, and were often asleep. Several times on the trip we wakened the sentinels by the doors as the corporal approached, thus saving them from punishment. Once Sergeant White laughingly told us that we could escape if we tried, but that he thought it would be more pleasant for us to ride around by way of Richmond rather than to walk over the mountains on our own responsibility. This very security lulled our suspicions, and made us shrink from undertaking an escape which would have involved severe hardship in mountain travel, if nothing worse. Besides, we no longer had the same homogeneous party as in Atlanta.

In the afternoon we passed Knoxville, and were glad to keep right on. Then came the town of Greenville, the home of our former companion, the heroic Captain Fry. About nightfall we reached the Virginia line, and ran steadily on. It was a beautiful night; the moon shone over the pale, frosty hills with a mellow radiance which made the whole landscape enchanting. The shifting scenes of mountain, stream, or ghostly wood seemed to me like a panorama of human life. The morning dawned upon us, still steaming slowly through the romantic valleys of Virginia.

The next day was wet and dreary. Our car leaked, our fire went out, and we were thoroughly uncomfortable. By evening we had reached the mountain city of Lynchburg, and discovered that we had missed the railroad connection. This led to a delay of twenty-four hours, which we greatly regretted, being very anxious to get speedily through to our own lines. We had all our plans laid for the happy day of our arrival at Washington.

We were quartered in a large bare room belonging to the barracks, where some of the worst criminals of the Confederacy were also confined. There was a great stove in the centre of the room, but, as no fire was put in it, we had to endure another night of dampness and cold. The only consolation was found in the thought that we would not have many more such nights to spend before reaching home. I paced the floor till nearly morning, and saw a good many amusing incidents. Many of the rebels were drunk and disposed to mischief. One man diverted himself by walking around the room on the forms of those who were try-. ing to sleep. In his round he stepped on Bensinger,— one of our party. The infliction was patiently endured the first time, but as the sot came again, Bensinger was on the lookout, and, springing to his feet, gave him a blow that stretched him out on the floor. Some of his companions rushed forward to resent the just punishment, but Bensinger's friends also were prepared, and there was a good prospect of a general fray. But, as soon as the ruffians understood the position, they retired to their own side of the room.

In the raw and chill morning I found here some of the most virulent enemies of the Union I had yet seen. A prisoner loudly declared that no quarter ought to be given in the war,—said that he had advocated raising the black flag from the first, asserting that "if it had been raised the war would have been over long since."

"No doubt of it," I replied. "In that case the whole Southern race would have been exterminated long before this."

That mode of ending the war had not entered his mind, and he did not appear pleased with the suggestion.

A little before dark the next evening we again started, and now had good, comfortable cars,—the best we had enjoyed on the route. But we only ran a short distance to the junction, where we had to leave them and wait the arrival of another train. Here was the best chance of escape we had yet found. The night was pitchy dark, and so cold that the guards built a great fire on the border of a strip of woodland, and allowed us to help in gathering withered sticks to replenish it. They scarcely appeared to notice us, and all that was necessary for escape was to give the word and run for it. Nothing held us but the absolute confidence of a speedy exchange, and, depending upon that, the golden opportunity was neglected. Of course, the perils and hardships of wandering through the Virginia mountains in the depth of winter would have been severe, but the start would have been mere child's play. Oh! how bitterly we afterwards regretted that we had not darted into the depths of the forest and sought to effect our own exchange!

CHAPTER XX.

LIBBY AND CASTLE THUNDER.

In a few hours the train for which we waited arrived, and, passing onward without further noticeable events, long before morning we were in Richmond. There was the same intense and piercing cold which had been the main element in our suffering during this journey, but the sky was clear, and the rebel capital was distinctly seen in the sparkling moonlight. Everything looked grim and silent through the frosty air, and our teeth chattered fast and loud as we walked up a street of the sleeping city.

But the sergeant in command of our party did not know what to do with us. We hoped that some arrangements had been made for forwarding us directly to City Point, the place of exchange, so that we might that very day behold once more the stars and stripes. Yet we knew it was more probable that some detention would occur. The sergeant left us where we were while he started in search of the provost-marshal's office for instructions. We endeavored to shelter ourselves as best we could from the unbearable cold, which really threatened to prove fatal. Two pieces of ragged carpet were all the protection we had, in addition to our well-worn summer clothing, and we spread these over our heads as we huddled together in a solid mass in the angle of a brick wall. It was astonishing what a

relief this afforded,—especially to those who were in
the inside of the *pack*, where I happened to be. Here
we shivered till the sergeant returned. He had found
the headquarters of the prison department and conducted us thither.

Several streets were threaded in the moonlight, and
when the office was reached, to add to our discomfort,
it was destitute of fire. We stood in the empty room,
looking at the grim portraits of rebel generals for an
hour or two, until the marshal entered. He did not
deign to speak to us, but broke open a sealed letter
Sergeant White handed him and read aloud that ten
disloyal Tennesseeans, four prisoners of war, and *six
engine thieves* were hereby forwarded to Richmond by
order of General Beauregard. The old name applied
to us was no small shock. We had hoped that the
title of " engine thieves" had been left behind, and that
from henceforth we would be only called " prisoners of
war." But we still trusted to be soon beyond their
lines, and it would make no real difference what name
they exchanged us under. The marshal then gave his
orders, and we were conducted onward.

By this time it was daylight, December 7, 1862.
Richmond looked still more cheerless in the cold morning than in the moonlight.

A long march through a number of streets brought
us to the banks of the James River, where we halted
in front of a most desolate-looking but very large brick
building, situated near the water, and surrounded by a
formidable circle of guards. This we supposed to be
a prison, and soon learned that we were right. It was
the famous LIBBY.

We entered, were conducted up a flight of steps, and
reached a vast, open room, where we saw, almost for
the first time since our capture, the old, familiar United
States uniform, and were soon in the midst of over a
hundred United States soldiers.

Our greeting at first was not very friendly, as we

still wore the ragged clothing that had served us all summer; but as soon as our true character and history were known, a most cordial welcome was extended. There was only one small stove in the cold, empty room, around which part of the inmates were huddled. But with the characteristic courtesy and chivalry of the American soldier they cleared a place beside it for us. When I got warm I had leisure to look around.

The prospect was not very cheerful. Above, the floor had been taken out, leaving only the rafters between us and the roof. The window-sashes were all removed, and the cold wind whistled in from the river far more sharply than was consistent with comfort. Only a very scanty amount of fuel was allowed per day, and when that was exhausted they had to endure the freezing as best they could. The room was too large and open to be warmed throughout, and only a few could gather around the stove. The food was neither better nor worse than in other Southern prisons. Probably among all the prisoners, past and present, we were the only ones who were glad to be there. We regarded it as the sure pledge that our foes had not deceived us in their promise of an exchange, for these men, with whom we found ourselves, were actually going northward on the next truce-boat, which was daily expected. What mattered the cold wind or the bare floor with such a hope? We felt that we were no longer held as criminals, but were now in the common prison, with other soldiers, sure that the day of final release could not be far off. What wonder if our joy was too deep for words, and we could only turn it over in our minds, and tremble lest it should prove too delightful to be realized? The vision of freedom was so warm and vivid that all hardships were forgotten.

It was also very agreeable to talk with our comrades who had recently been captured, and get news of the progress of the war from a Federal stand-point. All the intelligence we had obtained for a long period came colored by Southern prejudices. In such communion with friends who were still confident of success in the great conflict the time passed rapidly.

But in the midst of our conversation, probably two hours after our entrance, an officer came to the door and called for the men who had just been admitted. Every one in the room but ourselves had taken the customary oath of parole, not to serve against the Confederacy until regularly exchanged; and supposing that omission in our case was about to be supplied, we gladly responded. The guard led us down to the entrance hall and called over our names. The four prisoners of war who had come from Atlanta with us were sent up-stairs again, while we were turned into an immense, but dark and low, room on the left of the stairway and the door locked behind us.

This was an awful moment. The full meaning of this separation burst upon us. We had been taken away from those who were to be exchanged and put in a room reserved for those regarded as criminals. We had been bitterly deceived, and our hopes at once fell from the highest heaven to which they had soared. A cold sense of misery and despair came over us. No wonder we looked at each other with pale, troubled countenances in the dim light, and asked questions none were prepared to solve.

But for one moment only were we thus crushed; the next we eagerly sought an avenue for hope. Perhaps they did not choose to recognize us as soldiers, and merely wished to exchange us as civilians,—a matter of perfect indifference to us, provided we were exchanged at all. We looked around to see what foundation we could build on for this pleasant conjecture.

Our present apartment contained even more prisoners than that up-stairs. They were not Northern soldiers, but were from all parts of the South. Some of them had been in prison ever since the war broke out, while a few had been arrested for supposed anti-slavery sentiments even before that event, and had lived in loathsome dungeons ever since. There had been a reign of terror in the Southern States preceding the war, as well as after the opening of the contest, which differed from the similar terror in the French revolution mainly in being less theatrical, and in striking humbler victims. A few Northern soldiers were here who had been put in for attempting to escape or for other breaches of prison discipline. Every man in the room had some kind of "a charge" against him. These facts were not calculated to strengthen hopes of exchange, or even weaken fears of further punishment.

In the mean time breakfast was brought in. It consisted of a small quantity of thin soup and a very scanty allowance of bread. To our delight the latter was made of wheat flour instead of corn-meal; and all the time we remained in Richmond we received good bread, though it was very deficient in quantity.

While we were talking with our new room-mates an officer again entered, and inquired for the men who had last come in. We responded promptly, for hope was again whispering in our hearts that probably there had been some mistake, which would now be rectified, and we be taken up-stairs again. But no such good fortune was in store,—rather the reverse. We were taken out of doors, where a guard waited to remove us to another prison. Again our hearts sank.

We crossed the street and marched westward, halting at a desolate-looking building, a few hundred yards from Libby, which we afterwards learned was "CASTLE THUNDER," the far-famed Bastile of the South. Through a guarded door we entered a reception-room and waited for some time. In this interval a fierce-looking, black-whiskered, bustling individual, who I afterwards learned was Chillis, the prison commissary, came by and, looking at us, exclaimed,—

"Bridge-burners, are they? They ought to hang, every man of them; so ought everybody who does anything against the Confederacy." The latter proposition, with the change of one word, precisely suited my own feeling then.

Soon we were ordered up-stairs. Up we went, passing by a room filled with a howling and yelling multitude, who made such an outrageous racket that I was compelled to put my hands to my ears. A score of voices brawled with all the power of their lungs, " Fresh fish ! Fresh fish !" The same exclamations greeted every new arrival.

Here we were searched, as usual, to see if we had anything contraband, or rather, anything worth taking from us. I had obtained a large knife in Atlanta, which I managed to slip up my sleeve, and by carefully turning my arm when they felt for concealed weapons, succeeded in keeping it out of the way.

The examination over, I supposed they would put us in the bedlam we had just passed. They did no better, for we were put into a *stall* beside the large room. I use the word "stall" advisedly, for no other is so appropriate. It was one of a range partitioned off from the room in which were the noisy miscreants, and from each other, by boards nailed to the upright timbers, with cracks wide enough to let the wind circulate freely everywhere. Most of the windows of the large room were out, which greatly increased the cold. Our stall was only eight or nine feet wide, and perhaps sixteen in length. It was perfectly bare of furniture, —not having even a bench or any means of making a fire. It was in the third story, and had one redeeming quality,—it commanded a view of the street, but there was a guard below, who had orders to shoot at any head that might be protruded from the window.

In this cheerless place our party of six, with nine Tennesseeans,—fifteen in all,—were confined during the months of December and January. The first day our spirits sank lower than ever before. All our bright hopes were dashed to the ground, and there seemed

27

every reason to believe that we were doomed to this dreary abode for the whole duration of the war, if, indeed, we escaped sharing with our murdered friends the horrors of a scaffold. It was too disheartening for philosophy, and that day was one of the blackest gloom. We seldom spoke, and when we did, it was to denounce our own folly in suffering ourselves to be deluded to Richmond by falsehood. I cannot say at this time whether the false declaration concerning the exchange was intended to deceive or was only the result of some misunderstanding; but then we had no doubt it was deliberate treachery. Not being able to spare enough guards to make us secure, we felt that they had deceived us to this terrible prison, which we might have avoided by seizing one of the many opportunities for escape our journey afforded. But it was no use lamenting; all we could do was to register a vow never to be so deceived again. One resource remained. It was my turn to lead our devotions, which we had continued faithfully. If I ever prayed with fervor it was in this hour of disappointment and dread. I tried to roll our cares upon the Lord, and at least partly succeeded, for I rose from my knees convinced that we had one Friend who had not forsaken us, and who had often made His children rejoice in worse situations than ours. The next morning we awoke quite cheerful and nerved for any fate that might yet be in store.

The routine of prison-life here differed but little from that in Atlanta, though our condition was far less comfortable. In the morning we were taken down to the court (the building was square and built with an open space in the centre) to wash, and were immediately taken back to our stall and locked up. The principal difference arose from our lack of fire. No other physical suffering I endured in the whole imprisonment was more intolerable than this perpetual freezing. We had no opportunity for those pleasant fireside chats which had done so much to make our days endurable in the Atlanta barracks. In their stead, as the darkness and coldness of night drew on, we were compelled to pace the floor, trying to keep warm; and, when sleep became a necessity, we would all pile down in a huddle, as pigs sometimes do, and spread over us the thin protection of our two bits of carpet. Thus we would lie, until the cold could be endured no longer, then rise and resume our walk. When the weather became warmer than usual we would sleep much, to make up for wakefulness during the colder nights.

We never omitted our public prayers. For a while the crowd outside in the large room, which was composed of the very scum of Southern society, such as deserters from the army, gamblers, and cut-throats from the large cities, gave us all the annoyance in their power, by shouting all kinds of derisive epithets through the cracks in the board partition while we were kneeling; but, finding their efforts ineffectual, they finally gave over, and left us to pursue our own way in peace. We found, afterwards, when, for a short time, we were put in with them, that they respected us all the more for our perseverance.

A few days after our arrival we noticed a great stir at Libby Prison, which was in plain view. A truce-boat had arrived at the place of exchange. Soon a body of prisoners were marched up the street by us, and our four Atlanta companions with them. As they passed by they waved their hands to us in farewell and continued their journey to freedom. They were not disappointed, and, as I have since learned, they were soon with their friends at home. The representations made at Atlanta were true as regarded these four men; the falsehood was in making us believe that *we* stood on the same footing. We felt glad for their sakes; but the parting, to us, was very painful, and we turned away from the window with something of the gloom that had darkened the first day ᴎ ᴼᵛᴵ abode in this prison.

One great privilege we had here,—a delightful oasis in the dead sameness that settled over our days. This was found in reading the daily newspapers. We were not now forbidden their perusal, and some one in the large room had always money enough to buy a paper and charity enough to lend it. As soon as we received it, all the party would gather around while it was read aloud. Each item of importance was eagerly discussed. The news was often exciting, as the Union commander, Burnside, had just made an advance, and we breathed hearty prayers that he would be successful in reaching Richmond. Probably our enemies would, in that case, try to remove us farther South; but we had firmly resolved to escape in such a contingency or die in the attempt. We would not allow ourselves again to be moved from one prison to another without risking everything for freedom.

But soon came the sad news of Burnside's bloody repulse at Fredericksburg,—sad to us, but causing the greatest rejoicing among our enemies, who felt that they had escaped a great danger. If Union defeats diffused gloom throughout the whole of the loyal States, there was yet no place where they were so regretfully and bitterly felt as in Southern prisons.

Here I sold the hat I had obtained from Commander Wells in Atlanta, and made an effort to invest the money in books, for which I was more hungry than for bread. But the volumes I wanted were not to be found in Richmond. Chillis, the cross commissary who wished us hung on our first arrival, but who was, nevertheless, the kindest official in the prison, made the effort to obtain them; but when he failed, we took instead some very small cakes, at ten cents each. These were a great addition to our rations for a day or two.

The desire to escape once more became intense. Being in the third story, we could only get out by passing at each door successive relays of guards, all of whom had reserves ready to co-operate with them in case of alarm. Our room was nearest the jailer's office, and on the other side there ran a row of rooms filled with all kinds of prisoners,—some held as spies and others as murderers.

The nearest of these rooms to our own was occupied by Federal soldiers accused of various offences. Captain Webster was one of these. He had on one occasion been sent to capture a notorious guerrilla captain named Simpson, who was then hiding within the Union lines. When he was found, Webster summoned him to surrender. Instead of doing so he fired his pistol and started to run, but Webster also fired and mortally wounded him.

When Webster was afterwards captured by the Confederates, he was charged with the murder of Simpson, and confined in the room next our own. He was finally hanged, but in the official report the offence was changed, in a manner not uncommon with Confederate authorities, for the more plausible one of violating his parole. At this time Webster was very anxious for an attempt at escape. A plan was soon arranged, and the evening before Christmas selected as the time. The citizen prisoners in the room below were more favorably situated than ourselves for beginning the enterprise. We had opened secret communications with them, and the ramifications of the plot reached every room in the prison. The signal agreed upon was the cry of "fire!" When this alarm—always startling, but doubly so in a crowded prison—was given, we were to rush upon the guards and overpower them. They only numbered about thirty, while we had over a hundred and fifty men in the plot. After capturing the guard, we still had the very serious task of getting out of the guarded and fortified city. It is not probable that a very great number could have succeeded in doing this.

That Christmas-eve was not much like Christmas at home. We made everything ready, and anxiously waited for the thrilling alarm of "fire!" which we would have echoed at the top of our voices, and then burst off the door of our stall and flung ourselves on the guard. I had no doubt that we could thus break open the strongest prison in the Confederacy; but as to any large number escaping to the Union lines I was less confident. The hours rolled on and midnight came,—the hour fixed for the attack. But we waited in vain. No signal was given. The inmates in the room below had failed in courage at the critical moment and resolved to postpone the attempt.

Not yet discouraged, we determined to make another trial the very next night. Captain Webster was appointed leader, as we felt sure that he would not falter. The locks were taken off all the side rooms except ours, which was so near the station of the guard that it could not be removed without great danger of discovery. We cared but little for this. A long board which supported our water-bucket afforded a convenient battering-ram, with which we felt sure of being able to deal with our door.

Some of the inmates did not wish to run the fearful hazard, but were very kind to those of us who did, supplying us with serviceable shoes and taking our worn-out ones in return.

Again we waited for the signal. Four of us held the long board, and felt sure that one blow would dash our door into the middle of the room.

The other small rooms were soon vacated, the movement being concealed from the observation of the guards by the inmates of the large room, into which all the others entered, crowding up around the doors.

For an instant all was silent. We lifted our hearts in mental prayer to God that he would be with us and preserve us through the coming strife, and if consistent with his high will, permit us to regain our liberty.

What can cause the delay? Minute after minute passes, and the dead silence is broken only by the throbbing of our own hearts. We have counted the cost, and are ready for the strife which shall lead us to grapple, with naked arms, the shining bayonets of the guards. Some will certainly fall, but we trust that others will regain the unutterable blessing of liberty.

But now we see our friends *creeping back to their rooms!* We grind our teeth with rage and chagrin, but soon hear the explanation, which makes us believe that the Lord is indeed watching over us.

Just as the leader was ready to give the signal, a friend pressed to his side and informed him that we were betrayed, and that the enemy were on the watch for us. From a window in the far corner of the room a force of at least eighty men could be seen drawn up before the prison-door. The story continued that orders had been given to shoot down every one who attempted to escape, while another detachment was to close in behind and make an indiscriminate massacre. Had we carried out our plan, the guard would have yielded before our rush until we had been fully drawn into the trap, when they hoped to make such a slaughter as would be a perpetual warning to prison-breakers.

When I first heard this account I thought it the invention of some weak-nerved individual who wished to avoid the danger of our scheme. But it was perfectly true. The next day the newspapers of Richmond contained a full *exposé* of the whole affair, and Captain Alexander, the tyrant who commanded the prison, threatened to have every one engaged in it tied up and whipped. But he finally changed his mind. A nominal prisoner, who was really a spy in the service of the authorities, had contrived to get into the plot, and had reported it to his employers. This was the last attempt at prison-breaking in which I was concerned.

In Richmond there was a pretence of allowing prisoners to correspond with their friends in the North,—

of course, subject to the inspection of the prison officials.
From Libby Prison some letters did go safely. We
also tried writing, making our expressions very guarded,
but, so far as I have ever heard, none of our correspondence was forwarded beyond the lines. I was
providentially afforded a better opportunity. Some of
the prisoners captured at the battle of Murfreesborough
were brought to Richmond for exchange, and were
kept overnight in a room in the basement of Castle
Thunder. When in the court as usual in the morning, I asked a good-natured Irishman of their number
if he would carry a letter and mail it for me after getting to loyal territory. He cheerfully consented, and
I pencilled a note to my father on the fly-leaf of a
book and, watching an opportunity when unobserved,
gave it to him. He concealed it until out of rebel
power, and duly committed it to the mail. The sensation may be imagined which it produced among my
own friends and those of other members of the party,
as nothing had been heard from us since the October
escape, and we had long been given over as dead.
Though the note was very hastily written, I copy it
here without change, as showing the feeling experienced
at that time. Something of the hopefulness and lightness of the tone resulted from the wish to cheer those
addressed.

"RICHMOND, VA., January 6, 1863.

"DEAR FATHER,—I take this opportunity of writing by a paroled prisoner to let you know that I am well and doing as well
as could be expected. I have seen some rather hard times, but
the worst is past. Our lives are now safe, but we will be kept
during the war, unless something lucky turns up for us. There
are six of our original railroad party here yet. Seven were executed in June, and eight escaped in October.

"I stand the imprisonment pretty well. The worst of it is to
hear of our men [this refers to the Union army] getting whipped
so often. I hear all the news here: read three or four papers a
day. I even know that Bingham was beat in the last election,
for which I am very sorry.

"The price of everything here is awful. It costs thirty cents
to send a letter. This will account for my not writing to all my

friends! Give my sincere love to them, and tell them to write to me.

" You may write by leaving the letter unsealed, putting in nothing that will offend the Secesh, and directing to Castle Thunder, Va. I want to know the private news,—how many of my friends have fallen. Also tell me who has been drafted in our neighborhood, who married, and who like to be. Also, if you have a gold dollar at hand, slip it into the letter,—not more, as it might tempt the Secesh to *hook* it. I have tried to send word through to you several times, but there is now a better chance of communicating since we came from Atlanta to Richmond.

" No doubt you would all like to see me again, but let us have patience. Many a better man than I am has suffered more, and many parents are mourning for their children without the hope of seeing them again. So keep your courage up, and do not be uneasy about me. Write as soon as you can, and tell all my friends to do the same.

" Ever yours,
" WILLIAM PITTENGER.

" To THOMAS PITTENGER,
" New Somerset, Jefferson Co., Ohio."

The belief expressed in the above letter of imprisonment during the war was thought by the writer to be most probable. No word was spoken either of exchange or of court-martial. The prices referred to were in Confederate money, which was now greatly depreciated. The little we had brought from Atlanta rapidly melted away, procuring us very little addition to our meagre fare. We still hoped for great Union victories and a speedy termination of the war. But at the opening of the year 1863 the prospect was dark indeed.

About the 1st of February the range of side rooms in which we were confined was wanted for hospital purposes. The prison hospital had been located in the garret above, but disease increased to such an extent that its accommodations were no longer sufficient. These chill and comfortless rooms had but little adaptation to their new purpose, and hastened the release of many a poor unfortunate by the mercy of death. Disease was now making fearful havoc. The hardships of prison-life and the starvation diet prepared the way for every contagion. Smallpox broke out, and prevailed to such an extent that the whole town was alarmed. The prisoners were vaccinated by the wholesale, but this necessary precaution caused great additional suffering. Men died in every room, and the visiting physician came each morning to remove to the hospitals those who showed marks of the dreaded pestilence. It would scarcely be believed that some prisoners actually counterfeited smallpox in order to be sent to the smallpox hospital, where they would have a better opportunity for escape. But escaping had become a regular mania, and all possible means were employed to effect it.

No one of our party of six took the pestilence, though two suffered very severely from the vaccine virus. But the prevalence of disease did us a good service in securing our removal from the narrow stall to the comparative freedom of the room outside.

This was a great change, and did seem like freedom by contrast. From this time the isolation of our prison-life was at an end. I have spoken of the "room," but the term is scarcely accurate. The partitions had been taken out or never inserted in this upper floor, and the prisoners could go from one end of the building to the other, but with guards stationed at every door and watching every window outside. In a far corner there was a stove,—the first fire we had felt since leaving Libby two months before. It did not suffice to warm half the people around it, and these were very quarrelsome, but it was a great luxury to be occasionally warm.

The amusements of the hundreds who had been gathered into this receptacle of humanity were very *striking*, if not elegant. When a dense crowd had gathered around the stove, some person outside— usually one of a large group of very mischievous Irishmen—would cry, "Char-rge, me boys!" and a solid column of perhaps fifty men would rush against the group around the stove, knocking men in all directions, endangering limbs, and raising a perfect storm of profanity. Fights were very frequent, and it only needed the addition of intoxicating liquor to make the place a perfect pandemonium. As it was, the interference of the guard was often required to preserve order. Our party, however, always stood together, and were thus able to protect themselves.

The evenings were a compensation for the turmoil and quarrelling of the day. After all who possessed blankets had rolled themselves up and laid down to rest on the floor, some of the worst rowdies, who had been annoying and persecuting their fellow-prisoners all day, would gather around the stove and appear in a new character,—that of story-tellers. Old Irish legends, and some of the finest fairy-tales to which I have ever listened, were brought forth, and the greater part of the night was often passed in such discourse. But the approach of day put an end to the romantic disposition of these rude bards and left them ill ruffians as before.

We soon wearied of this perpetual ferment and excitement, and learning that there was one room in the prison occupied principally by Union men, petitioned to be placed with them. To our surprise this request was granted, and we were taken down to the ground floor, and placed in a large, dingy room on the level of the street. The windows were not only secured by crossing bars, but additionally darkened by fine woven wire. The refuse tobacco-stems—the building was an old tobacco manufactory—had been thrown into this room, and were now gathered into a great heap in one corner, occupying more than a fourth part of the entire apartment. This filthy stuff—for such it was, having been trodden underfoot for years—was not without its uses for the tobacco-lovers of the party.

But this dungeon had ample compensations for its darkness and dinginess. It contained a stove, and was

kept quite warm. Thus the terrible suffering from
cold was now ended. There was also good society
here,—nearly a hundred Union men from different
parts of the South,—all intensely patriotic, and many
of them possessing great intelligence. The rude, wild
element which dominated in the third floor was in
complete subordination on the first.

It would be easy to fill a volume with stories told
us by the loyal citizens confined in this room. One
or two may serve as specimens. I became very intimate with a Scotchman named Miller, from Texas.
He told me of the beginning of the reign of terror,
which prepared the way for secession. The rumor,
in Miller's neighborhood, was first spread of an intended slave insurrection. Weapons, and in some cases
poison, were secreted, to be afterwards found at the
right time. Some slaves were next whipped until,
under the torture, they would confess to the intended
insurrection, and implicate the most prominent opponents of secession. This was enough to drive the
populace to madness. The fear of servile insurrections
has always aroused the worst passions of slaveholding
countries. Slaves and white Unionists were now hung
up to the same trees, and the work went on until all
who opposed the withdrawal of the State from the old
Union were treated as criminals. It is not strange that
slavery thus furnished the means as well as the occasion
of rebellion.

Miller, being an outspoken opponent of secession, was
seized, and sent eastward, accused of treason against the
Confederacy. Twice he made his escape, and when recaptured told, each time, a different story. At Richmond, when brought up for examination, he merely
said, " I told you all about my case before." The ex-
amining officer, who was very busy and a little in liquor,
took him at his word and ordered him back to prison.
At length he was included with many others in a special
exchange.

A few Union so.diers, besides ourselves, were in this room. There was a young and adventurous scout from the Potomac army, Charlie Marsh by name, who had been sent a short distance inside the rebel lines to burn an important bridge. While on his way, with a gray coat—the rebel color—thrown over his own uniform, he managed to get some important information regarding the enemy, which he committed to writing. In this perilous position he was captured, and the papers, which he was not able to destroy, determined his character as a spy. A drum-head court-martial convicted him, and he was sent with a strong guard to Richmond for execution. While on the way the sergeant in charge got an opportunity to drink, and soon became very careless. Marsh could not escape; but, watching his chance, slipped from the sergeant's pocket the package containing the report of the trial and sentence, and dropped them, unobserved, into a ditch by the wayside.

When he arrived in Richmond, the sergeant could give the prison authorities no information further than that his prisoner was a Yankee he had been told to bring to them. The drunkard was reprimanded, and the authorities sent back to the army for the missing information. Pending its arrival, Marsh was put into our room, instead of being confined separately and securely, as would have been the case if his sentence had been known. When the evidence against him arrived, the commanding officer entered the room with a guard and called his name. This was Charlie's last chance for life, and shrewdly was it improved! A man had died in the prison the night before, and the body had not yet been removed. Charlie promptly responded, "Oh, that fellow is dead?" pointing to the corpse.

"Died, has he? the rascal! We'd 'a hung him this week and saved him the trouble if he had only held on," growled the officer.

No prisoner felt called upon to expose the deception,
28

and the officer departed and reported accordingly. Marsh continued to answer whenever the dead man's name was called, and was finally exchanged in his place. I once met him since the close of the war. He was then in congenial employment as a government detective.

CHAPTER XXI.

SICKNESS AND LIBERTY.

IN February the attempt was made to persuade the Union men of our prison room to enlist in the rebel army. Over twenty recruits were obtained. They were loyal in heart to the old government, but so worn down and dispirited by suffering that they could resist no longer. The refusal of the remainder to take the same step seemed to exasperate the prison officials, and new hardships were devised for us. Captain Alexander, the tyrant who had charge of the prison, issued an order for taking out a working-party to perform menial service each day. At first volunteers were called for, and the desire to be in the open air was so great that they were readily obtained, notwithstanding the conditions of the work were far from being pleasant. As soon as no more volunteers offered, a list was prepared, and a certain number of the names called daily for service. This was putting the matter in another light. One of the first called was a frank, brave Tennesseean named McCoy. He answered boldly, "I'm not going."

"What's the matter now?" demanded the officer who was calling the list.

"I didn't come here to work, and if you can't board me without, you may send me home," replied the fearless man.

"Well! well! You'll be attended to," growled

the officer, and proceeded with the roll. Four others on the list likewise refused. In a short time a guard entered the room and seized them. We feared that one of the terrible floggings, which were only too common in the case of prison insubordination, was going to take place. But another mode of punishment was devised. The four were taken before Captain Alexander, who ordered them to "the cell." This was a windowless place, beside the open court, only about four feet wide by six or seven in length. It had no floor but the damp earth, and was dark at mid-day. They were informed that they should remain here until they consented to work.

We found another alternative for them. There was a piece of file and a scrap of stove-pipe in our room, which we secreted, and, buying a piece of candle from the commissary, found an opportunity, when taken to wash in the prison-court, of slipping the articles into the cell. Thus provided, our friends began to dig their way out under the wall. All day and night they worked, but did not get through. We furnished another candle and they worked on. Towards morning of the second night they broke upward through the crust of the ground outside of the wall. The foremost wormed his way out and glided off. He was never heard of afterwards, and, I presume, reached the Union army. The next man was just under the wall, when the barking of a dog that happened to be prowling around drew the attention of the guard that way, and the hole was closed. This incident prevented the confinement of any others in the cell.

Yet the attempt to secure workers from the prison was not given up. I happened to be on the next list prepared. To work with a guard carrying a musket to enforce obedience did not seem to me a part of my business as a United States soldier. Carefully counting the cost, I determined to go any length in resistance.

On our refusal, we were ordered into the jail-yard.

It was a very cold, windy day in February, with abundant rain. We were nearly naked, having only the remnant of the rags that had already outserved their time. The bottoms were out of my shoes, and the water stood in the yard several inches deep. The yard itself was only a vacant corner in the building inclosed by high brick walls, on the top of which guards walked. The cold, wet wind swept down with biting sharpness, and almost robbed us of sensation. We paced the narrow bounds, through the mud and water, until too weary to walk any more, and then resigned ourselves to our misery. If this exposure had come earlier, when we were accustomed to the endurance of cold, it might have been less serious. But for several weeks we had been in a close, warm room, and the contrast was almost unbearable.

Here we remained from early in the morning until nearly dark in the evening. They told us we would have to stay there till we agreed to work or froze to death! The first we had resolved never to do. The latter seemed only too probable. I do not think any of us could have survived the night. We resolved as soon as it was fairly dark to scale the wall and seek our own deliverance, feeling that it could not be worse to die by the bullet than by exposure.

But we had help from an unexpected source. The old commissary, Chillis, had come out of his room, which was near by, several times during the day to observe us, and each time went away muttering and grumbling. We thought he enjoyed our suffering, but were greatly mistaken. In the evening he went to Captain Alexander and remonstrated with him in the strongest terms. Said he,—

"If you want to kill the men, do it at once! The rascals deserve it. Hanging is the best way. But don't leave them out there to die by inches, for it will disgrace us all over the world."

His remonstrance was heeded, and we were remanded

back to our room, which, with its warm fire,· never seemed more agreeable. We soon sank into a pleasant stupor, from which all awoke very ill. One poor fellow died within a few hours, and several more after a short interval. I was the only one of our railroad party who had been thus exposed. That day of freezing does not seem a worse hardship than many endured previously, but coming when already enfeebled, it was far more injurious. Pneumonia followed, and when I grew better a distressing cough continued, which has never left me. Ever since I have been a confirmed invalid. But the attempt to make us work was relinquished.

One day we were summoned into line, and the names of our railroad party, with a few others, called over. One of the prisoners who had not been called, asked the reason of the omission. The officer replied,—

" We can't tell, for this list came from Yankeeland."

This speech set wild conjectures afloat. Why should a list be sent from the North ? Was it for the purpose of exchange ? Had the Federal government made some arrangement at last which applied especially to us, and not to the mass of Union men in the prison ? We could not tell, but it was pleasant to believe that we were not utterly forgotten.

It was soon discovered that a special exchange of political prisoners—prisoners whose offences were of a civil and not a military character—was in contemplation. Soldiers were being exchanged frequently from the Libby on the other side of the way, but it had seemed as if we were altogether forsaken. Now the rumor was current that a large number on each side who were held for various offences were to be massed into one general exchange, and the including of our names in a list sent from the loved loyal States was sufficient fuel to rekindle the almost extinct fire of hope.

But the delay was long, and we grew very weary of waiting. Truce-boat after truce-boat went off, and week after week slid away, leaving us still in our dark and irksome prison. So completely did this damp our hopes that if any one referred to exchange he was laughed into silence.

One day, however, we received a most welcome token of governmental remembrance. An officer bustled into the prison and asked for the name of every one there who claimed United States protection. There was a general rush towards him, for, although we did not know how our government could protect us while in rebel hands, we were resolved not to lose anything for want of claiming it. It then transpired that the authorities at Washington, in order to relieve the sufferings of the Richmond prisoners, had offered to furnish a supply of clothing for them. The offer was accepted, and some of the clothing reached its destination,—not nearly all, as I judge from comparing the accounts given on the opposite sides of the line. My own portion was a pair of boots, which were sorely needed. We did not obtain a complete supply, but what we did get was very grateful, as a token that we were not forgotten, but that a great nation still cared for us.

I have said but little for some time past of our religious exercises. It must not be inferred that we had lost the zeal enkindled during the dark hours in Atlanta. Up-stairs we continued to pray, sing, and repeat Bible lessons morning and evening. When we first came into the room below, where we were strangers, and where the whole current of opinion seemed utterly irreligious, I did feel as if it would be impossible for us in the common room to worship publicly as before. At the arrival of the usual hour I was sorely perplexed, and almost persuaded to wait a day or two for better acquaintance with our new room-mates. But the matter was settled providentially for us. Mr.

Pierce, who had accompanied us all the way from Knoxville, and who was very profane in speech, had never shown any interest in our prayers beyond remaining silent when we were thus employed. But now he stepped on a box, and calling and stamping until he had the attention of everybody in the room, he said,—

"I have a matter to propose for our general interest. We have some preachers with us who are accustomed to sing and pray and read the Bible every morning and evening. Now, I am wicked enough myself, but I like to l ave something good going on; so I propose that we invite them to go ahead as they have done in other prisons. All that favor the motion say 'aye!'"

The response was most hearty. In a prison a proposition for anything which will break the monotony for even a little time is sure of favor. No one voted in the negative, and Pierce, turning to me, said, "Go ahead."

There were no preachers in our party, but, under such circumstances, we gladly embraced the providential opportunity. The majority of the prisoners gathered around in respectful silence, and seemed greatly pleased to hear, in that gloomy place, the voice of prayer and sacred song. Even the guards drew near the open door, and stood in reverent attention. But a small company of the more reckless of the prisoners regarded the whole matter in the light of a burlesque. One I especially noticed, who seemed to be their leader. He was quite young, had a confident bearing, and uttered great oaths on the smallest occasion. He watched us without making any disturbance while we read and sang, but, when we knelt for prayer, he knelt too, and became very noisy in his mock devotions, responding "amen" with more than Methodistic fervor and at the most inopportune places. This we endured patiently for that evening, but I resolved to win him over, feeling sure that we would thus do good and secure ourselves from interruption. On the next day I managed

to get into conversation with him, told him the story
of our adventures, which always commanded attention.
and asked the reason of his imprisonment. He gave
the story, and I afterwards asked after his friends in
his far-off Canadian home. He told me that he had
no near relatives except a sister, and his blue eyes filled
with tears as he spoke of his longing to see her once
more.   There were no interruptions to our evening
service; and I learned that my friend had taken occasion to say that those Ohioans were good fellows, and
that anybody who disturbed them would have to reckon
with him.   A number of other religious persons made
themselves known when the way was thus open, though
each one had supposed himself alone before. We formed
quite a church when all assembled, though there was a
great mixture of creeds, a Roman Catholic being one
of the most devoted of the number.

    A day now approached that had been longed for
ever since we first tasted the bitter cup of captivity,—a
day which yet shines golden and glorious in the light
of memory,—a day which I never recall without a
mental ejaculation of thanksgiving to Almighty God.
To have assured its coming I would at any time during
the preceding eleven months have unshrinkingly sacri-
ficed my right hand!

    On the evening of the 17th of March, 1863, when
we were sitting around the stove, discussing quietly
but not indifferently the siege of Vicksburg, an officer
stepped within the door and shouted the strange order,
"All who want to go to the *United States* come to the
office!"

    No more plans were laid for capturing Vicksburg
that night!   We thought we were in the United States
all the while, but had no objection to be still more so,
and at once fell into line, and walked out, between two
files of soldiers, to the office.   It seemed like a dream.
For a moment a delicious hope thrilled through my
veins,—a vision of happiness and home, dazzling as a

flash of summer lightning,—but it instantly faded before the remembrance of the manner in which we had been deceived in Atlanta. I did not doubt that an exchange had been arranged for some of the inmates of our room, but feared that the good fortune would not reach so far as our proscribed band. The oath of parole, binding each man not to serve against the Confederacy until regularly exchanged, was being signed as fast as the names could be written and the oath administered. To end the suspense, I pressed forward, gave my name, and held my breath, while fully expecting to hear " The engine thieves can't go,"—but no objection was made. I wrote my name, and watched each of my five comrades do the same, with growing hope, as still no objection was made. Then came the remembrance that our names were the first on the list, read a few days before, which, as we had been told, came from " Yankee-land,"—and I suspected, what I afterwards learned to be the fact,—that our government, in arranging this exchange, had specially stipulated that we should be included. Although a sickening fear would still intrude itself now and then, there was really no reason to doubt that all the preliminaries of our exchange were actually arranged.

When all the prisoners had signed the papers we were ordered to return to our room, and be ready to start for the North at four o'clock next morning. We could have been ready in four seconds! but we really needed the quiet night hours to realize the full magnitude of our deliverance. The wild excitement of that evening can never be fully described. The majority of paroled men acted as if bereft of reason. The joyousness of some found vent in vociferous shouts,—in dancing and bounding over the floor,—in embracing each other, and in pledging kind remembrances. Some seemed stupefied by their good fortune, others sat down and wept in silence, and still others laughed for minutes together. But in the room there were a few not permitted to go, and my heart bled for them. I remembered the hour when we had been left by our comrades on first arriving in Richmond, and now these friends sat cheerless and alone, seeming more wretched than ever amid the general joy.

But there was one expression of joy which it would have been the basest ingratitude for us to omit. It was near midnight before we became calm enough to offer up our usual evening devotions. But when all were wearied out by the very excess of joy, when the quietness which ever follows overwhelming emotion had settled upon us, we knelt in prayer,—a prayer of deep, strong, fervent thankfulness. We implored that we might not be deceived in our vivid hopes and dashed back from our anticipated paradise. Yet, if such should be God's mysterious will, and we should see these hopes fade, as others had faded before them, we asked for strength to bear the trial. Then, with solemn trust, we tried to commit the whole matter to the wisdom and the mercy of God, and lay down to sleep, if we could, and to await the event.

Few eyes closed during the entire night. Fancy was too busy peopling her fairy landscapes,—picturing the groups that awaited us, beyond that boundary which for nearly a year seemed to us as impassable as the river of death. But even as we muse we find that hope is not the only painter at work. What unbidden fears spring up to darken the prospect and stain the brightness of our joy! How many of those dear friends we were hoping to meet may now be no more! For a year not a whisper from them has reached us,—no letter or message from any friend, and we tremble as we think of the ravages of time and of battle. These and a hundred other thoughts whirled through our brains during that ever-memorable night. It seemed but a few moments after lying down until we heard the voice of an officer, who stood by the open door, and gave the thrilling order to—*prepare for our journey!*

Hurriedly we thronged to our feet. It was yet long before daylight, but the guard were in readiness, and they did not need to wait long for us. The visions of the night were swept away, but in their stead was the blessed reality. It was true! Freedom once more! Our terrible captivity ended! Oh joy! *joy!*—wild and delirious JOY!

There was a hurrying around in the darkness, illumined by the flashing of torch-lights,—a discordant calling of names,—a careful inspection of each man to see that none went except those who had been chosen; then, forming two lines in the court-yard, with bounding hearts we passed outward through the dreaded portals of Castle Thunder,—the same portals we had passed inward more than three months before!—passed out into the cool but *free* night air, and stood in the dark and silent street.

Beside us rose the tall, square, and ugly outline of the prison we had left. Not far away on the left was the shadowy form of the twin prison,—the Libby,—fit emblems, in their frowning blackness, of that system of oppression which had shed rivers of blood in a vain war, and was soon to pass away forever. But we could not pause to moralize even upon such a theme. As soon as all were out of the gate, and the column of prisoners duly formed, with guards on either hand, we marched onward through the muddy streets for many squares. There were with us a number of sick, who were too weak to walk unassisted, and yet unwilling to be left behind. As no conveyances were provided for them, we placed each of them between two friends, on whose shoulders they leaned, and they were thus able to totter the weary distance. A few had to be carried altogether by those who were themselves far from strong, but hope, and the exultation of liberty, made everything possible. After we were seated in the cars, which were waiting at the depot, and had begun to glance around with happy faces in the dim morning light, some Richmond papers were procured. Looking over them we found the very interesting news that " a large number of *engine thieves*, bridge-burners, murderers, robbers, and traitors will leave this morning for the United States. The Confederacy may well congratulate itself on this good riddance." The item was handed from one to another, and we recognized the names applied with quiet joy. Our congratulations were not less fervid than theirs, but we could not help thinking that the riddance might have been made long before!

With the rising sun we glided out of Richmond, and, passing fortifications and rifle-pits, soon reached Petersburg. Then, with but short detention and no notable incidents, we continued on to City Point, on the James River,—the place of exchange. It was not far from noon when we came within sight of the most glorious and fascinating object on the American continent!—the " Stars and Stripes," which we had not seen before for eleven months, floating in proud beauty over the truce-boat " State of Maine." It was a glorious vision. Cheer after cheer arose from the cars. The guard ordered the noise stopped, but the command was unheeded, and the officers did not try to enforce it.

The memories of that hour are indistinct from their very brightness. I seem to see again the great boat with its beautiful flag, the line of Federal guards with their bright blue uniforms, the gray-clad company for whom we were to be exchanged, and who did not seem nearly so glad as ourselves, and my own tattered and starved companions, some three hundred in number. I hear once more the seemingly interminable reading of names, the checking of lists, the wrangling over trifles, and at last the order—which needed no repetition—to go on board. There was still a sense of trembling and apprehension until the boat actually pushed off and we were on our way down the James.

Then our delight was boundless. We had awakened from a hideous nightmare-dream to find that all its shapes of horror and grinning fiends had passed away and left us in the sunlight once more. Our hearts kept time with the glad threshing of our wheels on the water, and sang within us, knowing that each ponderous stroke was placing a greater distance between us and our dreaded foes.

The hearty, cheerful welcome we met on board was no small element in our pleasure. We were hungry—no wonder after a year's fasting—and we were fed,—the only difficulty being to avoid hurtful excess. With a full supply of provisions and a large tin cup of coffee—I am not sure that so good a cup of coffee has been made since—I sat down and ate slowly, as if I could never have enough. Then I wandered all over the boat, from the upper deck and the cabin down to the hold, in the mere wantonness of liberty. To go about with no guard watching me was as strange as it was delightful. The act of going up to, and passing unchecked through a door, was a great pleasure! I saw little of the country through which we passed, for the mind was too busy. No emotion on earth has the same sweep and intensity as the throbbing sensations that rush through the bosom of the liberated captive!

I have no recollection whatever of the lower James, of Fortress Monroe, of the Chesapeake. In all my memoranda no word occurs of these things. Whether the hours were spent in sleep or waking, whether the monotony of happiness obliterated memory, or nature, weakened by disease and exhausted by too great a multiplicity of sensations, refused to receive new impressions, I know not; but not until we were near Washington can I again recall passing events. Then we thronged to the vessel's side, and bent loving eyes upon the snowy front of our beautiful Capitol. It seemed a far more grand and fitting emblem of our country's power now than when I had first looked upon it, an inexperienced boy, in the far-away opening of the war, though only two years had elapsed since that time. In those two years the whole country had learned many lessons, and to me they were an age!

Here a brief controversy arose with the commander of the truce-boat. He had orders to forward all the exchanged soldiers to the parole camp at Annapolis, and wished to send our party with them. I demurred, feeling that it was right for us to report at Washington, at military headquarters. General Mitchel, who sent us forth upon our expedition, was dead. Our leader, Andrews, was no more. How many of our officers had fallen in the sanguinary battles of the West we knew not; possibly we had been reported as dead and our places filled. This, we afterwards learned, was actually the case. The right place for us to report, in order that everything might be put in proper shape, was at Washington, and to the Secretary of War, Hon. Edwin M. Stanton, in person. Our case, as the rebels had been showing to our cost for the past year, was not that of ordinary prisoners of war, and we thought ourselves entitled to claim the same distinction on Federal soil. I therefore informed the commander that we had urgent business with Secretary Stanton, and must be sent to him. He was a little incredulous at first, but as soon as I gave my reasons he gracefully yielded.

Our reception in Washington was even more cordial than it had been on the truce-boat. We were provided with most comfortable quarters, and literally feasted on the best the city afforded. Secretary Stanton asked us to go before Judge-Advocate-General Holt and there give our deposition, that the full particulars of what he was pleased to consider our extraordinary adventures might be given to the world on an unquestionable basis. Our first visit to Judge Holt was merely friendly, at which Major-General Hitchcock and Mr. J. C. Wetmore, Ohio State Agent, were also present. We were invited to come again on the morrow, when we found a justice of the peace and a phonographer to take our testimony. I was questioned first, and the examination covered all the outlines of the story. All were sworn except Mason, who was unable from illness to be present. The result of the examination, together with Judge Holt's comments upon it, were published in the *Army and Navy Gazette* of that date.

General Hitchcock then accompanied us in our call upon Secretary Stanton, where we enjoyed a most delightful interview. At its close he brought out six medals which had been prepared according to a recent act of Congress and left to his disposal. He said that they were the first given to private soldiers in this war. Jacob Parrot, the boy who had endured the terrible beating, received, as he well deserved, the first one.

Secretary Stanton next presented us one hundred dollars each from the secret service fund as pocket-money, and gave orders for payment to us of all arrearages, and for refunding the full value of the money and arms taken from us at our capture. This was not all. He tendered us, each one, a commission in the regular army, and on our expressing a preference for the volunteer service, he requested Governor Tod, of Ohio, to give us equivalent promotion in our own regiments. These commissions were promptly given, but through ill health, some of our number, myself included, were not able to be mustered as officers.

Stanton praised the bravery of Mitchel in the highest terms, and stated that he had been aware of our expedition, but, until the escape of our eight comrades in October, had supposed that we had all perished; that he had then threatened retaliation in case any more of us were executed, and had demanded to know the reason for the execution of the seven who had been put to death. It was answered that the Confederate government had no knowledge of the death of any member of the party. Since that time he had been most anxious to effect our exchange, and by special effort had at last succeeded in arranging it.

We were then escorted to the Executive Mansion, and had a most pleasing interview with President Lincoln. We told him many incidents of prison experience and received his sympathizing comments in return.

After taking our leave of the President we received transportation at government expense to our homes. The joy of our reception in our own Ohio and among our own kindred I will not attempt to describe.

APPENDIX.

EXTRACTS FROM THE REPORT OF JUDGE-ADVOCATE-GENERAL HOLT TO THE SECRETARY OF WAR.

"JUDGE-ADVOCATE-GENERAL'S OFFICE,
"March 27, 1863.

"SIR,—I have the honor to transmit for your consideration the accompanying depositions of Sergeant William Pittenger, Company G, Second Regiment, Ohio Volunteers; Private Jacob Parrot, Company K, Thirty-third Regiment, Ohio Volunteers; Private Robert Buffum, Company H, Twenty-first Ohio Volunteers; Corporal William Reddick, Company B, Thirty-third Regiment, Ohio Volunteers; and Private William Bensinger, Company G, Twenty-first Regiment, Ohio Volunteers; taken at this office on the 25th instant, in accordance with your written instructions; from which the following facts will appear:

"These non-commissioned officers and privates belonged to an expedition set on foot in April, 1862, at the suggestion of Mr. J. J. Andrews, a citizen of Kentucky, who led it, and under the authority and direction of General O. M. Mitchel, the object of which was to destroy the communications on the Georgia State Railroad between Atlanta and Chattanooga.

"The mode of operation proposed was to reach a point on the road where they could seize a locomotive and train of cars, and then dash back in the direction of Chattanooga, cutting the telegraph wires and burning the bridges behind them as they advanced, until they reached their own lines. The expedition consisted of twenty-four men, who, with the exception of its leader, Mr. Andrews, and another citizen of Kentucky, —who acted on the occasion as the substitute of a soldier,—had been selected from the different companies for their known courage and discretion. They were informed that the movement was to be a secret one, and they doubtless comprehended something of its perils, but Mr. Andrews and Mr. Reddick alone seem to have known anything of its precise direction or object. They, however, voluntarily engaged in it, and made their way, in parties of two or three, in citizen's dress, and carrying only their side-arms, to Chattanooga, the point of rendezvous agreed upon, where twenty-two out of the twenty-four arrived safely. Here they took passage, without attracting observation, for Marietta, which they reached at twelve o'clock on the night of the 11th of April. On the following morning they took the cars back again towards Chattanooga, and at a place called Big Shanty, while the engineer and passengers were breakfasting, they detached the locomotive and three box-cars from the train and started at full speed for Chattanooga. They were now upon the field of the operations proposed by the expedition, but suddenly encountered unforeseen obstacles. According to the schedule of the road, of which Mr. Andrews had possessed himself, they should have met but a single train on that day, whereas they met three, two of them being engaged on extraordinary service. About an hour was lost in waiting to allow these trains to pass, which enabled their pursuers to press closely upon them. They removed rails, threw out obstructions on the road, and attained, when in motion, a speed of sixty miles an hour; but the time lost could not be regained. After having run about one hundred miles they found their supply of wood, water, and oil exhausted, while the rebel locomotive which had been chasing them was

ın sight. Under these circumstances they had no alternative but to abandon their cars and fly to the woods,
which they did, under the orders of Mr. Andrews, each
one endeavoring to save himself as best he might.

"The expedition thus failed from causes which re-
flected neither upon the genius by which it was planned,
nor upon the intrepidity and discretion of those engaged
in executing it. But for the accident of meeting these
trains,—which could not have been anticipated,—the
movement would have been a complete success, and the
whole aspect of the war in the South and the Southwest
would have been at once changed. The expedition
itself, in the daring of its conception, had the wildness
of a romance; while in the gigantic and overwhelming
results which it sought, and was likely to accomplish,
it was absolutely sublime.

"The twenty-two captives, when secured, were thrust
into the negro jail of Chattanooga. They occupied a
single room, half under ground, and but thirteen feet
square, so that there was not space enough for them all
to lie down together, and a part of them were, in consequence, obliged to sleep sitting and leaning against
the walls. The only entrance was through a trap-door
in the ceiling, that was raised twice a day to let down
their scanty meals, which were lowered in a bucket.
They had no other light or ventilation than that which
came through two small, triple-grated windows. They
were covered with swarming vermin, and the heat was
so oppressive that they were often obliged to strip themselves entirely of their clothes to bear it. Add to this,
they were all handcuffed, and, with trace-chains secured
around their necks by padlocks, were fastened to each
other in companies of twos and threes. Their food,
which was doled out to them twice a day, consisted of
a little flour wet with water and baked in the form of
bread, and spoiled pickled beef. They had no opportunity of procuring supplies from the outside, nor had
they any means of doing so,—their pockets having been

rifled of their last cent by the Confederate authorities, prominent among whom was a rebel officer wearing the uniform of a major. No part of the money thus basely taken was ever returned."

[The report narrates the continued sufferings of the adventurers in prison substantially as they are given in the preceding pages, and concludes:]

"So they remained until a few days since, when they were exchanged; and thus, at the end of eleven months, terminated their pitiless persecutions in the prisons of the South,—persecutions begun and continued amid indignities and sufferings on their part, and atrocities on the part of their traitorous foes, which illustrate far more faithfully than any human language could express it the demoniac spirit of a revolt, every throb of whose life is a crime against the very race to which we belong.

"Very respectfully, your obedient servant,
"J. HOLT,
"*Judge-Advocate-General.*
"HON. EDWIN M. STANTON,
"*Secretary of War.*"

No. II.

A SOUTHERN ESTIMATE.

THE following extracts from an editorial published in the Atlanta *Southern Confederacy* of April 15, 1862, will serve to show the intense excitement of the hour:

"THE GREAT RAILROAD CHASE!

"THE MOST EXTRAORDINARY AND ASTOUNDING ADVENTURE OF THE WAR!!

"THE MOST DARING UNDERTAKING THAT YANKEES EVER PLANNED OR ATTEMPTED TO EXECUTE!

" *Stealing an Engine—Tearing up the Track—Pursued on Foot, on Hand-Cars, and Engines—Overtaken— A Scattering—The Capture—The Wonderful Energy of Messrs. Fuller, Murphy, and Cain—Some Reflections, Etc., Etc.*

" Since our last issue we have obtained full particulars of the most thrilling railroad adventure that ever occurred on the American continent, as well as the mightiest and most important in its results, if successful, that has been conceived by the Lincoln government since the commencement of this war. Nothing on so grand a scale has been attempted, and nothing within the range of possibility could be conceived that would fall with such a tremendous, crushing force upon us as the accomplishment of the plans which were concocted and dependent upon the execution of the one whose history we now proceed to narrate.

" Its *reality—what was actually done*—excels all the extravagant *conceptions* of the Arrowsmith hoax, which fiction created such a profound sensation in Europe.

"To make the matter more complete and intelligible, we will take our readers over the same history of the case we related in our last, the main features of which are correct, but lacking in details which have since come to hand.

"We will begin at the breakfast-table of the Big Shanty Hotel at Camp McDonald, where several regiments of soldiers are now encamped. The morning mail and passenger train had left here at four A.M. on last Saturday morning as usual, and had stopped there for breakfast. The conductor, William A. Fuller, the engineer, J. Cain,—both of this city,—and the passengers were at the table, when the eight men, having uncoupled the engine and three empty box-cars next to it from the passenger and baggage-cars, mounted the engine, pulled open the valve, put on all steam, and left conductor, engineer, passengers, spectators, and the soldiers in the camp hard by, all lost in amazement, and dumbfounded at the strange, startling, and daring act.

"This unheard-of act was doubtless undertaken at that time and place upon the presumption that pursuit could not be made by an engine short of Kingston, some thirty miles above, or from this place; and by cutting down the telegraph wires as they proceeded the adventurers could calculate on at least three or four hours the start of any pursuit it was reasonable to expect. This was a legitimate conclusion, and but for the will, energy, and quick good judgment of Mr. Fuller and Mr. Cain, and Mr. Anthony Murphy, the intelligent and practical foreman of the wood department of the State Road shop, who accidentally went on the train from this place that morning, their calculations would have worked out as originally contemplated, and the results would have been obtained long ere this reaches the eyes of our readers,—the most terrible to us of any we can conceive as possible, and unequalled by anything attempted or conceived since this war commenced.

" Now for the chase !"

[The account, which fills a whole page of the paper, is omitted, as it differs in no essential particular from that given in the foregoing pages. In concluding, the editor gives his estimate of the purpose and magnitude of the expedition.]

" We do not know what Governor Brown will do in this case, or what is his custom in such matters, but, if such a thing is admissible, we insist on Fuller and Murphy being promoted to the highest honors on the road,—if not by actually giving them the highest position, at least let them be promoted by *brevet.* Certainly their indomitable energy and quick correct judgment and decision in the many difficult contingencies connected with this unheard-of emergency has saved all the railroad bridges above Ringgold from being burned; the most daring scheme that this revolution has developed has been thwarted, and the tremendous results, which, if successful, can scarcely be imagined, much less described, have been averted. Had they succeeded in burning the bridges, the enemy at Huntsville would have occupied Chattanooga before Sunday night. Yesterday they would have been in Knoxville, and thus had possession of all East Tennessee. Our forces at Knoxville, Greenville, and Cumberland Gap would ere this have been in the hands of the enemy. Lynchburg, Virginia, would have been moved upon at once. This would have given them possession of the valley of Virginia, and Stonewall Jackson would have been attacked in the rear. They would have had possession of the railroad leading to Charlottesville and Orange Court-House, as well as the South Side Railroad leading to Petersburg and Richmond. They might have been able to unite with McClellan's forces and attack Joe Johnston's army front and flank. It is not by any means improbable that our army in Virginia would have been defeated, captured, or driven out of the State this week.

" Then reinforcements from all the eastern and south-eastern portion of the country would have been cut off from Beauregard. The enemy have Huntsville now, and with all these designs accomplished his army would have been effectually flanked. The mind and heart shrink back appalled at the bare contemplation of the awful consequences which would have followed the success of this one act. When Fuller, Murphy, and Cain started from Big Shanty *on foot to catch that fugitive engine,* they were involuntarily laughed at by the crowd, serious as the matter was,—and to most observers it was indeed most ludicrous; but *that foot-race saved us,* and prevented the consummation of all these tremendous consequences.

" We doubt if the victory of Manassas or Corinth were worth as much to us as the frustration of this grand *coup d'état.* It is not by any means certain that the annihilation of Beauregard's whole army at Corinth would be so fatal a blow to us as would have been the burning of the bridges at that time and by these men.

" When we learned by a private telegraph dispatch a few days ago that the Yankees had taken Huntsville, we attached no great importance to it. We regarded it merely as a dashing foray of a small party to destroy property, tear up the road, etc., *à la* Morgan. When an additional telegram announced the force there to be from seventeen to twenty thousand, we were inclined to doubt it,—though coming from a perfectly upright and honorable gentleman, who would not be likely to seize upon a wild report to send here to his friends. The coming to that point with a large force, where they would be flanked on either side by our army, we regarded as a most stupid and unmilitary act. We now understand it all. They were to move upon Chattanooga and Knoxville as soon as the bridges were burnt, and press on into Virginia as far as possible, and take all our forces in that State in the rear. It was all the deepest-laid scheme, and on the grandest scale, that ever emanated from the brains of any number of Yankees combined. It was one, also, that was entirely practicable for almost any day for the last year. There were but two miscalculations in the whole programme: they did not expect men to start out afoot to pursue them, and they did not expect these pursuers on foot to find Major Cooper's old 'Yonah' standing there already fired up. Their calculations on every other point were dead certainties.

" This would have eclipsed anything Captain Morgan ever attempted. To think of a parcel of Federal soldiers—officers and privates—coming down into the heart of the Confederate States,—for they were here in Atlanta and at Marietta (some of them got on the train at Marietta that morning, and others were at Big Shanty); of playing such a serious game on the State road, which is under the control of our prompt, energetic, and sagacious governor, known as such all over America ; to seize the passenger train on his road, right at Camp McDonald, where he has a number of Georgia regiments encamped, and run off with it; to burn the bridges on the same road, and go safely through to the Federal lines,—all this would have been a feather in the cap of the man or men who executed it."

No. III.

A FRENCHMAN'S VIEW OF THE CHATTANOOGA RAILROAD EXPEDITION.

THE following extract from the "History of the Civil War in America," by the Comte de Paris (vol. ii. pp. 187, 188), is suggestive and characteristic, though erroneous in many particulars. The numbers of those who escaped and of those who perished are reversed, and the cause assigned for the failure of the expedition is purely imaginary; but the local coloring is exquisite:

"Among the expeditions undertaken by Mitchel's soldiers at this period, we must mention one which, despite its tragic termination, shows what a small band of daring men could attempt in America; it will give an idea of the peculiar kind of warfare which served as an interlude to the regular campaigns of large armies. An individual named Andrews, employed in the secret service of Buell, and twenty-two soldiers selected by him, went to Chattanooga under different disguises, and thence to Marietta, in Georgia, which had been assigned them as a place of rendezvous, and which was situated in the very centre of the enemy's country. Once assembled, they got on board a train of cars loaded with Confederate tr... ps and ammunition. During the trip this train stopped, as usual, near a lonely tavern close to the track; everybody got out, and both engineer and fireman went quietly to breakfast. Andrews took advantage of their absence to jump upon the locomotive, which was detached by his men, with three cars, from the rest of the train; they started off at full speed, leaving their fellow-travellers in a state of stupefaction. At the stations where they stopped they quietly

answered that they were carrying powder to Beauregard's army. Presently they began the work of destruction which they had projected; they cut the telegraph
wires, tore up the rails behind them, and proceeded to
fire the bridges which they reached on their way to
Chattanooga. They hoped to arrive at that city before
the news of their expedition had spread abroad, to pass
rapidly through it, and join Mitchel at Huntsville.
But it was necessary to avoid the trains running in the
opposite direction. One of these trains, which they
had just passed on the way, after exchanging the most
satisfactory explanations, reached an embankment,
where Andrews had torn up the rails and made every
preparation to throw the cars off the track. The conductor discovered the trap in time, and backed his en
gine instantly, in order to overtake those who laid it.
At his approach the Federals made off in great haste,
throwing out of the cars everything that could embarrass their flight. They at first got a little ahead, and
the few occupants of log huts lying contiguous to the
railway track looked on without understanding this
strange pursuit. But, being short of fuel, they soon
began to lose ground; they could not stop long enough
to tear up rails; they tried in vain to keep up the fire
of their engine; they were about to be overtaken; their
oil had given out; the axle-boxes were melted by the
friction. The game was lost; they stopped the engine
and rushed into the woods, where they hoped to conceal themselves. Meanwhile, the telegraph had everywhere announced their presence, and the entire population started in pursuit. A regular hunt was organized
in these vast forests, and Andrews was captured with
all his men. The majority of them were shut up in
narrow iron cages and publicly exhibited at Knoxville,
to intimidate the Union men, after which fifteen of
them were hung; the remaining eight were spared, and
had the good fortune to survive and relate their strange
adventures."

No. IV.

OLD SCENES REVISITED.

NEARLY twenty years after the events narrated in the preceding pages the writer passed over the same ground again. Many of the prisons in which he had been confined were no more. In some cases even their sites had been so changed by the altering and grading of streets as to be undiscoverable. But the railroad from Chattanooga to Atlanta continued to be one of the most important in the whole South, and the memory of the captured train and the stirring events connected with it had become a cherished local tradition. The principal pursuers were also found, some of them being still in the employ of the same railroad, and others located in Atlanta. From these former enemies nothing but kindness was experienced. The very locomotive which had been captured was repaired and continued in use, the writer having the pleasure of once more riding over the road on a train drawn by it. The same stations were passed. Many of the smaller towns were externally almost unchanged. Yet everywhere there was a new atmosphere. War and slavery had vanished, and the enterprises of peace were in the ascendant. Chattanooga and Atlanta displayed wonderful improvement, having become like Northern towns in the rush of their business and the character of their population, —the latter city, however, to a less degree than the former.

But a still deeper and more melancholy interest was felt in seeking for the bodies of those who had perished so tragically in Atlanta while rebellion was still in the plenitude of its power. Of the grave of Andrews, himself, no trace could be found. Many old citizens could point out the spot where his scaffold had been erected, and near which he had been buried. But that portion of the town had been entirely burnt by Sherman, and when rebuilt the streets had been raised to a higher level and rearranged, so that the precise location of the grave is probably forever lost.

The scaffold of the seven soldiers was erected in a little wood directly east of the Atlanta city cemetery, about an acre of ground being cleared for that purpose. On this spot, which is now included within the bounds of the cemetery, the terrible tragedy took place. The heart of the writer was almost overwhelmed as he stood there on a peaceful Sabbath afternoon and brought back in recollection that hour of horror! When the work of death was completed the bodies were placed side by side in a wide trench at the foot of the scaffold and covered over. So profound was the impression made by their heroism that the place of burial could not be forgotten, and was often visited by sympathizing friends even during the continuance of the war. But this rude grave is now empty, and for a time the writer could not ascertain what disposition had been made of its contents. An old man formerly connected with the cemetery at length supplied the information that the bodies had been removed, not to the Federal cemetery at Marietta, as had been first conjectured, but to the more distant and larger one at Chattanooga. Here, in probably the most beautiful of all the National cemeteries, the graves were found. In Section H, placed in the open space about the centre, which is usually assigned to commissioned officers, the seven heroes have obtained a final resting-place. There is a headstone, with name and rank, at each grave, and the seven are arranged in the form of a semicircle. This part of the cemetery overlooks a long stretch of the Georgia State Railroad, the great prize they struggled to seize for their country

and thus lost their lives. From this spot the frequent
trains are distinctly visible. Watched by the mountains and undisturbed by the passing tide of human
activity, they rest here as peacefully as if death had
stolen upon them in the midst of friends at home instead of rushing down amid the gloom and horror of
that memorable Atlanta scaffold.

THE END.

www.ingramcontent.com/pod-product-compliance
Lightning Source LLC
Chambersburg PA
CBHW071313090426
42738CB00012B/2691